This book is due for return on or before the last date shown below.

Don Gresswell Ltd., London, N.21   Cat. No. 1208   DG 02242/71

Queueing
for a Living

Paddy O'Gorman

POOLBEG

Published in 1994 by
Poolbeg,
A division of Poolbeg Enterprises Ltd,
Knocksedan House,
123 Baldoyle Industrial Estate,
Dublin 13, Ireland

A catalogue record for this book is available from the British Library.

ISBN 1 85371 355 4

Cover illustration by Jon Berkeley
Cover design by Poolbeg Group Services Ltd/Red dog Graphics
Set by Poolbeg Group Services Ltd in Garamond 10/13
Printed by The Guernsey Press Company Ltd,
Vale, Guernsey, Channel Islands.

CONTENTS

Chapter One

BEGINNINGS; THE NEW EMIGRANTS

London; 7-11 December 1984

I got off the Slattery's bus at London's Victoria Coach station at around six in the morning. I enjoyed the journey on the ferry from Rosslare and the bus trip to London even though I didn't meet any emigrants I could interview. Mainly shoppers going over for Christmas. But I sat next to a nurse through the long, dark hours across Wales and down England's motorways. She'd been out of work for a few months, lying on her back after a car accident. She was three or four years older than me. She had a lot of stories to tell from her years in the casualty department of a London hospital. About the fellow who came in with an electric cable that he had shoved up himself for self-gratification. They thought of wiring him into the mains. A fellow came in attached to his dog. A woman sounded almost normal after these two. Her lover had put a miniature bust of Julius Caesar into her person and, you guessed it, what went up would not come down.

The nurse and I got on well and had a good laugh over the hours. Our conversation was intimate. No, she didn't miss sex in those months after her accident. We started kissing. We shared blankets and then we fumbled under each other's clothing.

At Victoria the nurse told me she had never done anything like that before with a stranger. A relative came to meet her and I've never seen that nurse since. The first marital infidelity in my life and I'd achieved it within hours of kissing goodbye to my wife and my eighteen-month-old daughter. At the time I thought it was harmless fun but nine years later my attraction to other women would lead to the break-up of my marriage. I would meet a lot of women over the next nine years. I've introduced myself to so many now, out with a tape-recorder, working for RTE. I came to have a lot of women friends and these almost always stayed just friends. I never again had a one-night-stand but I had two love affairs. First with a woman I interviewed. And then with a friend of my wife's. That second love affair broke up my marriage.

I was excited and anxious that morning in London. For the first time ever I was making a programme that would be all my own work, instead of producing for John Bowman or Pat Kenny or whoever. The programme was about the new wave of young Irish emigrants in London. Over the previous couple of months I suggested to reporters in RTE that emigration was back with a vengeance and that it was a story worth covering for John Bowman's *Day By Day* programme. I got no enthusiasm from the reporter staff. Then the department head, Michael Littleton, suggested that I should go to London. I'm forever grateful for his suggestion. It changed my life. People find it hard to believe it now but at that time I was a shy person. I lacked confidence.

I headed to Kilburn to keep my first appointment. I don't bother setting up interviews in advance these days. I much prefer to arrive in a place, ask around and see where my luck takes me. But in 1984 I was inexperienced. I hadn't yet developed my own style of work. I'd set up an interview with a priest in Kilburn who was one of the usual alleged spokesmen for the Irish in London. The interview turned out to be a waste. He talked about lifting border security and using the money saved to finance job creation in Ireland. A Provo without a backbone. I didn't use any of this in the programme. It was boring rubbish which had no bearing on the experience of young emigrants. Also that priest was on the airwaves and in the papers every other day, spouting off about emigrants. I wanted the real thing, not a spokesman. That Thursday morning in London was when I decided that I would always go for the real thing.

Out of the Presbytery into the cold and rain of Kilburn High Road. There was one Irish emigrant in Kilburn I wanted to see even though I was scared of what I might find. I'll tell you about her now because she was an important part of my life up until her death in 1986 at the age of twenty-eight. Since then there has rarely been a day I haven't thought about her.

Niamh was from my home town, Cobh in County Cork. We had been part-time teenage lovers and full-time friends. I had a steady girlfriend from Cobh, Jacinta, who moved to Dublin in 1973 and whom I joined in Dublin in 1977 and married two years later. But I stayed close to Niamh. We always got on well and had loads to talk about. We went through University College Cork together. She was a year junior to me. In her first year, my second year, we saw a lot of each other. My friends became her friends. Then after a year Niamh changed. She became a drug addict. She rarely attended college. She had no time for me any more. She hung around with a completely different group of friends. This was the crowd who drank in a particular pub in Oliver Plunkett Street. Not students. They were young working-class men from Cork City and from Middleton. And they used every sort of drug, including heroin.

I lost contact with Niamh when she became a drug addict. Then one weekend in Cobh a gang of us went back to a friend's flat after closing time and Niamh turned up. I told her I missed meeting her in college and asked her about the stories I'd been hearing. Had she really robbed chemist shops in Cork and a vacant house in Wellington Road? She said it was all true. Then Niamh was gone and so was a nice jumper belonging to one of her old friends, that is, one of her non-drug-using friends. And so I learned a life-long lesson. You should never trust a junkie. A junkie cares about drugs more than anything else. Shitting on old friends is only a minor consideration.

In 1978 Niamh astonished everybody except me when, after barely attending lectures for two years, she coolly dropped into UCC to do her finals and came out with an honours degree in History and English. The same degree I got the previous year but I worked my ass off for it. Niamh was extremely bright. I always knew that. Some people assumed that because Niamh was wild she was also thick. That was very stupid of those people. I knew Niamh well and I used to defend her reputation. I was Niamh's greatest admirer.

Late in 1978 Niamh visited Jacinta and me at our flat in Rathmines in Dublin. She invited us to a Prisoners' Rights Organisation meeting at Liberty Hall. Niamh was secretary of the Cork branch. She spoke well. She gave a report on helping Cork people visit relatives in Portlaoise, the Curragh and so on. After the meeting, next door in Barneys, I got to meet some of Niamh's pals. They were an odd mixture. Drug-users, semi-political types and straight criminals. Eddie Hogan was there. Years later he was part of a kidnap gang who cut two fingers off their victim, a dentist. Hogan is doing forty years now for shooting a detective who helped spring that dentist from his captors. And there was Tommy, whom Niamh loved and who, like

4

Niamh, would eventually die because of drug addiction. Tommy was smoking dope in Barneys which I thought was pretty bloody stupid.

Niamh was still in Cork in 1979. When Jacinta and I got married that year she came to the wedding. Sometime after that she moved to London with a lot of her Cork drug friends. She gave birth to a daughter in 1981. She no longer cared much for the father. She wished the father had been Teddy whom she loved for a long time. I never knew Teddy but I'm told he was the brightest and the nicest of Niamh's drug-using friends. But there was one problem. Teddy was bisexual. Niamh reckoned he was mainly homosexual. Teddy lived with Niamh and her daughter after the real father had gone. Niamh only wanted Teddy. I remember Niamh telling Jacinta and me that she and Teddy and Teddy's boyfriend had gone on holidays to Italy together. Sure Teddy was on his holidays and she couldn't begrudge him his boyfriend. Besides, the Italian men were delicious.

Teddy seemed to make Niamh very happy but sadly he died. It was one of those old London buses which had no doors at the back. He got off when it was moving and banged his head on the ground. He seemed okay going home but that night, sleeping next to Niamh, Teddy died.

So now, December 1984, I hadn't seen Niamh for two years. How was she? Was she still on drugs? Was she still at the address I had for her in Kilburn? I walked up Shoot-Up Hill and then turned in to Maygrove Walk and reached the house. It was in a quiet cul-de-sac of recently-built, two-bedroomed council houses and there was a nice playground. Not bad, Niamh. I rang the doorbell.

Through the glass panel in the door I saw her coming. She was in her pyjamas. She was frowning. Then she smiled. It's Paddy. Come in. It's great to see you. I thought first it was the probation officer calling. Her hug was boney. Her skin pale and sweaty. Her teeth nicotine-stained. She called Tommy down from upstairs. It's Paddy. You remember Paddy? But Tommy wouldn't come down. Never mind Tommy. He's not being rude. He usually locks himself away when there are strangers around. Then I noticed the blood trickling from a puncture in Niamh's wrist. Yes, she said. She had just turned on.

I told her why I was in London. She was impressed, as I hoped she would be. And yes, she could help me. There was a young Corkman who was working as a rent boy to pay for drugs. She'd ask Tommy to talk to me about drug addiction and she could tell me about single parenthood. Niamh was a good contact and wanted to help. Wonderful. And then she said she would love to do be doing the sort of work that I was doing. Do you know, Paddy, I have an honours degree? Of course I knew that. And over the next few days I began to imagine Niamh with a different life. Not in the world of drug addiction but in my world again. Journalism, current affairs, things we were both interested in. I really thought I could help her get away from drugs but I vastly overestimated how much help I could be. I know a lot more now about drugs and drug addicts than I did then.

Niamh brightened wonderfully when I told her I was meeting Pauline, an old College friend, on Saturday night. Niamh would come too. She would love to see Pauline again. Pauline was, I think, the most beautiful woman I had known in University College Cork. We had been good friends and regular companions but there had been no romance because I was committed to a woman in Dublin.

Niamh followed me down Maygrove Walk. She directed me towards the Bridge Tavern on Kilburn High Road. I would meet some young Irish in there. Then I broached the subject of Niamh's drug addiction. Please Niamh, I would hate to go to your funeral. That won't happen Paddy. Drug addicts who die usually do it through overdosing. She was too careful to let that happen. Then she said it was lovely to see me again. We said goodbye for now and a few moments later she chased after me again to bum a fiver. Bloody drug addicts. They never miss a chance.

So don't worry, she told me. She could handle heroin. As it turned out, Niamh had less than two years to live.

When I visit Kilburn now I sometimes go to that spot on Maygrove Walk where she told me everything would be okay. I can't pray to you Niamh. You were an atheist as I am. And I won't go back to the crematorium in Essex where I watched your coffin slip behind the curtains. You're not there either. All I can do is keep my memories of you. In Cobh, in Cork, in London. And I want to remember you with this book. You maddening fool. You drug addict. You told me how much you always loved me. Well you could hardly share a life with me if you were a drug addict, could you? You killed yourself Niamh. You fool. I miss you terribly.

I cried walking down Kilburn High Road after meeting Niamh that morning. I couldn't stop thinking of the blood running from the needle-mark in her wrist. I hated that house. I hated and feared Niamh's world. I was so shaken I didn't feel a bit like working. I had to remind myself I had a job to do.

I followed Niamh's directions to the Bridge Tavern. There was a gang there from Carrick-on-Suir, including a young couple who had got married a week before at the church at Kilburn's Quex Road. One man couldn't afford to work because he would lose his rent allowance so he did the double. He signed on and also took casual work from the sub-contractors (the "subbies") at the morning hiring fair outside the Crown in Cricklewood, a place he thought I should visit. The married couple were here because they were fed up with Carrick-on-Suir. They enjoyed the freedom of London. And yes, there was plenty of work. London was good as long as you could put up with the accommodation problem. This gang from Carrick-on-Suir were glad they were in England, they were street-wise and they had no over-optimistic expectations.

Hold on. This doesn't sound right. The social-worker-and-poverty-nun version of emigration which was dominating the media that year argued that young people arrived in London expecting the streets to be paved with gold. They got an awful shock in the cold light of dawn. They probably got picked up under the Prevention of Terrorism Act and were subjected to vicious anti-Irish prejudice. Eventually they would expire on the streets for want of a priest or social worker to rescue them.

But this crowd from Carrick-on-Suir didn't fit that picture. I realised then why the social workers used to sneer at the emigrants' grapevine as a source of information for young people going to London. Tut tut. Those young people listen to their friends home for Christmas in pubs. Of course they should come to us professionals instead. The social workers were painting as bad a picture as possible in order to justify the need for their services. (There was never yet a report written by social workers that didn't conclude there was a need for more social workers.) And the media lapped up what the social workers fed them. Shock horror. The plight of the Irish in London. I remember the *Sunday World* reported on a mass murderer in Cranley Gardens at Highgate who chopped up homeless young men and shoved their bodies down the sewer outside. Nilsen was his name. The *World* described this as the sort of fate that could be expected for an Irish emigrant in London.

No wonder I got on the wrong side of the social

workers when my programme was broadcast. I undermined their authority. This was to be the start of a pattern that I have observed ever since. I report on an issue like emigration, unemployment, travellers or whatever. I speak to the people directly concerned, that is, the emigrants, the unemployed, the travellers. And afterwards the social workers or community representatives come back at me and complain that they weren't consulted. Social workers, I was to learn, are very arrogant people.

The Bridge Tavern was good. The first lesson I learned was that people are willing to be interviewed. I've often been asked how I get people to open up to me on the programmes I make. And the only answer I can give is that I ask the questions and people are willing to answer.

I would speak to the builders the following Monday morning. I would do more pubs. A bit of music. And Niamh's contacts might work. And get an Irish stripper in Soho. Serious? Yes. Colm Keane, my mentor in RTE at that time, had discussed my programme ideas in detail with me the week before. Get as much variety and interest as possible into the programme. And make it move fast. But Colm, how will I meet a stripper? Go to Soho, for fucksake, and ask around. I didn't think I could do it. The idea of sordid Soho frightened me but now I was determined. Soho it would be.

After two good days around Kilburn and Archway I took the tube to Picadilly Circus. Out from the station into the roar of traffic of London's West End and then around the corner to Soho and the Live Girls, Peep Shows and the Adult Books and Mags. The peep shows of Soho were a lot ruder and more revealing in 1984 than they are now. I went in with my 50p. There were cubicles to stand in and you could bolt the door behind you. There was a smell of disinfectant and I suppose it was just as well the floor and (I hope) the walls got scrubbed after customers had been in there. I put the coin in the slot and a letter-box size viewer opened up. Just in front of me, behind the perspex, a young woman performed a display that couldn't have been more revealing. Then after thirty seconds the letter-box closed and I realised I should have had a supply of 50p coins if I wanted to fully enjoy the show. With only one coin you had barely time to get your fly open.

Back out on the street. Who could I speak to? I was too scared to go into any of the sex clubs. Young Irishmen in Kilburn had warned me that you pay two pounds to get in and twenty pounds to get out. After you get past the door there's a membership charge of a fiver. They offer you beer which you have to buy at six pounds a pint. (The beer was usually non-alcoholic. The clubs didn't pay a drinks licence.) Then a tip for the hostess. And you wait for the show that never happens. Some Corkmen told me all about it. There was no strip, the beer was cat, it cost twenty pounds a man and everybody left in bad form.

I decided to record some sound effects of Soho. There were people canvassing passers-by. Come on in mate. Live show inside. Two pounds.

There was a young woman with a Dutch accent. You like to come inside see the show? I showed her my tape-recorder and asked if I could talk to her. I was scared she would call on some dress-suited gorilla to deal with me but she turned out to be friendly. Yes, she would talk. Tell me what happens in here in the peep show? You put fifty pence in the slot, a little window opens up and a naked girl will dance in front of you for thirty seconds. Thirty seconds? That sounds expensive! She laughed. This is Soho. Everything is expensive around here.

I asked her if she knew any Irish women working the Soho sex scene. She had one Irish friend. Her boyfriend stripped in a gay club. Ask for Dave at the Manhattan Male Revue bar in Rupert Street. She was sure he'd like to talk.

This I had to see. The bar was just around the corner. A tall, dark-haired, good-looking young man was sitting by the door. Are you Dave? Yes. I was apologetic to Dave. Could he see his way to doing an interview with me? But Dave was only too delighted to talk. I've learned a lot of things about people in the years since 1984 and one of those things is that some people are very vain. For Dave a media interview was the high point of his stripping career. His big break.

Dave brought me into a club next door and behind one of the areas for the peep shows. A woman in a dressing-gown sat smoking a cigarette. 'Allo Dave. 'Allo luv. She was on her break from performing in front of the letter-boxes. Dave led me up the stairs to his room.

Dave had a drawly, middle-class Dublin accent. (He was from Blackrock, as I learned the next month when his horrified sister contacted me in RTE to say that his family had recognised his voice on the radio. They hadn't seen him for a long time. I told her where his club was in London.) I think Dave was gay, even though he had a girlfriend whom I met. He was affected and a bit camp. He told me he was straight but I still can't believe somebody would do his job if he weren't homosexual.

"I enjoy dancing. I definitely could say that I'm a good dancer so, the audience enjoy that and they give you tips as well. Usually the wage is twenty pounds for a six hour shift which is a half-an-hour dancing, a half-an-hour break, a half-an-hour dancing and so on for six hours.

"I myself have enjoyed very much being a male stripper and a male dancer as well. For one thing I like dancing and also, I suppose, it's a maybe narcissistic feeling or whatever, to have people looking at you and getting excited by your presence or whatever."

This guy was brilliant. I was calm on the outside but inside I was jumping up and down saying, yippee! It was

11

the first time I experienced the thrill of going in somewhere difficult, finding the bottle to do my job and then getting something really good on tape. Something listeners would remember and talk about. Something colleagues would ask about and critics write about.

I pushed Dave further. If he was really straight, did it trouble him to have an audience of homosexual men watch him strip?

"Not at all. I like working in gay places. One of the things about my own club, which I'm interested in, is that it actually gets young people off the streets. There's five of us dancers work here. We've a very friendly atmosphere. We all get on very well here. We're all friends. And it's actually very enjoyable to dance. A lot of people think it's very dark and shady and sort of perverted and corrupt and whatever, and it's not at all. As far as I'm concerned it's just a completely normal, healthy desire. I'm not gay. I just like working a gay club."

As I listen to my tape of Dave, I hear myself handling this sort of interview just like I do now. Don't challenge him too much. Wouldn't we all love to make our living by stripping off in front off a bunch of queers in a seedy London sex club? A completely normal, healthy desire. Just nod along and then gently prompt him to give away a bit more.

I had enough on tape. I hated this place. I wanted to get out again. Like Jack getting back down the beanstalk once he'd stolen the giant's gold. Goodbye Dave. It was really nice meeting you. I won't tell you that I find this place oppressive and sordid and I don't want to stay in your company for any longer than I have to.

Back to the tube station and onto the Bakerloo Line. I listened to snatches of my tape of Dave. Yes. It was all there. You did it Paddy. Yes. I felt very good about myself. Change at Baker Street and take the Jubilee to Kilburn.

Niamh and I were going to meet Pauline in town. A Saturday night off for me, good work done and I would enjoy myself that evening in the company of two of my favourite women friends.

Niamh and Pauline had been pals in Cork. They knew each other through me. But they hadn't kept in touch in London. They had different lifestyles. Niamh was into drugs. Pauline was into having a good time. And because Pauline was, and is, so good-looking she's never had any shortage of men to take an interest in her.

Niamh and I found the pub near Victoria where we were to meet Pauline. Niamh saw her first. I'm sick, said Niamh. What's wrong with you? I thought it was some kind of drug problem. No. Not that. Niamh felt sick because Pauline looked so stunningly beautiful. Pauline can outshine every other woman in her company by wearing jeans and a jumper but that night she had gone to the trouble of looking her best. Niamh suddenly realised how she had neglected and abused her own body with drugs. Niamh's teeth were rotten. Her cheeks hollowed. Her body skeletal.

We enjoyed ourselves that evening. I told the girls about my stripper in Soho and Pauline kept us laughing with stories about the wealthy Arab men she met through her work in the Kuwaiti Embassy. The Arabs spent lots of money on her. She had been to Ascot and all that. But no, she wouldn't marry. The rebellious, fun-loving Pauline could never be a Moslem's wife.

I think meeting Pauline was good for Niamh. Going back to Kilburn on the Underground, Niamh told me how much she enjoyed the evening because, for the first time in years, she hadn't been in the company of junkies. Well, good for you, Niamh. She told me she was fed up with Tommy. He was no good at his trade any more. That was robbery. He sat in front of the telly all day. She would come back to Ireland with her daughter. She would change her life. She would get off drugs. She would use that honours degree to try to get a job.

Niamh, I can't tell you how happy you made me feel that evening. Back in the house we hugged each other. It's so good to see you again Niamh. It's great to be your friend. I lost you for too long.

I know, Niamh, you meant what you said about giving up drugs and I believed you. But I understood so little about drug addiction. I didn't realise just how hard it would be for you. I couldn't know then that you would fail.

I stayed in Niamh's house for the next two nights. It was in the heart of Kilburn and it suited me. I've come to recognise drug-user's houses because of my experience then. The people living there were runny-nosed and shivery. They sat for hours in front of the telly. There was a smell of dirty socks. There were blackened spoons everywhere. That was because the spoons were used for cooking the heroin, or something like that, before it could be injected. Apart from these spoons there was an almost complete lack of cutlery or delph.

The most telling thing about a drug addict's house is that it is clear that money is available for nothing else except drugs. Niamh had only one light bulb upstairs. It was transferred around from the bedroom to the bathroom to the loo or wherever. The kitchen had the remains of two leaky washing-machines from skips. One for washing. One for spinning. There were two televisions in the front room. One with sound. One with vision. I remember I got a Sindy doll in Argos for Niamh's little girl to help say thank you for putting me up. Niamh seized the doll and hid it. She had a present now for Christmas.

Niamh told me about drugs. She explained that the first thing she did in the morning was to arrange her fix. She

14

could cope with everything else after that. She looked after her daughter well. She didn't care for the bunch of Cork city and county drug morons who were always in her front room watching telly.

I interviewed Niamh for my programme. That tape is very precious to me. Niamh talked about the housing list. She got a good house for her daughter and herself but she resented Brent Council who categorised her as an ethnic minority. She saw no reason why she should have got better treatment than an English girl in the same circumstances. Brent's argument is that they monitor ethnicity so that discrimination does not occur. Niamh said if they applied the rules fairly there would be no need for ethnic quotas. She told me why she came to London.

"I was pregnant and I decided I couldn't stay in Ireland and London was the only, the best possible place for me to come to. When I arrived here first of all, being pregnant I was classed as a homeless family, so it was the responsibility of the borough council in which I was living to house me. I was put in a bed-and-breakfast until a flat was found for me. I was given three offers. You don't have to take the first one. And I was given a very nice flat."

(How things have changed. These days she would be offered a flat in the tower blocks of Stonebridge Park in Wembley and if she didn't like that it would be the streets.)

"Here I'd be called a single parent or a single mother. At home I'd be called an unmarried mother. You can see the difference in attitude in those very terms. There's no stigma attached to being a single parent in Britain, in modern Britain. There is still in Ireland. That's one of the reasons why girls leave Ireland and come to live here."

She was right there. In the Archway Tavern on Friday night I met a young woman who told me it was obvious why she was in England. Take a look at her belly. The father worked in a chemical company in Castlebar. He wanted nothing to do with her. The pregnancy would get her out of the hostel. And, off the record, she told me she was providing urine samples for her friends. They would be diagnosed pregnant and present the results to the local council.

Niamh's male prostitute from Cork turned up to meet me on Sunday. Niamh was out when he arrived and I didn't realise that this fellow was the interviewee I was expecting. It never occurred to Tommy to tell the guy who I was. This rent boy got tired of waiting for the RTE man to turn up. Niamh came back after he was gone and probably a good interview was lost.

My last job in the Kilburn area was outside The Crown in Cricklewood. At six-o'clock on Monday morning I went into the Cricklewood Cafe. The men, young and middle-aged, were having breakfast and waiting for the "subbies", that is the sub-contractors, to come by to hire them.

One young man had the classic accent of the West of Ireland. The Wesht.

"I'm here looking for work myself. For labouring. The subbies'll be coming by, in their vans, and you'll have to ask him if they'll be any oul' job going."

Your first time here?

"Oh Chrisht no. I'm coming here a while now. If I don't get shtarted up with the first subbie, I'll try agin."

I went outside to the darkness on the Broadway. This was exciting. A whole world I knew nothing about even though my father had worked for many years as a builder with Wimpys in London. Hundreds of men in the darkness waiting on the vans. You could just see the subbies through the van windows having a look at the labourers on offer. A hiring fair. I've heard a lot about this place in the years since but I knew I had a good and original bit of work done that morning. Not bad for a first-time attempt at making a radio programme.

By nine in the morning I was in McDonald's on Kilburn High Road having breakfast. I bought the *Daily Mirror* instead of *The Guardian* or *The Times*. I liked the idea of being a tabloid journalist. My programmes would be high quality but they would be listened to because they were interesting and entertaining.

I knew I had a good programme under my belt. I had surprised myself with my success. I never knew I would be good at that kind of thing. I mean look at me. A university graduate with a sort of English middle-class accent and here I had been listening to rural and working-class Irish people as they experienced the sharp end of making their way in London. And, do you know, people were so nice and so friendly? I had been nervous coming to London but I had really enjoyed myself. My life was changed by those few days. I've never looked back.

Niamh came back to Cobh for Christmas in 1984 but she could never settle. She went to London for St. Patrick's weekend to see Tommy. He was on remand in Pentonville. It was for stealing a handbag. Afterwards, I'm told, she couldn't wait to get back to London. I felt exasperated. What did she see in Tommy? Had she forgotten all she said about making a new life for herself? I was really disappointed that Niamh was gone to London by the time I came to Cobh at Easter. I could only hope she would stay off drugs.

I saw Niamh again in August. Jacinta and I were in London on holidays and we called to see Niamh in Kilburn. She was still on drugs and looked it. We stayed with her for a few nights and we did our best to persuade her to come back to Cobh again so she could try to get off drugs. She said she would come to Cobh to see her family but then she would go back to London. That was good enough for me. At least we were getting her out of that house of heroin addicts.

As we drove the M4 headed for South Wales Niamh's little girl and our little girl fell asleep. Niamh told us about drug addiction. When she took heroin the first time it was the best thrill she ever had. When she stuck the needle in, the immediate physical feeling was like taking off in a plane, being shot backwards in your seat. The mental feeling was an indescribable elation. She had found the drug that was for her and yes, she wanted to do it again.

She used to tell herself she wasn't addicted to heroin. It was just a thrill that she enjoyed when she could. Addiction crept up on her without her realising it. Her life soon reached a stage where heroin became the first priority of the day. Where am I going to get a fix? How will I get the money for a fix? And everything else took second place to heroin. Once the fix was sorted out the rest of the day, parenthood, money, dealing with the police, could all be seen to. Niamh said heroin gave her a tremendous feeling of confidence in coping with whatever else the day might bring.

We reached Pembroke Dock that evening and drove into the queue for the car ferry. Niamh said she needed to go to the toilet. Jacinta and I stayed in the car for more than half-an-hour with the two children. The rest of the cars went on board and we waited for as long as we could. Fuck you Niamh and your fucking drugs habit. And of course you're bringing enough gear with you to keep you well for your stay in Ireland. If the customs search us I swear you're on your own. Jacinta went to the ladies and called out for her. I'm coming now Jas, came a voice from a cubicle. Back in the car she had a sheepish look about her. She didn't want to talk about what she was at. I felt depressed.

We reached Cobh the next day and enjoyed ourselves there for a few days. Then Jacinta and I and two other old friends of Niamh went off to West Cork for a few days. Niamh chose not to come with us. She had to get back to London. Damn you Niamh and your drugs.

When we came back from West Cork my dad told me that Niamh's brother had been phoning for me. He was the eldest of the family, eighteen years older than Niamh who was the youngest. I phoned him and he told me Niamh wasn't going back to London. I said that was the best news I had heard for a long time. Then he asked me if I was a drug taker. I told him I was not. He said sorry for asking but he had to find out. He had been away at sea most of his adult life and had never really known much about his baby sister or her friends.

He organised medical help for Niamh. She got a place in St. Martha's Therapeutic Community in Jonstown, Co. Meath. It was a centre for drug addicts, like Coolmine, near Dublin. Before she went there Niamh told Jacinta and me that once she was off drugs she would go back to London and Tommy. After all, she just wanted to get off drugs, not change her whole life. No Niamh. Please don't go back to London. To get off drugs you have to change your whole life. Stay away from London. Stay away from Tommy.

A few months later Niamh was allowed out of the drug centre for the first time. She came to Dublin. Jacinta and I brought her little daughter, then aged five, to see her. The little girl had been living with relatives in Skerries. Niamh stayed with us sometimes in Dublin. She told us a lot about the centre. She said she had learned that she had an addictive personality. She stayed off alcohol because it might lead to drugs. She told us that she had learned she had low self-esteem. This had never occurred to me before but it rang true when she said it. Niamh was highly intelligent but always seemed most comfortable in the company of the virtually brain-dead. She never stood up for herself. She always tried to gain the approval of others. When she got over drugs, she said, things would be different.

It was heartbreaking when Niamh had to say goodbye to her little girl to go back to St. Martha's. Once Niamh visited us with a young Spanish friend. A very beautiful girl from Madrid whose wealthy parents had sent her to Ireland for treatment for her drug addiction. The Spanish girl hugged Niamh when she cried as she said goodbye to her daughter.

Niamh told Jacinta and me about AIDS. It was a nightmare when they were tested in St. Martha's. People were scared to ask each other the results. Niamh was lucky. She had used needles and had once loved a bisexual man but she had escaped the virus. Looking back on it, I realise now how little I had thought about AIDS in those days. When I'd called to Niamh's door in London in December of 1984 and I'd seen the blood running from her wrist, it never even occurred to me that she might be in danger from this new, exotic condition called AIDS. I was just terrified of what she would do to herself through drug-abuse.

Niamh and I talked about making a radio documentary about drug-treatment. When she had recovered from her drug addiction I wanted her to take a tape-recorder to St. Martha's and ask all her friends there about trying to get off drugs. Of course you would be a good broadcaster, Niamh. I'll be the producer of the programme and help you all the way. Just get yourself clean of drugs and then there's nothing you won't be able to do.

In June of 1986, about eight months after she first went to St. Martha's, Niamh arrived at our door in Devenish Road in Crumlin and said she was going back to Cobh. She was off drugs and wanted to be a mother again. Niamh, are you sure you're able? Please finish the course of treatment first.

She couldn't be persuaded. She rang her brother in

Cobh, to tell him she was coming. Then she said he wanted to talk to me. Paddy, either you drive her back to Navan now or I will as soon as she reaches Cobh.

I feel the same as you do but I can only plead with her. She's twenty-eight years old. I can't force her.

Niamh moved to Cobh and Tommy came from London to visit her. They went to West Cork together for a few days. Tommy made more of these visits over the next few months. I used to speak to Niamh about Tommy. If you're with him, please stay away from heroin. That's okay, Paddy. Tommy's been attending a clinic in London. The only drugs we would get in West Cork would be a bit of blow.

Niamh phoned me in Dublin on 10 October, 1986. She had heard I wasn't well. It was my usual problem. Eczema on the soles of my feet which had left me crippled for a couple of weeks. She told me she was going to West Cork again to meet Tommy. I'm glad Niamh lied to me. If she had told me the truth, that she was going to London, then I would have been burdened forever after with the knowledge that I could have tried to stop her.

A few days later, the evening of 15 October, 1986, we got a phone call in Dublin from my brother in Cobh. Jacinta took it. Niamh was dead. She died in Tommy's sister's flat in London. She died of a heart attack after injecting heroin.

Chapter Two

IN A BOOKIE SHOP

Killinarden Estate, Tallaght, Dublin;
27 May 1986

It was Wednesday. Dole day. The men moved between the Killinarden Inn and the bookie shop next door. I was talking to people in the bookie shop.

Just one woman in there among the press of men. She was middle-aged and faded-looking with long greasy hair and nicotine stains up her fingers. Six months later I saw a woman like that in a bookie shop in New York. Perhaps every bookie's has one. It was the men I was interested in today. This man was in his late thirties. He looked pale and sickly. How were the horses going for him?

"Not very well. Lost a few shillings. Came up for a few pints and watched the races on telly."

Is that an expensive way to spend the day when you're on welfare?

"Of course it is because you have all day to do it and every day. Unless you sit in the house and looking at the missus. So you take a chance. If you have a few shillings you can have a bet. If you don't win you go home. If you win you have a few pints. Then you go home."

So no more pints today?

"No. I'm afraid not. Not even for the weekend. I'm afraid I'll be in now all weekend."

So you have to go home to your wife later and say, look I'm sorry, we have no money left for the weekend. Does she mind you gambling?

"She minds all right. She goes mad if I go to the bookies. Usually she takes her chance of getting the money first. If I get it first I'd be gone, you know?"

You're serious?

"Yeah I'd be gone. Be gone with the money if I got it first. I'd say, to hell now. I'm going to have a good time today and worry about the consequences after, you know?"

Does that put your marriage under strain?

"It's bound to. What chance have you got? If you have a job, fair enough, it keeps you out of harm's way. But if you haven't a job you go for a few pints or go for a bet. When I had a job it didn't worry me because I used to have the few shillings to spend. But now it's putting an extra strain on her cos I expect the same spending power as I had before but now I ... it means that I have to hit her money, you know?"

When will you finish betting today?

"Me last race is run, I'm afraid. I'm after blowing the lot on the last one. Money is gone now for the week. It will be next Wednesday before I'll have another bet. I'll just expect her now to buy cigarettes for the week and that's it after what I gave her."

And can I ask you how you and your wife split the welfare money for the week?

"I gave her sixty-five and that leaves me with twenty for myself. That's gone now. I had two pints and a few bets."

Does it get you down?

"Of course it does cos I wake up in the morning and what am I going to get up in the morning for? I'm just going to stay in bed now. At least I have the television to watch but otherwise than that I just stay in bed until half-two, three-o'clock and then I get up and have a bit of dinner and whatever is on television, watch it then. It means I won't go out now until next week. I'll just stay in the house."

His face was familiar. He told me he used to be a bus conductor. That was it. It was a route I'd travelled on for years. Other busmen have told me since that he was always in trouble at work because of his gambling. The offer of a redundancy package had been like an offer of heroin to a drug addict.

Another man I spoke to in the bookie's was given fifteen pounds by his wife for himself. She looked after the bills. And so it went. Grown men reduced to the status of youngsters waiting on their pocket money. The woman in an unemployed household has still got a job and responsibility. The man has no job. No responsibility. Over the next few years I came to realise why so many mothers on welfare choose to stay single or feel they are better off deserted. Unemployment makes men useless.

Bernard was in his mid-thirties. He had five children. He told me about his day out.

"I do two lucky fifteen bets. It's like a Yankee. I do 5p each way. It'll cost me one pound odd. That's it. You just hope for the big one. This is the one day of the week that I can afford to have two pints. That's it. Wednesday. This is labour day. Collect our few bob today. That's the big thrill for the week."

Bernard must have been proud of Christine, his wife. That's the only way I can explain why he wanted me to meet her. I think another man in his circumstances would have felt that he had a lot to hide. Later that day I called to see Bernard and Christine at their home in nearby Cushlawn Park.

"My husband is unemployed four years. It's not for the

want of trying. But no go. It's got to the stage now where he's lost all ... you know the age thing. They just don't want to know. They want the young kids."

"It's very hard for me, a man, to have to stay at home, do the washing-up, take care of the kids. It's very hard for a man to face that every morning and every night for most of his married life when all he wants to do is go out, do an eight-to-five job and be happy with that."

"Some days we've had no dinner. I'd be waiting for him to get paid or maybe some weeks I have an ESB bill. You've got to give them so much off. Right. You buy a few packets of soup and that'll have to do us for the week. Packet soup and potatoes. The schools they want money. Every second week they do be sending the kids home. They need such a book cost one pound twenty, two quid. We need copies. The teacher said we need copies and you haven't got it. You've to cope with that as well."

"On the first two years after I lost my job with the Port and Docks we weren't too bad. We were holding our own. We were paying our bills. But then it starts to get worse. You start to borrow off Jewmen. And finally when you get rid of the Jewmen you start to go to anybody you can get money off. I'm up to my eyes in it. Credit unions. Banks. Anybody who comes to the door, I owe to."

"Most times I would go without rather than have anybody go without, including him. But I'd have to pretend to him that I had something to eat. Sometimes he'd know. He'd say that's stupid. He'd suss out after a few days that I hadn't been eating. And then he'd start giving out to me and one thing leads to another thing then everything is brought up and it's, who are you going to pay this week? I'm not answering the door for you, I haven't got the money. I'm ashamed to answer the door. I know how the men feel coming to the door. I hate that. Not being able to pay them."

"Well there's a simple rule for answering the door that I find simple. The wife doesn't find it that easy. If you don't feel like facing them yourself you send one of the kids out. Tell them you're not there. Mammy and Daddy has gone out. That's normal procedure. If you do face them it's the credit union or the Jewman or the coalman or the milkman. It's very embarrassing to tell them you don't have the money to pay them. But me and her do row. Your marital status becomes two people putting up with each other. It can get violent because the man tends to go out and drink and get into what sort of different divilment and he'd come back and probably clatter the wife."

"There's a lot of violence. From him. Not as much as it was. But the chances are there that it could get worse. There was a lot of violence at the start of me marriage. Basically through drink. On his behalf. Getting involved with the wrong people. Coming in well on. Locked. And of course, three-o'clock in the morning, course you're going to say to your husband, where the hell have you been? Or whatever. And that's all you'd have to say and then I'd get bet up. I've had many, several hidings. I used get terrified of him. Even when he was sober then I got it. Even today. Even today. He's out and when he walks in I tense up. I just tense up. There's always that chance there. He can be very violent on drink. But he can also be violent when he's sober. I can never relax."

"It's something I'm not proud of. Never will be. I mean I'll have to live with that for the rest of me life. But at the time it happened ... you're not hitting out at your wife and your kids. You're hitting out at yourself. You're the one that suffers in the end. But just like my wife's breakdown, that was my breakdown, when my reality disappeared. It's a time when you lose all your pride. You lose all interest in yourself and in your family. That's when the violence comes in. Because you have no answer for anything and

26

the only way is to strike out. And unfortunately you're not out mixing with people. The only one you're talking to is your wife and she's the one that gets the brunt of it. I've lived to regret it. Yeah. I was ... I was in court over hitting my wife. It's probably forgiven but never forgotten. It's in the background. It's something that's with you all the time. It's something that you have to live with. And you know that it could happen again. As you get older, you can restrain yourself a lot easier. I mean I find it a lot easier to restrain myself. I don't get so hot-headed. But I used to lose the head very easy. Especially with the frustration of debts and Jewmen and your wife nagging you for money and you're not working, you haven't got it."

"There was very few good times in our marriage. We've been married thirteen years and most of our married life he's been unemployed. He's had jobs but they never lasted long. It's been pressure all the time. I've had to go out to work when I can. I haven't got a happy marriage."

"Since I became unemployed the good times have been few and far between. Maybe once I could say there was a really good time. We missed all the bills. The debt men. We sacrificed our labour. We went to Butlins for a week. We came back different people. Literally different people. She got pregnant. We had a high time."

"What is there for us? My children. They're not going to get nowhere. You go looking for a job. Lower class area. That's it. I hate this. What we've got."

"Only recently, she couldn't take the pressures of debts and bills. We knew that court proceedings were being taken against us and fears that she had from her childhood with police dealings ... without the actual proceedings the knowledge that they were there was enough to drive my wife to her breakdown."

"I've got scars on both wrists. It was ... just everything got on top of me. February it was. Just everything.

27

Arguments over money. Him arguing with me over nothing. I've got brothers as well. They're unemployed too. And they'd come out, stay for days. They can't take a hint. I only had so much money and they smoked a lot. And you couldn't sit there and not give them cigarettes and the extra plates of food. It just all come on top of me. Him arguing with me and telling me to tell them to go home. And I was trying to tell them and not hurt their feelings, y'know? All this. I just couldn't take any more. I knew what I was doing. I knew what I was doing now. I went up to the bathroom. Everyone was asleep. I went straight into the bathroom. I just wanted to finish it. That was it. I couldn't see nothing to life. The way I looked at it was ... of course later on psychiatrists told me think about your children, think about your husband, think about all this ... but at the time I didn't care. Me mind went blank. I thought about nobody. I just cut me wrists. I wanted to finish it. I cut my wrists and I needn't tell you there was blood everywhere. I went into me bed. I lay at the side of the bed. I just put me hand out the side of the bed to let the blood drip. That's what normally you do I suppose. I don't know. And I cried a little bit. I cried because I was saying goodbye to the kids in my mind. You know that type of a way? That's the way it was. Cos I was sure I'd be full dead. I'd be dead in the morning and that'd be it. Course at the time I made a mistake. I suppose it's as well now it didn't happen but I did. After about an hour I was losing that much blood that I got cold. I was freezing. I just happened to take me hands up and I did this. I put me hands up against me chest. I dropped off asleep then I thought I was going. This is it. Me hands up ... it stopped the flow of the blood which saved me life. The next morning he woke up and the blood had stopped. Had congealed. He found me. Sent for the ambulance. I don't even remember much of what he said to me. I was in a world of my own. I was raging I was still there. I can't even do this right."

"I had cooked the supper for her. Myself and the wife had our supper. She had a bath and went to bed. I stayed up. I played darts. In the house I have an old dart board and I throw the few darts. I never noticed anything strange. I went to bed late. And the following morning I discovered it. Lucky enough it wasn't too late to do something about it."

"I survived. I remember I woke up. I was looking at the ceiling and when I heard him, he was beside me and he said what the ... he went mad. Me brother and all was here. I didn't say anything. I was just gone. I was too depressed. I was still here and I was going to have to face the consequences and all because I was still here. The questions. The asking. The snooping. The neighbours. He was a nice doctor. He was talking to me. I didn't answer him. The ambulancemen were very nice. They brought me to James's. They fixed up me wrists there. I heard the doctor say she's very badly depressed, we'll have to admit her to Loman's. I was there for two weeks. Depressed and crying and the usual. My wrists was sore. I had to get them dressed every day. They were fairly deep and they'd put stingy stuff on them. The people that were there, they were depressed as well and I thought, I'm in a madhouse. They put me on tablets. Anti-depressants. They put me on antibiotics for these, they got infected. I was home after two weeks. Me husband dressed these for me every day."

"That was three months ago. Things have been fairly good since. But the danger is still there. You can sense it. The least pressure now on her can bring it back on again."

"I couldn't say I wouldn't do it again."

Three months later Bernard phoned me to ask me to visit Christine in hospital. She was back in St. Loman's after another suicide attempt. One day, the following year, Christine opened the door to me at her home. Her face was blackened with bruises. One eye was nearly closed and there were finger marks on her throat. He had beaten her again.

The interviews in the bookie shop and with Bernard and Christine formed the first programme in the series I called *Faces of Unemployment.* Over the summer of 1986 I made thirteen programmes in this series. I dealt with the black economy, emigration, crime, debts, mortgages, job schemes and other things. I tried to plan the series in advance but I kept finding that the programmes would take on a life of their own that was different to what I intended. When I went into that bookie shop in Tallaght I meant that to be part of a programme on how unemployed men spend their time. Pool halls and so on. But I met Bernard and he brought me home to meet his wife and the programme took on that shape instead. I was fascinated that it was possible to make a radio programme by using a bookie shop as a starting point and then just seeing what happened after that.

I was surprised by how candid people were prepared to be for a microphone. Not just Bernard and Christine but men in the bookie shop as well and other people I would meet on dole queues. While I was doing the *Faces of Unemployment* series, colleagues in RTE and the public in general began to ask me how I managed to get people to be so open with me. It's a question I'm still asked to this day and I still don't know the answer. I just ask people to talk to me, that's all.

Chapter Three

Europe

West Germany,
Arbeitzamt, Goethe Platz,
Munich; 25 April 1988

It was six in the morning. The place was full of winos. I'd never really thought about poor Germans before. I had some notion that only the Turks and the blacks would be poor here. But these were rough-looking, white-skinned men with the dirty smell of homelessness off them.

The Arbeitzamt is the labour exchange. Men come here to pick up casual work. Employers phone in and the job is announced over the public address system. If you want the job you put up your hand and the official calls you forward. But a lot of the men here, I guessed, were just looking for a place in from the cold.

I'd been told back in Dublin that this would be a good place to look for Irish workers. I flew in to Munich the evening before and now I was starting work. I'd already made programmes about emigrants in Britain and the USA. So now try Europe. Starting with Germany.

I wandered among the jobless men. There were Poles, Turks, Yugoslavs. And there were Irish.

You're from where? RTE? They couldn't believe it.

Rodney was about twenty-one. He had a strong Cork accent.

"I left home. I went to America first and I lived in New York for almost seven months. And I was deported from America. And then I was back home in the Lough in Cork for two months and I couldn't get work back in Ireland. I had friends here in Munich so I came out. You can make better money in the States but you take bigger risks."

How did you come to be deported from America?

"I was working with the horses around Central Park. I came home for a holiday for ten days but on the way back emigration gave me some fair old stick because they saw that I had been already over there and that my passport was stamped. You're back for another holiday after only ten days? The last straw was they found me with a cheque from work.

"I was put into jail over there because I had to fight my case. I had a work contract for two years and I thought I could fight it. I was deported for five years. They stamped my passport. The worst of it when they do deport you is they make sure they really catch you. They put me on to a British Airways flight. They handcuffed me up to the moment of the deportation. You can imagine arriving on a flight in handcuffs. You can imagine what people thought."

Meeting Rodney was one of the moments in my life when I asked myself if I'm just very lucky or truly talented or maybe a mixture of both. I was thrilled. My gamble coming to Europe had paid off on my first morning's work. I knew from dole queues back home that West Germany was becoming an important destination for jobless Irish people. I'd already reported many times on deportations of illegal Irish immigrants from America. Now I was exploring an alternative to the USA. With Rodney I had made a damn good start.

Work was slack in the Arbeitzamt that morning. I stayed with Rodney for about two hours. Nothing doing. Then

Rodney saw a man he knew who ran a furniture-removal business. Rodney intercepted him before he approached the Arbeitzamt officials. He was taken on. I don't know where Rodney is now (he said he would get back to his girlfriend in New York when he could find a way) but I think with his attitude he's always going to get on okay. Rodney told me to come along to Jollies pub near the Goethe Platz that night. Like everywhere else in Europe, the local English pub was a good place to meet Irish people.

Jollies was good. There were English, Irish and English-speaking Germans. Did Irish people like Germany? This man came to Germany after he had given up training for the priesthood.

"It's different. Marriage is seen as a very old-fashioned, traditional thing. I work in a bakery. The man I'm with has his wife and he has his sweite frau, his second woman and the two women know all about each other. It's not something that appeals to me. It's a German way that marriage won't last. You're going to be divorced. If I get married I want it to be the giving of all. This isn't a place for families either. There's the culture of kinderfeindigheit which translates as enmity towards children. The Germans have their one point two children and they think having more than that is really anti-social. It would be hard for an Irish family to get a flat here. That's why you'll find it's mainly single, childless people here."

There's a colony from Thurles in Munich and a lot of them were in Jollies that night. Friends have followed friends over the years. They have each other for company but romance with Germans happens too.

Over his pint, Frank told me about German girlfriends.

"They go out on a night and they expect you to go home at ten-o'clock. I'm not into that crack. Like if I go out on a weekend night, I'm after working a hard week, I want to go out and enjoy myself. Have a good few pints. And I don't find going out until ten-o'clock my idea of enjoyment. The Germans have a different view of enjoying themselves. They go home earlier. There's a reason for that too but I'm not going to say in case my mother's listening."

I realised that in Germany the main connection between drink and sex was simply that the pub was a good place to meet. Then go home at ten-o'clock to enjoy yourselves. A German doesn't have to get drunk before sex is allowed. Not like Ireland where casual sex generally happens after closing time.

My Cork friend Rodney pointed out to me that Munich is full of queers. The homosexuals wander naked in a part of the Englischergarten, Munich's huge municipal park. I was shocked the first time I came across these men on a Sunday afternoon. I'm not making a value judgement on them. I just found that kind of public nudity hard to take. Rodney, talking to me in the pub, made what I thought was a very perceptive observation about German culture. In a men's toilet in a pub in Ireland it's considered polite to make small talk with the man standing at the urinal next to your own. It might be a remark about sport or maybe the weather. The conversation goes on while you're washing your hands. (I've found that a strong, working-class accent is the one you're supposed to use in Irish public toilet culture. It pays as well to have at least some knowledge of sport so you can bluff your way with the fellow at the urinal next to you.)

The rules of behaviour in a German public toilet are quite different. As Rodney said to me, if a German leans over to you from the adjacent urinal he is not making small talk. Your only response must be to clench your buttocks tight together and get out.

That's the way with German culture. Not at ease with casual conversation. Not as friendly. Much more formal than Irish culture. It's rude in Germany, as in France or North Europe generally, to speak to a stranger. In Ireland it's nearly rude not to speak to a stranger you find yourself in company with. I'm not saying that the Irish way is better. More than once I've had long train journeys spoiled by a stranger who wants to talk when I would rather read a book or just look out the window and enjoy my own thoughts. But over all I prefer the Irish way. I love the informal atmosphere of an Irish pub. You meet people, drift off into other company and so on. The pub is neutral territory. In North Europe people do a lot of entertaining at home where much more restrictive rules for socialising must apply.

Irish culture is much closer to British culture than we admit. True, the English are more reserved and private than the Irish but once you've met the Germans, the English, by comparison, seem like positive fireballs of spontaneity and passion.

Netherlands
Den Haag; 10-11 May 1988

I had one address for Den Haag. (I'm following the example of the Irish here in calling this city by its Dutch name, Den Haag, rather than the English version, The Hague.) I'd got the address two weeks earlier from an Irishwoman in Madrid. Her boyfriend, Tony, was one of a colony from Rathdrum, Co. Wicklow, who have settled in Den Haag. She'd written to him so the men were expecting me. Thirteen of them sharing a big, old, red-brick house.

The men were from all over Ireland. They ranged in age from their twenties to their forties. Some single. Some married. What they had in common was that all thirteen had been unemployed back in Ireland.

I was touched by the welcome they gave me. I was only doing my job but these men seemed to really appreciate me coming to speak to them.

"I was unemployed at home. A few of my friends from Rathdrum were working out here so I phoned the company in Dublin. They said sorry Tony, you're too small for that sort of work. I think they must have only wanted big Mayo men or something like that. So I forgot all about it. Then one day last September the phone rang. There was two jobs going in Holland for myself and my brother if we came out the next day. I'd been unemployed two years at home so I jumped at the chance."

Michael had a wife and four children in Mayo.

"I don't like working away from home. The days are very long when you're away from home. You miss out on an awful lot. The children miss out. Maybe I can put up with it but they don't understand it. And in later years when you think the family should be close and it's not, it's split up, then you've nobody to blame only yourself because it's you that left it."

Do you get back to Mayo much?

"Every three months you get a break of a week. Then you come back. There's nothing in Ireland."

Pat had a wife and two children in Millstreet, Co. Cork.

"You can't live on fresh air. What they give you on the unemployment back home, it wouldn't keep the kids. My kids are so young like, they don't even understand where I'm gone to. They're too small to understand that I had to go. I phone my wife twice a week. She's had to adjust to living alone ... I hope."

There was general laughter at that. But marriages can be strained by this type of split. John was from Kilkenny.

"I have the same story as the rest of the lads. I was unemployed back home. I'm here four and a half years."

Are you married or single?

"Married ... well ... married, yes."

What do you mean?

"Ah, we got separated. But I think we're probably going back together again now. I was at home a few weeks ago and we discussed things and I think we're going to try it again. I have five children. I came here after we separated but my contract is finished in the summer so, get a few pound together and go home for a few weeks."

Can you put your marriage back together if she's in Kilkenny and you're here in Holland?

"She's willing to come here. We're going to try it somewhere. We've talked about it. It's difficult for the kids but I'd like to raise my family in some kind of decent standards and I can't do that in Ireland."

This surprised me a bit. There's plenty of visible drugs and prostitution in Den Haag but John's idea of a decent upbringing was that the children should not live in poverty. Good for you, John.

Michael had a strong, West of Ireland accent.

"I was ten years in England. I have four children. I lived in London with my family and I moved back to Ireland because I got a small farm of land and that was the sorriest thing I ever done was to leave London. In Ireland I couldn't make a go of it."

Michael was bitter about what had happened to him. He didn't want to spill his sadness on tape. He waited until we were all in the pub. Recently he had to miss the eldest child's Confirmation. Every three months there were tears at the airport. Then he cried on the plane. I felt sorry for Michael and the other older, married men. Working down holes in Holland. Work that Dutchmen won't do. And living like billetted soldiers, three and four to a room. Denied the privacy of their own home and the company of their wives and children.

I got drunk. Of course I wanted a big glass of beer. Not

those little measures that the Dutchmen were drinking. I think my Irish hosts decided not to warn me how potent the damn stuff was. No. I couldn't make it back to my hotel at the Holland Spoor. It was, as they told me, a dangerous part of town at night. So they put me up in their house.

I remember vomiting in the shower. I couldn't find a toilet. I barely knew where I was.

In the morning the men had gone. They left at five, as usual, and were now digging up the roads of Den Haag. Gerry, a young man from Kilkenny, stayed behind. We wandered downtown to get some breakfast.

Den Haag is a nice kind of town. Lots of red brick and greenery that made me remember the part of London I spent my childhood in. I had a hangover but I felt good about my work so far.

Gerry showed me the sights. The biggest culture shock is sex for sale. Some apartment blocks have a resident prostitute. She normally has an advert in the foyer. Reduced rates for OAPs.

There's the street with the women in the windows. I don't usually record people secretly but I had to get a sound effect of this. I had my tape-recorder in a shoulder bag.

"You like to come inside?"

Sorry?

"You speak English?"

Yes.

"So you come inside?"

You're very nice. How much are you?

"Hundred guilders. A fuck or a suck."

A hundred! The other women are charging fifty!

In a cafe, Gerry said she probably thought I was a rich American. That's why she tried twice the going rate. She was trying to charge me all of thirty four Irish pounds rather than seventeen.

"On this street it's all legal. We're often down here because we drink in a pub near here. A Scottish pub called the Peter Pan. There's never any trouble down here, even at night time because the pimps make sure nobody gets bothered. And there's no danger of AIDS or anything else because you must wear a condom."

I said to Gerry that I thought the arrangement here was much better than in Dublin where women hang around the canals or the quays at Benburb Street. It was obvious as well that Dutch prostitutes were healthy women, not like the beer-bellied, leathery-faced women who were on Dublin's streets to pay for a drink or drugs habit.

Gerry agreed that the Dutch prostitutes we saw were very attractive. Like models. But, he said, there are other streets where sex is sold much cheaper by drug-addicted women. So whether or not you have prostitution legalised and supervised, as it is in Holland, you're still going to get the poor drunks and drug addicts who will sell themselves in the back streets. A Benburb Street in every city.

Denmark
Copenhagen; 14-17 May, 1988

I had no contacts for Irish people in Copenhagen but I knew by now just to look for the local English pub. I found the John Bull. Near the city centre.

It was about seven in the evening. Happy hour, which meant that the drink is only very expensive instead of being totally prohibitive. It was a lovely, sunny evening and people were sitting at the tables outside. There were Dublin accents here. Two men in their thirties. It turned out they had been here eleven years. I asked them if they were married or single.

"That's a terrible complicated question. I've been married here. I've got a five-year-old son. I'm separated from my wife. I would probably feel I've got a better relationship with my wife since I'm separated. We've both decided we don't need a divorce because we get on well anyway. I mean we go with the child, meet, go and eat together. There's no problems there."

I saw that in other parts of Europe too. In Johnny Granville's bar in Paris an Irishwoman introduced me to her ex-husband. They were out together in company.

"People should not dislike one another just because they've decided not to stay on the same path."

Who has your son?

"She has him on a daily basis. I have him every second weekend or whenever I want to. On occasions when she's going somewhere I just look after the kid."

"Just as a coincidence I have the same situation but my son is two and a half so I started a bit later than Eamonn. You split up and afterwards you realise that the child's happiness depends how you get on together. There's no point in arguing with each other. And then you put that above your personal differences. And then the same situation. I have my son four days a fortnight and he seems quite happy."

As I listen to my tapes of these men now, six years on from that evening in Copenhagen, I envy them the relationship they described with their wives and children. My own marriage break-up is full of pain. I often meet the kids, maybe go to the movies, take a walk or whatever. I've decided as a result of these meetings that family quality time is crap. The real way to be a father is to be there for routine things. Making lunch. Helping with homework. Just being there to talk and to experience them growing up. I'm not that sort of father any more. I'm glad for those men in Copenhagen that they seemed so happy now but I feel the whole thing must have involved more pain than I understood when I spoke to them six years ago.

A Dublin man brought me to a bloody boring part of the city called Christiania. It's an old fort and it's full of hippies. They sell dope openly here. Like Amsterdam that I was glad to leave earlier that morning. Dope smokers are bores. This Dubliner was a bore. An aged hippy. He was getting me a world exclusive, man, on Christiania. He knew people on the committee for the area. If I stayed with him he could help me apply for permission to interview people. Because I'm telling you man, nobody's going to talk to you anywhere in Copenhagen because they don't trust the media here. And your radio programme will be shit.

Thanks for your help but I really do need to get back to my hotel to get more tapes. No. No need to come with me.

It was a great sense of relief to shake this fellow off. He was the sort of person I could imagine getting his way with young, impressionable people. A creep. He was like the parasites who tried to latch on to me in Amsterdam.

The hotel receptionist was an unexpected bonus. She spoke Danish so I didn't realise at first that she was Irish.

Geraldine joined me after she came off duty. We spoke in the hotel bar.

"I came over here as a student and during one of those summer periods I met a Danish man, fell in love. That broke up. Then I met another one and I live with him now and we have a baby."

Will you marry?

"No. I'm not marrying because if I marry, the father is named as the father of the child. And who's to know that our marriage will last? If we separate now he has no rights over her. If I marry he gets custodial rights also. And I know that he loves his daughter very much and would never allow me to take her out of the country."

You were back in Ireland for nine months teaching. What are your feelings about Ireland now?

"The mentality of Irish men I found very hard to cope with having come from Scandinavia. I find they have very little respect for women. They don't mind paying for your drink. In fact they take insult if you offer to pay for your own drink. But they have very little respect for the woman as a person."

You've had two strong romances here in Denmark ...

" ... and a lot of casual relationships."

Do you like Danish men?

"I prefer their attitude to women. They have more respect for women than Irishmen do. Because sex is not a big deal here, it's just part of life, they're not looking to ... how do you put this on Irish radio? The only thing an Irishman is thinking of the whole night he's with you is, are we going to get to bed? Or is it up against some wall somewhere? Whereas here it doesn't really enter into things."

Two days later, Sunday, Copenhagen Celtic had a match. That was a team made up of Irish and British emigrants here. I realised when I met the team that I'd already interviewed a lot of them in the pubs and fast-food restaurants where they worked around town. A lot were from the Crumlin\Walkinstown area of Dublin. Colonies of Irish tend to come from particular localities. One or two start the trend and a lot more follow.

It was a beautiful, hot, sunny morning. The girlfriends were there at the sideline, sunbathing in their knickers. The bikini top seems to have become a redundant piece of clothing.

Your name is?

"Gida."

What's it like to have an Irish boyfriend?

"It's tough. They're spoiled. And they have their religion. They're brought up different to what we are. We are more free."

What do you mean spoiled?

"They don't do any work. They're used to their mother goes home and do the work. He's changing a little bit."

And your name?

"I'm Shenna. That's my boyfriend. The bloke over there. I'm with him three years. Compared to Danish behaviour and Danish attitudes, Irishmen are a bit brutal. What fascinated me was they took things a bit for granted. Whether that's life or girlfriends. When it's girlfriends they just expect things to be a certain way and there is no two ways about it. It can be a bit difficult to cope with."

I knew what she meant here. Shenna's boyfriend was from Crumlin. I think that Dublin men can be particularly blinkered about things. "End of bleedin' story."

"Culturally we differ. You don't at first notice it. Then after a while you get close. The behaviour in the home. They don't do anything in the home. Over here you have a Danish boyfriend he helps you. With the Irish you're sort of a housewife."

So what attracts you to him?

"His brutality. He's different from a Danish guy. That's the challenge. I know Irish guys think the Danes are weak and soft. It's hard to explain. The Irish are different. They are running away from any conflict. They find it hard to sit down and say, listen we've got a problem, we need to talk about this. It's easier to go out on the piss. Sorry. And just come home a day or two later and think everything is okay again."

He's done that?

"That happens. I think I accept more with him being Irish than I would from a Danish bloke. Perhaps because

I'm still fascinated by what is his real personality. The Irish are not so open. They talk a lot and they're jokey and they're extremely friendly but they don't actually tell anything about themselves whereas Danes tend to talk a lot about themselves and their lives, you know?"

Do you think you might settle with him? Marry? Have children?

"Ooo ... I don't know. The future is too uncertain ... "

YAHOO! WHOA!

Copenhagen Celtic scored. The match ended soon after. A draw.

Chapter Four

THE WOMEN OF TALLAGHT

Post Office-cum-grocery, Kiltalown Housing Estate, West Tallaght, Co.Dublin; 6 July 1989

I was nervous. This was my first day on a new radio series for the summer schedule to be called *Queueing for a Living*. Whatever I got on tape over these next couple of days would form my programme on the Monday. I'd made lots of programmes about joblessness over the years but this would be different. I would simply find a queue where poor people wait (and there are plenty of such queues) and I would see what people might talk about. *Adventures with a Tape-recorder* had been a sort of working title in my mind over the previous months. I knew that what we call "vox pop" work, that is, just meeting people at random, had worked well for me. I'd often found that the most remarkable story that people would have to tell was nothing to do with what I was asking about.

I'd chosen Kiltalown post office in West Tallaght because I'd meet deserted wives there. Thursday is the day when post offices throughout the country pay out Lone Parents Allowance. Up until 1990 this payment was called either Unmarried Mothers Allowance or Deserted Wives

45

Allowance depending on which sort of lone parent a woman was. The women queueing here from the housing estates of West Tallaght were mostly deserted wives. The unmarried mothers, who usually have only one child, are more likely to be found in corporation flats such as those of the tower blocks of Ballymun.

This is the very edge of Dublin City, in the foothills of the mountains that stretch into Wicklow. Beyond the last concrete blocks and paving there are grass, heather and sheep. And up Killinarden Hill are the fields where, in September, the children collect magic mushrooms, or psilocybin as this hallucinogen is scientifically called. There are farmhouses and sheds from a bygone age when Kiltalown and Killinarden were the demesnes of wealthy landowners. Today these names belong to the vast, bleak housing estates that are the welfare ghettoes of West Tallaght.

The men in the queue were collecting dole money. They had already queued earlier in the week at the dole office in Tallaght village to sign on. The queue from the post office hatch inside the shop stretched around a corridor surrounding the grocery area then out onto the road and up the hill.

The first person I spoke to was a man of about forty with a strong Dublin accent. He'd been a barman all his life but had been unemployed for two years. Publicans can always get younger workers who will work for nearly nothing. This ex-barman was one of those men who had never lost his anger about unemployment. He loathed this Thursday ritual.

"This is Kiltalown. I live over in Fettercairn which is about two miles away. When you come over here it's at least 150 people in front of you. In the winter you'd be drown-ded. You wouldn't see it in Russia."

There were two Soviet dissidents in the queue. Her

name was Tanya and she was from Moscow. His accent wasn't Russian.

"I am from Mexico. I was a student of politics in Moscow. The KGB wanted to recruit me to work in South America but I refused."

This couple had jumped plane in Shannon in 1985 en route from Moscow to Cuba. Her father's academic career had suffered because of her illegal exit from the country and now they were both facing expulsion from Ireland as they had only working visas, not resident visas. I tried to find out what I could for them from the Department of Justice. I could find out nothing. The Department wouldn't even discuss the case with me. It's my belief that at that time, in return for Aeroflot business in Shannon, our government was turning a blind eye to human rights abuses in Russia. This cynical auctioning off of Irish foreign policy used to be lauded by the Left as standing up for Irish neutrality.

People in the queue told me they would prefer to have been able to collect payment in their local post office. For a lot of them this would have been Springfield. Later I phoned An Post who assured me that people can choose to collect their money in whatever post office they wanted. A puzzle. Either the hundreds in the welfare queue were grossly mistaken and were putting themselves to unnecessary trouble every week or I was getting the wrong information from the confident, well-educated press officer of An Post. This press officer was the sort of person whom journalists get their information from all the time.

The press officer was adamant. She had checked with the section concerned and had no doubt. Eventually the Department of Social Welfare solved the mystery for me. It was on their insistence that people could not choose the post office in the privately-owned Springfield housing estate. As a matter of policy, welfare queues are confined to council estates such as Kiltalown. So An Post was at least technically correct and could carry on claiming that people were jamming into the grocery in Kiltalown on a weekly basis because they liked collecting their money this way.

I interviewed one woman as the queue made its way into the grocery shop and along the makeshift corridor. I found myself squashed between two women in their mid-thirties who didn't know each other then and still don't. I have remained friends with them both ever since. The more reserved of the two, whom I'll call Margaret, spoke about the poor queueing arrangements. She had heard discussions on the *Gay Byrne Show* about how these things could be improved. She used to be a shop steward in Cadbury's. All right. I could do with speaking to somebody like her for the programme. I made an arrangement to meet her that evening. I expected the interview to be confined to an earnest and considered set of views on welfare matters. As it turned out, I couldn't have been more wrong.

The other woman I was squashed against, I'll call her June, was a hit with me from the start. Would it be better for her husband if there was a purpose-built welfare office as Margaret wanted?

"I haven't got a fellah. He deserted."

Do you think that unemployment led to his desertion?

She laughed. No. That wasn't it. And then she gave me her address. I called later and she brought me in.

"I was in hospital having our last baby and my husband left me for another woman."

Is that what broke up your marriage?

"Partly. It was an awful lot to do with the likes of blue movies and porno magazines in the house. He watched them rather than sleep with me. He'd wait until I was going to bed and he'd get out of bed and he'd come down and watch them on his own. He got great joy out of them. It annoyed me because I had no husband in bed with me when he should have been there. He was downstairs all the time. And I won't tell you what he was doing with himself and I caught him but ... "

And did you say to him that he should be more interested in you and less in his porn movies?

"Oh, he'd say there was nothing wrong with it, y'know but, it's wrong when you're watching them over and over again. It started four years ago. He got money and got a video. He started off getting maybe one movie a day, and then it worked out that he was paying thirty pound and more out of his redundancy and he just kept watching them and watching them."

And did you ever watch them together?

"I watched them at the beginning. I thought they were funny but then I saw how warped he could get from them. I mean, when we were together first he'd never do that on his own. We had a good sexual relationship and when he started watching these, that went out the window. It started off as a joke but then it got very, very serious. I think anything for a laugh, but not that. When it interrupts my sex life, that's serious."

You have a steady romance with a man now, but because of the cohabiting rule you would be cut off your deserted wife's money if he were to move in with you. How do you feel about that?

"Well you can have a boyfriend but you can't have him staying with you so therefore your sex life is non-existent unless you have it when your children are out. You're like an unpaid whore. Your boyfriend has to slip in and slip out without neighbours seeing."

So sex is a day-time thing?

"It's a morning-time thing when they're at school. And then you've got your knocks on the door, neighbours coming in for cups of tea and they're disturbing you. It's frustrating. And you have the guys from the Department of Social Welfare watching the house in case you have a man with you."

She described the social welfare officer who was checking up on deserted wives for cohabiting. The description fitted one given to me by my Soviet friends earlier who thought the KGB had followed them to Tallaght.

I heard a lot more about cohabiting over the next few days. I don't think it's acceptable that a lone parent can have her money cut off "pending a Departmental investigation" on the charge that she is claiming fraudulently. I have met those women at community welfare offices, queueing up for reduced money until they get their payment book back for the post office. No proof is necessary. Just an anonymous allegation from a begrudging neighbour. Lone parents have plenty of those. Most of us have to have a crime proven against us before we are punished. The welfare recipient can have his or her money cut off on the basis of a suspicion. It's just one of the many ways in which poor people find their lives ruled arbitrarily by middle-class professionals.

Let me bring you back, June, to your husband. When you were in hospital, having your baby, he took the chance to sleep with somebody else. Did that hurt you very much?

"It was more hurtful than anything. It was because I was having his baby. Pity it wasn't somebody else's. It was like losing a child. Now I still have that hatred. I'd like to see him getting killed by a car and I'd laugh. That hatred is so bad."

And did you say this to him?

"It was after I came out of hospital with the baby. I'd found out for definite what he'd done. I was looking for my wages and he told me he hadn't got any. I had no money for nappies or anything. He was after bringing her off for meals, out drinking. He had a good job at this time but I had no money."

So what did you do?

"I threw him out."

How did you do that? How do you force a man to leave?

"I told him if he didn't go I'd stab him in his sleep. He knew I'd do it. Because I would have."

June went on to give me an example of just how odd her husband had been. One day she found her family photographs piled in a drawer. They had been kept in a photo album which had gone missing. Her husband explained that he'd sold the album which struck her as very odd. Eventually she found it. He had used it to keep a collection of his favourite pornographic pictures which he'd cut out of magazines. June took the album from the shelf to show me. Her family photos were back but you could still see the outlines of naked women. The colour had come off the pages and stuck to the plastic overlay. Me mother and father in with all the nudes.

I still see June from time to time. She's a woman who has seen a lot of life. She once worked as a prostitute in a massage parlour. She wouldn't talk about this on tape because even now, she's afraid the social workers might try to take her children. They wouldn't even have to show neglect and certainly in June's case, that would be impossible to show. And June doesn't want her children to know that she was a prostitute. At least not until they are old enough to understand. Which is why she has asked me not to call her by her real name in this book.

June enjoyed her work in the massage parlour. She liked the men as well. A lot of them were court officers as the brothel was near the Four Courts. She used to whip their bottoms. One fellow would crawl round and round a couch as she stood still in the middle with her whip. June said it was easy money. Any time she got a big ESB bill it was a case of getting out her whip and letting the brothel manager know she was available for work. She's retired now and resists all overtures from her old boss to come back. I can imagine he wants her. Her good-humoured approach would be very appealing to customers. For myself, while I have no interest in suffering pain, I find the thought of having to bare my bottom for her discipline to be strangely exciting.

The other startling thing about June is her appetite for sex. Once I called to her mid-morning and she hitched her skirt to show me her sexy knickers and stocking tops. No, she wasn't expecting anybody that day. She just enjoys dressing in a way that makes her feel ready for sex.

At one stage she seemed to be running a number of lovers simultaneously. One was a prison officer from a Co. Kildare town. Whenever he wanted to stay with June he would tell his wife that there were particularly important IRA prisoners being moved and he would have to work nights. So June would have her night out, lots of vodka and lots of sex. She has that sort of attitude to men. Her most remarkable lover is a deserted husband with children. I've often met him with June and I like him. He loves June and he accepts her as she is. I understand his feelings. June is great fun to be with.

One more thing I'll tell you now and this includes something that it's difficult for me to talk about. June's story about the pornographic films sounded familiar to me and to others who would hear it on the airwaves the following Monday. One listener even asked me if June was the same woman, known as Caroline, whom I had interviewed two years earlier for the *Pat Kenny Show*. She wasn't.

I'll tell you first how I met Caroline. In 1987 I was working on John Bowman's *Day by Day* programme. On 1 April, the day after Budget Day, the then Finance Minister, Gene Fitzgerald, came into studio to answer listeners' questions. This post-budget phone-in has been a tradition on radio since 1973. I was the producer on the 1987 programme and I was particularly interested in one caller from Tallaght who spoke about the effects of the budget on a low-income, but non-welfare family such as her own. It was Caroline. I phoned her afterwards and got to know her well over the next few months. Caroline and I grew close to each other. She began to tell me about her unsatisfactory sex life and eventually, using a slight voice distort, she gave me an interview about this on tape for the *Pat Kenny Show.*

Caroline and June both disliked their husbands' tastes in films and their addiction to masturbation. The two women also gave remarkably similar accounts of how pornographic films had gone from being a source of pleasure, or at least amusement, for both man and woman to being a source of conflict between them and an obsession of the man. But whereas June was ignored sexually, Caroline had been under pressure to take part in sexual acts which she hated.

I love to be kissed, Caroline told me. I'll never forget the way she said that. Her eyes were full of expression, her voice full of longing. She had a beautiful mouth and beautiful teeth. But kissing had ended in Caroline's sex life. If she cried with pain from her husband's version of lovemaking then that was so much more of a turn-on for him. Her only relief would come when he had satisfied himself. Afterwards he was ashamed and made the excuse that he did not want to make her pregnant.

Then one morning I called to Caroline and she was in the kitchen in her dressing-gown. I forget what I was trying to talk about but I remember how we read the look in each other's faces. So began a love affair in the Autumn of 1987 that would last just under one year.

I found myself thinking about Caroline all the time and my wife seemed to realise this from the start. Caroline and I used to have long phone conversations and we got on well with each other. Not since Niamh who died in October 1986, six months before I first met Caroline, had there been a woman who interested me so much. I used to joke with my wife and others that Caroline was now the SOP, that is, the Significant Other Person in my life, that Niamh had once been. But whereas Niamh and I had not been lovers since our teenage years the attraction between Caroline and I was strongly sexual.

It was Caroline who finished our love affair. She decided she wanted to make a go of her marriage. I found that hard to accept and eventually she fell out with me. She told me to stop bothering her. So we didn't speak for a long time. We're on talking terms again now, although Caroline has a rule that we don't talk about our past. I'll never forget Caroline.

Fettercairn Estate, West Tallaght, the next day

This was Friday. Day two of working on the first ever *Queueing for a Living* programme that was to be broadcast on the Monday. I'd had a very good and very long Thursday talking to people I'd met at the post office and I'd put off calling to Margaret, the former shop steward, until this, the next morning. When I knocked at the door a tall man in his underpants looked out the window upstairs. I told him I was from RTE and I was looking for Margaret. Yes, she had been expecting me the evening before and was disappointed I hadn't called. Come in. He was her brother, by the way. I was polite enough not to laugh at that. I'm sure he's laughing now as he reads this. Donal and I are good friends today.

Margaret told me she had been thinking through the things she wanted to say to me and had really had to prepare herself mentally. I apologised for not having turned up when I said I would. I wondered what she had been working herself up about. After all, I thought, we were only going to discuss how facilities for unemployed people could be improved. She was a former trade unionist and would be well able to speak on things like that.

Margaret brought me in to her sitting-room and told me about the husband who had left her.

"He had a drug habit when I met him. And I really thought it was such a shame. And he was a different person on drugs. He was a much gentler person [when he was on drugs, but not on drink, she meant] and I remember going with him to Jervis Street and I was Florence Nightingale and I was going to help him off drugs. But then he was okay till after we got married. He hit the drink really hard and it was like a different person. The drink just turned him into some sort of crazed animal or something.

"And I think myself now if he had been drinking when I met him I wouldn't have liked him because I used to run a mile from men who drank. But eh, I really tried. I tried everything. We went to the Rutland Centre, Stanhope Street and every time he drank after doing something like that he'd get worse. So the only thing he could do in the end was to run away. And I think now that it was he couldn't face the guilt of what he had done to me and the kids and all that."

What had he done?

"Well we learned so much in those centres about the damage that could be done to our children by his drinking and my reaction to it. It went into an awful lot about how he was affected as a child in his home and how I was affected as a child in my home. And it helped you to get in touch with some of the pain you felt as a child and just blocked down and ... I know with me now I can feel so guilty with the kids and that's another problem with me now that I might feel guilty one week about their father being gone and I'll go out and I'll spend extra money on them, y'know, which is wrong really." (She was laughing at herself here.) "I'm lavishing it on them trying to cover this guilt I do feel."

You say you came from a home background in which there was a lot of drink and yet you married a man who also had a drink problem?

"A lecture I heard. Usually in a home where there's an alcoholic parent, say there's nine in my family, well some of them will become alcoholics and some will go on to marry alcoholics. It's some sort of mood habits you pick up from your family. You may have picked them up from your mam or your dad. It's usually the mother comes off worst because she's reacting to the father. The father'd come in drunk and the mother'd start shouting. Then the kids'd say, I hope she doesn't start!"

You were twenty-nine when you married. Should you have stayed single?

"The whole thing was crazy. Before he ever left I used to leave and run to me mother, run to someone and then I'd bad-mouth him but then I'd go back. And when he finally left people were saying, ah, he's a bastard you're better off without him, but I was really hurting inside."

Did you say earlier that he was not violent on drugs?

"Yeah. I don't know why that is. He needed someone I think when I met him and he was so nice to me, even taking drugs. And he always had plenty of money and at the time I really didn't know where the money came from when I met him first. He was into fraud, like kite books [stolen chequebooks]. And he lorded it all over me. He gave me flowers and brought me for meals and stuff like that. I'm not making excuses. It was just part of my life."

How long did the marriage last?

"We were together five years and he's gone two."

Do you still think about him now?

"Yeah. I still think of him an awful lot."

Do you know how he is? How is his health now?

"Ehm ... I have a sister in London and the last time she saw him ... I believe he's very ill, with drugs ... ehm ... " (her voice was dropping now, then came back with a determined whisper) "he's HIV positive. And I have went and had tests done and we're okay. I've had two. They came back negative. It was only after I had the last baby that I started worrying about it and thinking about it, y'know, because the publicity started getting a bit more about AIDS and he had used then. He had mainlined. But y'know, that was a big trial for me but I got an awful lot of support from people while we were waiting on results and that. It took six weeks the first time. It was horrible. It was a horrible wait. But I went through an awful lot at that time. I nearly had a nervous breakdown and I nearly went into hospital but I didn't. I had to go on anti-depressants. And that was a horrible time for me because I always hated drugs. I could never understand people who took drugs. But I had to co-operate and take them and I got through it and I didn't go to hospital and I didn't leave me children. I couldn't go out for about three or four weeks. A friend of mine used to do the shopping. I couldn't bring the child to school. But they say if you come through something like that and you survive that you will never get that bad again." (She laughed.) "At least I hope not. But it was horrible. A horrible time."

I'll tell you one more odd thing that happened after I visited Margaret and Donal's house one day a few months later. I'd noticed an unmarked police car cruising and they had taken down the number of my Kadett when I went in to see Margaret. Later, out on the dual carriageway, the same car gave me a hell of a fright when it trapped me to the hard shoulder and forced me to pull in. The copper on the near side pointed to the kerb. I suppose his one visible epaulette gave him sufficient authority to do this. If I hadn't noticed them earlier, there's every chance I wouldn't have realised it was the police who forced me off the road.

Who are you? What's your address? Where do you work? The chief interrogator really seemed to feel he was on to something here. Then one of the policemen remembered me from outside Kiltalown post office in July. He had tackled me over the *Sunday World* coverage of a suicide in the area. A man went missing for weeks and was eventually found hanging in the waste ground where the Square has since been built. The body was found by an amateur botanist. My former friend Caroline had told me all about it. But a few weeks later the *Sunday World* thought it would be better to pretend that this horrible discovery was made by children out playing. Children still nightmaring as they remembered his blackened hands and so on. The policeman had made me carry the can for the *Sunday World*. Why do you journalists make up stories like that?

So the same garda couldn't forget me now. He thought it had been a very good radio programme that I made at Kiltalown. And he told me and the chief interrogator to be friends. Sure weren't we both Corkmen after all? We were all friends now and the police told me sure don't they know Donal well, the man I was visiting. That's a bad sign of course, as I well realised. Why did they know Donal well? What had he done to be on first name terms with the guards in Tallaght?

A few weeks later Donal told me the answer and I couldn't have been more shocked. Donal was an alcoholic and a heroin addict and had been using drugs all his adult life. I had never suspected it of Donal. For one thing he seemed too old. He was forty. Most Dublin junkies are much younger. And he didn't look a bit like a drug addict. Donal is a big, fit-looking man. I was astonished that Margaret had once again taken up with a drink and drug abuser but, even as this sank in, I remembered what she had told me about childhood experiences guiding your behaviour in later life.

I told Caroline about Donal. She was shocked. You didn't meet him did you? Stay well away from him, Paddy. He was a notorious drug addict back in the seventies. It turned out that Caroline and Donal had once been lovers. She was a homeless teenager and he had promised he would leave his wife. Caroline jumped Donal one day when he and his wife were out shopping in the supermarket in Ballymun. She hit him and smashed his glasses. You lied to me you bastard. Donal remembers the incident too. He told his wife he hadn't a bleedin' clue who this mad woman was.

Caroline was, I think, disturbed that I had met Donal. He represented a part of her life that she had left behind. Caroline would have preferred me to know her only as a responsible person who could do research for RTE and hold her own with the Finance Minister on radio. But I didn't think any less of Caroline when I found out that she had once associated with drug addicts. Rather I felt a sense of admiration for her. She had got out of all that. She had certainly not become a drug addict herself.

Caroline was right about one thing though. If you associated with Donal you'd end up in trouble. A well-known retired guard told me the same thing. Patrick, if you have Donal with you in the car then the guards will stop you. (The guard was a drinking buddy of Donal's and some sort of in-law of Donal's ex-wife. From his years in the drug squad I suppose he and Donal had a lot of stories to swap.) As it turned out I did eventually run into trouble with the law when I was with Donal. It was my own fault and I'll tell you about it later.

Donal and I are close friends now which makes him one of the very few men I know whom I can call close. Usually my closest friends have been women. Donal is in Alcoholics Anonymous and I think I believe him when he tells me that he no longer takes drugs. Pity he has to stay off drink. He was fun to be with and I love to have a pint in good company. But I suppose it's just the lot of the alcoholic that he can't keep drinking under control and therefore has to cut it out altogether.

Margaret and Donal moved to the West of Ireland in 1991. I often see them when I work in the area. Margaret loves getting out for a pint still, something Donal can't do. Both are working, at least part-time. They say they miss Dublin but would not be prepared ever again to live and to raise the children in any of the areas that they would be offered by the Corporation. They have had enough of drugs, crime and joblessness.

Eastern Health Board Office, Tallaght Village, Dublin; 25 August 1990

The welfare office at Tallaght Village is a handy place for me to work. It's back from the traffic and down a long gravel path, beside a garage that fits tyres. I can sit on the low wall of the garage and, from the time people come out of the office to when they reach me, I have a chance to introduce myself and explain what I am at before they have gone by. My microphone and tape recorder are on view. People are usually at least curious enough to stop and hear me out. Some post offices or welfare offices are jammed up against main roads or narrow pavements which means I can't get my pitch in before people have walked past. And people will always try to walk past when I first speak to them. They think you're some kind of beggar or somebody selling flags or lines or something. Or just a nut.

I settled down on the wall, happy to spend the next several hours meeting the women of Tallaght. I was in good form anyway because I was taking holidays in a few days after I had finished this programme, the last in the second series of *Queueing for a Living*. The sun was shining too.

My opening line was on the school uniform vouchers that were due that week. An Eastern Health Board industrial dispute had delayed this payment in Dublin, Wicklow and Kildare. The hope generally was that school principals would take an understanding attitude when the schools re-opened the following week and pupils attended in jeans.

One woman had recently come back from Kuwait. Her husband was still there. Iraq had invaded Kuwait a few weeks before but she didn't seem too concerned. She was more worried about the school uniforms.

"Well I'm just after moving in to the area and I need the whole uniform and I won't have the uniform for them by the time they go back to school next Monday cos it's not coming out till the end of September. They'll have to go in to school in what they have on them. It's either that or keep them home and I can't keep them home."

I was still curious about her husband in Kuwait. Was she not worried about him? She made me turn off the tape-recorder. Hopefully her husband would be blown up. He was a Moslem, you see, and you would have to be married to a Moslem to know what was involved in that. I told her

I wanted to speak to her about it. No, she wouldn't. I asked her to think about how it might help other women in the same situation. No. That didn't work with her either.

I met a Welsh woman with two dark-skinned children.

"Yes, I've applied for school uniforms. It will be the end of September."

The word "uniforms" sounds something like "YOU-NEE-forms" in her Welsh accent. Each syllable distinct. I love accents.

"I come over to Ireland for the first time in May, went home and packed and come here for good. I didn't come here to be on welfare. I want to get a job. I have a sister here."

And have you a man to go with those children?

"Their father and I was together for six years. Then when our first daughter was born, things just didn't work out."

Your children are of, I think, Indian appearance?

"That's right. They're half-Asian."

That you were from mixed racial backgrounds, did that contribute to your break-up?

"It did, yes. Their father was Moslem. He has totally different religious views to my way. And totally different way of life to mine, you know, and sometimes it doesn't work out. When somebody's very much, you know ... I'm not putting this over very well."

No. You're doing fine.

"When you live your life you think that's perfectly normal. And somebody who's got a totally different way of life, they think that's perfectly normal. And sometimes you clash."

Can you give me an example of that?

I knew the answer I was angling for here. I've come across the wreckage of Western-Moslem marriages too often not to know the pattern. I got the answer I expected.

"Well, women, to an Asian fellah, are second-class citizens. They're there to cook, clean and produce their children. They're not there to socialise. They're not there to have friends or go out. They're strictly for their man, to be there at home and for the children. And the way I was brought up was, yes, I can be a good mother and a good housewife, but I could also go out and have friends."

What about when you were dating him? Did you not realise what he was like?

"No. It's a totally different story when you first meet somebody and you go out together. You always see the best side of somebody in that sort of state. That first date you first meet. And it doesn't cause any problems at all cos you're trying to bring out your best in yourself and you don't bring any religious, political views into your relationship at first. It works out quite well in the beginning." (She was laughing.) "Very romantic."

So you don't recommend marrying a Moslem?

"Not very clever. No."

This was the familiar pattern of Western-Moslem marriage.

I had heard it before and have heard it many times since. Everything is fine during courtship but after marriage and parenthood a different set of attitudes begins to emerge from the man. This is something which the Western woman can't accept.

It's not just a problem with Moslems. How often have women married to Irishmen told me that everything was fine until the ring was on her finger? Among travellers, particularly, I find the attitude of men towards their wives to be one of ownership. But Moslems are the worst.

Would I want my daughter to marry a Moslem? If, some day, Kate wants to marry a black Irishman, Englishman, American or whatever I won't be concerned. But if she wants to marry a Moslem I will be extremely worried.

I said I would tell you again about Donal, whom I mentioned before and about the time I ran into trouble with the law. Now is a good time to tell you because the story, in a small way, involves the Welsh woman I have just told you about.

It was 1991, the 22 January to be precise. I know this because it was the eve of my thirty-fourth birthday. I bumped into Donal in town as he was bringing his son to the railway station. This was a teenage son from Donal's marriage in the distant past. Donal has fathered children for four women. His wife in Wexford had asked him to try to exercise some influence on his eldest son who had begun to get into trouble with the law. I walked to Amiens Street with them and, after the boy left on the train, Donal and I had a pint in the station buffet.

I gave Donal a lift to Tallaght and we stopped off in the Belgard Inn and had another couple of pints. Okay. You have to be careful about drinking and driving. Just a few weeks earlier I had interviewed Donal for the *Pat Kenny Show* about his experience of arrest and subsequent conviction for drunk driving. The Garda spokesman on the programme told Pat Kenny that he had to admire the candour of that drunk driver.

We were standing at the bar of the Belgard looking at the latest news from the Gulf War which had finally erupted a few days previously. We were on our way out when I heard a familiar Welsh voice from behind me. I would know that hat anywhere, she said. We chatted with the Welsh woman and her friend. She had loved doing the interview the previous summer and had got to know lots of people in Tallaght because of it. I bought a round of drinks. You're sort of expected to do that if you get a chance to thank an interviewee in a pub. Donal bought a round. He was terribly interested in the Welsh lady, he told me, and he thought her pal was interested in me. For fucksake Donal. Stop dreaming. I'm dropping you back to Margaret now.

We drove through West Tallaght. We were in Fettercairn Estate when Donal told me the police were following us. And the fellow driving was an officer he knew well. He's a complete bollocks, by the way, so be careful.

Great. How many pints had I drunk? Three was it? No, four, I think. It was over a lot of hours but I was surely over the limit. As the car turned into the cul de sac the blue beacon started flashing behind me. I don't know if I took a corner badly or what. I pulled in. Oh God. Is this happening to me?

They got out with their torches and came up to the car. Hello Mr.K----. And who are you? I gave my name. Have you been drinking? One or two low alcohol, I think. Will you breathe into that bag? A bit more breath please. He held up the crystals. Right. I'm arresting you for drunk driving.

Donal got them to agree to park my car in his driveway. Fettercairn isn't the best place to leave a car at night. I got into the back of the squad car for the short drive to the police station. I turned out my pockets at the reception then I was brought in. They would make a phone call for me if I wanted. I got them to ring Jacinta. Look love, I'll be a bit late. I'm in Tallaght Garda Station. I've been arrested for drunk driving. I know now that Donal rang her a few minutes later to tell her as well.

Then they brought me down a corridor. Everyone was quite pleasant and polite. It was a shock when they banged the door behind me and I was alone. So this is a prison cell. A bench with a thin mattress on it and a blanket that smelled of vomit. Graffiti all over the walls. I suppose I had probably interviewed a lot of the young men who had autographed the walls. I didn't feel a bit like leaving my own name there. There was a sort of sunken toilet which wouldn't flush. A guard looked in and told me the doctor would be along in an hour or so to take a sample. Just relax. Great. It was a freezing January night but there was no way I was pulling that blanket over myself. It occurred to me that it must be gone midnight by now. Happy birthday.

The doctor came. I opted for a urine sample rather than blood. I walked home to Crumlin, too agitated to want a lift in a taxi. Then I got up early and put together a successful report for the *Pat Kenny Show* on a welfare-related subject. I confided in a colleague in RTE who, I guessed, might know about these things and sure enough, he knew all too much about these things. It might never happen he said. Wait until your sample comes back from the lab in Athlone. But I felt I must surely have been over the limit. Jacinta set about learning to drive and I set about worrying how I would work without a car, not to mention the money we would lose on mileage claims.

About ten days later a registered letter came in the post. It was the test results from Athlone. I had been within the legal limit for driving.

I've digressed a bit. Let me go back to where I was before, that day the previous August outside the welfare in Tallaght Village.

Roisin was a noticeably good-looking woman. Late twenties, black wavy hair, ready smile and a friendly manner. She had a slightly more middle-class accent than most of the people here. It turned out she was from Rathfarnham originally. Certain words she said had a touch of New York.

Yes. She would love to speak to me. Like most people she was there for the school uniform grant. Roisin's eldest child was of school-going age. Roisin hated being on lone parent's pay and would much rather be working. She had a lively response to every question. Roisin was definitely somebody whom I would visit later at home.

There are so many things I could tell you about Roisin. She joked about coming back from New York, pregnant. She thought first her sickness was caused by jet-lag. When she realised the truth she wrote to the father, a young Italian. He arrived in Dublin but she made him stay in a B&B in town. Roisin pointed to the poster on her kitchen wall. It was a Levis ad. One of those hunky-looking fellows wearing only his jeans. That's as close as she would get to having a man in the house, she told me. The Italian had always treated her well but she couldn't live with him. No more than with the father of her first child.

"I just didn't like a man living in the house with me. I feel like I'm under a lot of pressure if there's a man around. Besides the fact there's ten times more work to do. I get real edgy."

Why is that?

"I'm not as comfortable when I'm living with them as when I'm going out dating. It's easier to go out and date and come home than to live with somebody and wake up beside them."

Why do you feel this way about men?

There was a long silence this time.

"I don't know how to answer that one."

Roisin laughed nervously, then she regained her confidence.

"Well my father used come home, say Thursday, drunk, Friday drunk, Saturday drunk. Sunday, like hangover day. Sometimes he wouldn't go into work Monday because he'd be spending the whole weekend drinking. And he was a gambler and if he lost on the horses he'd come home broke and really angry and take it out on my mother and give her hell. Sometimes you'd come home from school and this was going on."

You'd hear your mum crying or being beaten?

"We'd see her being beaten. I've seen him throw knives at her. I've seen him punch her. I've seen him put his hands round her throat, you know? And I don't mean he wouldn't just give her a slap he would really give her a beating. She's a very frail woman, sickly."

And what about you?

"These are just things I've seen all my life. And then there was my brother. He was very violent as well, you know, with everybody and ehm ... he used to give us a rough time. If he didn't get his own way he used to put his fist through the windows and stuff like that. This is how I ended up an unmarried mother that people are giving out about. It's because I can't live with men. I've had too many problems with them. Because if I could get out tomorrow and be like them ... most of my friends are married ... if I could get out and be like them, if I could live their lives it would be great but I can't do that now at the moment."

There was a question hanging in the air. Sometimes in interviews you can only skirt around a subject for so long.

Were you sexually abused?

"Yes. When I was seven years old or younger probably, I don't remember when ... for a long time."

By whom?

"One of my brothers."

Tell me what happened.

"Ehm. I can't really get into the details of that. I'm still kinda dealing with that. I'm still getting help today, you know, for ... my psychiatrist is still trying to get that out of me cos it's inside. I can't put it into words. It's not easy."

What kind of a scar does that leave on you, being abused sexually as a child?

"I wouldn't like to live with a man and have to have that kind of a relationship all the time."

You mean it put you off sex?

"I wouldn't say it puts me off. I just had no interest, just

68

isn't something I think about. I don't get frustrated in other words." (She laughed here.) "I don't sit around thinking, *I need a man tonight.*"

This is something that happened twenty years ago and you're saying it still has an effect on you today?

"It paved out the path for my life really, because if that hadn't happened I'd have had better relationships with men. And I probably wouldn't be a single parent."

Okay, so you're suffering still because of the abuse you saw your mum suffering, the sexual abuse you suffered as a child, you're suffering still. What can you do about that now? How can you help yourself?

"Just try to learn to accept it and put in the past, you know? I used to think I'd accepted it until I got into a relationship again and when the relationship got serious I'd run like hell, you know? Ehm ... I'm fine when I'm not having a relationship with anybody but when I am having a relationship with somebody it frightens me. As soon as it starts getting serious, I start getting scared. I'm trying to learn to trust and I'm just going through that and I hope that someday I'll get to the end of that road."

What you're telling me is that you and people like you who have suffered that way, even twenty years on, it still affects you ?

"It affects you I think for the rest of your life. I don't think you ever get over it and I don't think you should sit around feeling sorry for yourself all the time. I don't. But ehm ... I think I should have felt sorry for myself at one stage and maybe I wouldn't be the way I am now. Maybe I would have accepted it before. Instead I used to blank it out and I couldn't understand why I couldn't have a relationship. I couldn't understand why every time I got serious with somebody I'd just kind of freeze. I didn't know why I was doing that. I only know now because I'm going to get help."

You say you'd freeze. Do you mean when he'd put his arms around you?

"I'd just shiver, you know? As if, you don't touch me. It's like this guy ehm ... I used to go out with. He just used to reach up to get something and I used to duck and he'd say, I'm not going to hit you. And he'd get really annoyed because it was as if every time he lifted his hands I thought he was going to hit me. Subconsciously that's the way I reacted cos I spent all my life ducking from people and watching the blows."

Does it make you angry that you're still suffering for something that happened so long ago?

"It makes me very angry now cos I'm starting to think about it. Whereas before I used always say, ah, it's just me, I can't blame everything on that. But now I know that is the cause of all my problems. I think it'll always leave the scar. Depending if they get help on time or not. I didn't get help in time."

The brother who abused you, he was a good few years older than you. Have you ever said it back to him?

"Yeah. But you see when you grow up, what happens to you is you're totally convinced it was your own fault and you're told it's your own fault. You get told things and you believe them and you grow up believing them."

Your brother told you it was your fault?

"He said he was going through puberty when it happened. He told me I was exaggerating, that it had that effect on me. He didn't believe it had that effect on me and he still doesn't believe it."

Did it shock him when you brought it up?

"It frightened him. In case it would disrupt his life. In case I'd start telling people. But I'm not looking for revenge. I just wish I could take a tablet that would make it all never have happened but you can't do that either."

(Months later Roisin told me about her history of drink

70

and drug addiction. She had indeed taken a tablet to make it all never have happened. She wouldn't come for a drink with Jacinta and me because she stays out of pubs now. It was a part of her life that she had bravely put behind her.)

What do you think we can we do Roisin, to help protect our children from abuse?

"There are signs. I was very moody as a kid and my mother used to give out hell to me because I was so moody. But nobody understood why. Or if your kids don't like a certain person or are coming into money that you didn't give them. These are all signs. It's very hard for a mother to see but I still don't know how my mother never saw it. Because it happened during my lunch hour from school when he'd be on his lunch from work. It happened in the day-time. It happened at night-time. It happened at any time."

(Her voice was shaking here. But she was speaking with a steady nerve.)

"And I'd be crying and it would be, why are you crying? And I wouldn't say. Cos I was afraid to say. I was afraid of what would've happened if I told anybody. I was afraid I'd get into trouble. That's why people should listen to the children. A seven-year-old doesn't ask somebody to do things to them. A seven-year-old is innocent. You just don't think of things like that. You just want to play with your doll and pram."

Roisin told me she felt great after speaking to me. We stayed on, chatting for hours about everything. We liked each other. When I called a few days after the broadcast she told me her psychiatrist had heard her on the radio and had been delighted with her. A social worker from the North Western Health Board asked me for a copy of the interview to help him with his work with sex offenders. Roisin agreed and the tape was sent.

In 1992 I met Roisin while I was doing a report for the

Today at Five programme. It was the launch of an enterprise initiative by a body called Tallaght NOW. That stands for New Opportunities for Women. The venue was Kiltalown House, an old ascendency home now in community use. Roisin was there. She looked radiant in her black dress, outshining everyone else in the room.

I didn't like most of the women I met that day and they didn't like me. There were resident association types, welfare groups, poverty nuns, social workers, counsellors, aspiring politicians and individuals who introduced themselves as "resource persons". These were the women who claim to speak on behalf of the women of Tallaght. So you're Paddy O'Gorman. You're the one who is always doing down Tallaght, always reporting negative things like social welfare, drugs and unemployment. You never talk about the positive things like the shiatsu and aromatherapy groups that they run and could do with more government funding for. They accused me of damaging job prospects for Tallaght people.

Radio Soviet Union I call it. That is, the expectation that the media should not reflect reality in all its diversity but should instead broadcast material designed to help achieve socially desirable ends. It's a totalitarian attitude. No doubt, Russian radio listeners used to hear that Moscow's equivalent of West Tallaght was a wonderful place that everyone wanted to live in. What social problems? The result of this approach was widespread cynicism and disbelief among ordinary Russians about anything in the media. People knew they were being fed a line.

It would be very hard to find anyone in the welfare ghettoes of West Tallaght who wouldn't prefer to live in a private house on a middle-class estate. But according to the totalitarians this is not to be said. The alleged community representative for the area is to be regarded as the voice of the people. Journalists like me should not exploit poor, ordinary residents with no media experience. (One of the written complaints against me to RTE that I treasure most is from a community group who accused me of having interviewed people with no previous media experience.)

The poverty nuns seem to have a permanent hotline to RTE. The newspapers are just as bad. I call it In-Tray Journalism. Have a look at what's in the post and phone up whoever's name is at the bottom of the page.

The laziness and timidity of In-Tray journalists fits in with the aims of the Radio Soviet Union brigade. No need for journalists to visit welfare queues. That would be an invasion of privacy. Poor people don't want that. Let us tell you about poverty. Let us speak on behalf of the unemployed. Let us give you the line.

That's why the poverty nuns hate me. Because I don't take my line from them.

Roisin has talked to me a lot since about business ideas. It's fair to say that she shares my scepticism about some job initiatives. There can be only so many jobs in aromatherapy around Tallaght. But she says that Tallaght NOW helped her to get off welfare and become her own boss, something which she seems to be succeeding in doing. Her most recent venture in arts and crafts looks like it might work.

I hope Roisin has every success. I'll always be her biggest fan.

Post Office, The Square, Tallaght, Dublin;
30 July 1992

The Thursday morning queueing arrangements have improved for the deserted wives in Tallaght since I made the programme three years earlier at the Kiltalown post office. The Square has a purpose-built post office.

Some of the deserted wives I met in 1989 have got jobs in the shops here, as have the wives of unemployed men. This is part of a general tendency for men's work, that is work that would support a family, to be replaced by low-paid women's work. Throughout the country and, I suspect, throughout the Western world, families on welfare are finding that the woman is the partner with the best chance of getting work.

I like working in Tallaght. Over the previous two days I had been outside the dole office at Anne Street in Wexford town. Of the hundreds of unemployed people I met there, three were willing to speak to me. One was drunk, one was an eccentric Englishwoman and the other was a likeable young musician just back from Spain. He was good but I could hardly run a programme just about him and I needed something on the air for Friday.

Wexford had not been one of my better ideas. I had grown tired of repeatedly introducing myself and getting nobody to speak to me. I decided that Wexford people must be the most rude and boorish people in Ireland. (I had yet to try working in Tuam.) By Wednesday evening I was badly stuck. I had only one full working day left and decided I could take no chances. The women of Tallaght had never let me down in the past so the post office there the next morning, lone parents day, seemed to be a good bet.

My opening question was about divorce. They were almost all in favour. That's the way with separated people, not like the mixed feelings shown by the public at large. I wasn't really all that interested in divorce. For me this is just an opening line. I'm trying to find people who will talk to me about anything. And then I try to spot the women who I think have more to say and I ask if I may call to see them later at home. (Deserted wives are good candidates for this because they don't have suspicious, possessive husbands living with them. Men almost always come over all authoritative when I try to speak to their wives.)

I'll tell you first about a woman who invited me back to her home and who I liked to begin with but ended up feeling angry with as the afternoon wore on. She was back from London after her separation. She had gone on the housing list and had accepted a house in Jobstown, one of Tallaght's welfare ghettoes. I felt that she would have a lot to tell. I wasn't wrong.

I met you this morning at the Square in Tallaght. Can you tell me from the start what your story is?

"Well I have three children and he was eh ... he's Egyptian and he was just ... it was his culture. He was Moslem. And I wasn't allowed to talk to men. I wasn't allowed to ... you know the usual. So this was great at first. I was only seventeen when I met him so this was great cos he put me on a pedestal and I thought this was lovely and everything else and then all of a sudden I couldn't go out anywhere, you know."

What was the all of a sudden?

"When I married him."

You say "the usual". I know what that is because I've heard this story from other women who've married Moslems. But could you explain it for people who don't know?

"Well he ... for instance if his friend called to the door, he said to me you only have to open it half ajar, like a little bit. He said you don't open it the full, if it's one of my friends. And if I ever did there'd be war in the house. You know, he'd call me names and say you shouldn't have brought anyone in. Things like that. So I took that then. I thought, well that's good. He's only respecting me. And with my mother and father dead and this man all of a sudden coming along, seven years older than me, I was only seventeen, and taking me to dinner, treating me well,

I said, oh well, that means he must love me a lot. But he was, I didn't know at that time, he was having affairs, left, right and centre, you know? And then he said to me that certain clothes I'd wear ... like I wouldn't be able to wear what I'm wearing now ... "

You're wearing shorts ...

"Shorts and a T-shirt. He wouldn't have it. He'd say no. It came to the stage that I started to wear my dresses really long. He'd say to me, you'd be thought a lot of, you're decent and all this business. That was it, we'd had the two girls and then he said he'd love to try for a son. And then I ... me friends asked me to go out for a drink with them and when I said this one night to him he just said only prostitutes and whores go out, you know, and things like that and their husbands don't love them like I love you and you stay. So he convinced me, right, I'm not going out. So really for the years I was married to him I never went out until one day I rebelled. I went for a drink and got drunk and came in and he just looked at me and made me feel that I was a tramp even though I hadn't done it. And he'd been going out to clubs with all these women. And then ehm ... "

Irishwomen was it? Where were you living at the time?

"No I was in England. He was going out with eh ... Brazilian women. It didn't come out when I was married to him. It came out three years after I'd left him. He said I could have had any women. I could have had beautiful women. Not like you. Tall women. All this business. He said they weren't like you. Fat and all this business. So he justified himself walking out on me. So that was it and I just had it and I said to him, you know, I don't think I love you anymore, you know ... "

Tell me some of the other things about being married to a Moslem.

"Well when you're married to a Moslem you have to

respect them. They are the man and whatever they do goes. My husband never beat me but ... mental cruelty. If I talked to a maintenance man in the lift ... I needed my sink fixed once and all the man said to me was, I'll be up to you later on to fix the sink. And my husband went wild in the lift. He said, who are you? You don't talk to my wife. I mean the result was, I used to always keep my eyes to the ground and used never look up into any male's eyes at all because I knew an argument would break out. Then if his friends came and I gave them up a meal and if one of them dared to stare at me or to even ... I lost a lot of weight one time cos I couldn't eat and all his friend said to me was, you look well. And he just threw him out of the house. And he said to me, why did you answer him? I only said thank you to him and he went crazy because his friend commented on that you know."

Could you wear make-up?

"He told me I didn't need it. I used to put it on and then he said you don't need it and I said to him, well, I like wearing it cos I like to brighten myself up. I have brown hair but I used to always have highlights. I had highlights when I met him. And then he made me ... he said to me grow them out and have your natural hair. And my hair was so dark and everyone I met said it was horrible but no, Mohammed said this is how I want you. It's natural. This is how you should be. Eventually I didn't wear make-up. It was only a bit of lipstick and eyeshadow, but no."

In Moslem marriage when you have your period that has an effect on a man?

"Oh yeh, they don't come near you. They don't like cuddling you. They don't like anything like that because you're dirty, you know? And I begged him. I sat down one night and I said listen, I'm gonna stop loving you because you don't ... And he said you'll never stop loving me cos who'll want you with three children? Who'll want you? And, he said, you're fat. So he had me looking in the mirror saying that I was nothing. I didn't look nothing, you know?

"And then I just ... I left after I had my son. I went to social services and they put me into a battered wives home which is the only place I could get. Although I wasn't battered they put me there. And from there I went to a rat-infested B&B. And I said no, I'm gonna go home to Ireland. I hadn't been here since I was nine years of age and I didn't know what to expect ... "

It must have been a great relief for you when you finally got the courage to leave him.

"Ah yeah. I just didn't love him. The love had gone. Although his people, I'd been to Egypt twice and his people were very good to me. I lived with them in Alexandria. I loved them. Well I ... I couldn't go out in the sun, cos they wouldn't let me. I couldn't wear ... I had to wear the sleeves down to my arms and things like that. Eventually they convinced me, so I covered my hair as well. Now they didn't say I had to. They convinced me so I did it. I had a wonderful time with them. But you're totally in the house. I asked to go out one day. I said I'm going. I told his mother in Arabic, I'm going, I won't stay here. And they barricaded the door. They wouldn't let me out. Even New Year's Eve. He went out and didn't come in until twelve. I know it's silly to other people but to me it was important. It didn't matter to them. What are you upset about? But you're barricaded. They didn't let me go out at all without someone. Constantly."

This interview was about to take a turn for the worse. For reasons I'll explain, I decided not to broadcast any more of this.

"But I got on great with them. And they learned what I could do. Speak to people ... you know, life after death you know. I do readings. I've had this gift since I was sixteen. It's contacting people that have passed over. What happened was they found this out and I got frightened then and they decided they'd have to take me to a priest. A Shak. So they took me there. He turned all the lights off and started shouting at me and holding his hand to my head. He says, now she's supposed to faint. I had an evil spirit in me and I'm supposed to faint. It didn't happen. I just sat there. So he said it must be very evil. I was terrified. And he said to me, you tell me something about me. So I concentrated and tuned in and I got that he had stomach problems. And he said to my husband in Arabic, that's right, I have got stomach problems. So he came on again. Started screaming that I had this evil in me. And my husband never let me do readings again and I never forgave him for that. He used to say to me, you're a witch. What I think is he was scared I'd find out he was having an affair. Like what I do is like Doris Stokes, you've heard of her ... "

Yes I have. I've always thought she was a fraud.

"Really? I only gave her as an example. Like I only had people here before you came. Like I might only get three pound or four pound ... "

We decided it wouldn't be a good idea to let it be known that she had another source of income. It might affect her welfare pay. We talked about mediums. She knew a man in Dublin. I knew him too and I'll tell you a bit about him before I tell you any more about this woman in Tallaght.

The male medium, I can't remember his name, phoned me at work one day three years earlier. One of his customers had given him my name. I was, at that time, a producer on Marian Finucane's *Live Line* programme and he was looking to get into studio to do his thing on air with listeners phoning in. He had already had an outing on the *Gerry Ryan Show* and had got a lot of business as a result. I told him I didn't think it would suit *Live Line*. He said he had been called in by the guards to help in the search for a missing schoolboy, Philip Kearns. I said, tell me something about myself.

Well nobody close to you has died in the last two weeks. He was right. And you have a male relative, or a relative of your wife's, who is waiting for a heart operation or for whom there is some suggestion of heart problems or high blood-pressure. I thought through my own male relatives a generation older than myself. Then I went through Jacinta's uncles and her uncles' in-laws and sure enough, I think one of them was on some kind of pills for blood pressure. It's uncanny, but you're right again.

And he said you're thinking about getting glasses. No. You get headaches from reading? No. Now or in the past, some kind of eye infection or irritation? No. He guaranteed me that in the future I would wear glasses.

I'm told afterwards, by the woman who gave this man my name, that he told people the reason he didn't get on to *Live Line* was that Paddy O'Gorman was a Catholic bigot.

Back now to the woman in Jobstown. I said to her that people often long to speak to loved ones who have died. Their grief could make them vulnerable. I had a friend whom I loved very much. But she died through taking heroin ...

But she didn't kill herself deliberately, said the woman.

No. It had never occurred to me that she did.

She wants you to know that she didn't take her own life.

I explained that Niamh's boyfriend, Tommy, told me that he thought Niamh died because she took her habitual dose of heroin one day even though she had been off drugs for over a year.

She said to me the anniversary of Niamh's death was just coming up, or had just gone by. I told her Niamh died in October of 1986. It was July as we were speaking. Well there you are, she said.

I don't get anything from this Tommy person. (That's how she put it). I feel he must be dead as well.

I said that Tommy was a drug addict and there was every possibility that he was also dead by now. Every junkie's like a setting sun, as Neil Young sang. I hadn't seen Tommy since September of 1988 when I met him by chance one day in Kilburn.

Then the woman told me she kept seeing a black-haired woman. I didn't tell her that Niamh had light brown hair but I think she read my face and told me that some woman close to me has black hair. I didn't bother saying that Jacinta has black hair. I was beginning to get annoyed. It seemed to me that if something sufficiently general is stated then somebody is bound to fit the bill.

Then she told me that a male relative of my own or my wife's was expecting either a heart operation or had a blood pressure problem. Now where had I heard that before? I told her I wouldn't broadcast anything about her alleged psychic powers because I didn't think I should promote her trade when I didn't believe in it.

She seemed to respect my decision and I don't think her interview with me was a premeditated attempt to get publicity for herself as a psychic. But I still feel angry that people could be taken in by her. I wondered if she genuinely believed in her own powers. Or was she just a cynical confidence trickster as I believe Doris Stokes was? I'm still wondering.

One last thing. Three months later I was in London and I learned that Tommy, Niamh's boyfriend, was indeed dead. He died in Kilburn the previous year from drug abuse. So my Tallaght psychic was right on this at least. Was that just a shrewd guess about a drug addict? Probably.

Back to the car and I checked my diary. One more person I'd met earlier at the post office whom I said I would call to that day. She was in her early thirties, strongly wished to be divorced and would be pleased to speak further. Late that afternoon she brought me into her house in the shabby Tallaght housing estate known as Glenshane.

"Yes I would like to be divorced. For the simple reason is I feel I am attached to a piece of paper for the last six years since my separation. And I don't feel that there's anything there. Like he doesn't even see the kids any more. I don't see him. I haven't seen him in about six or seven weeks so for the way it is ... I don't know who he is. I don't know what he is. I don't care what he does. He doesn't care what I do. All I know is he sees the kids, I have the kids and that's it. There's nothing there. It's stupid. You're still married to this person but he's leading his own life. He's been living with somebody else. He's been seeing someone else same as I have. There's nothing there. There's absolutely nothing there. And eh ...

"The reason why I got married was because I was the oldest girl at home. I had a lot of hassle in the house and I thought, oh ho, this is my ticket to freedom. Get married, get out. And that's the reason why I got married. It wasn't for love nor money. I didn't know what love was. I didn't know what it was to love another man as a man loves a woman. I hadn't a clue. I hadn't a clue."

What age were you?

"I was twenty. But I was a kid at twenty and that's all I can say."

Can you say what broke your marriage up?

"What broke us up was because, when I was pregnant on my first child, my husband was off with other women. He was leading his life, what we should've been leading when we were kids, when we were married. I couldn't handle it. He dared me go and I left. Because ...

"I had a very strict father. Now I'm not saying I don't love him cos I do. I had a very strict father and I wanted to get out of the house cos I couldn't handle the hassle at home. I was sick of it. Stay in Tuesdays and Thursdays. Do your ironing, wash your hair and blah blah blah. You're not going out, you're not doing this, you're not doing that. I wanted to go away to start with my husband. I'll tell you this. I'll ... and this is for real. I was a virgin when I met my husband. I was a virgin when I married my husband. As far as I know he was the same. We never had sex before. Neither of us had a clue what it was about.

"After I left my husband I lived with a man for four years. I had a baby for him. And my sexual life with him was totally different. He showed me how to love as a man loves a woman. With my husband I never had that. I never had that attraction. And maybe my friends had with their husbands. I don't know. But I never had it with mine."

The man you met after your husband was someone you had a better sex life with?

"Oh God. Oh yes. Much ... jaynie mac. There was nothing in comparison. I don't know. I can't explain it to you. With my husband it was zilch, nothing. Nothing."

But you had a baby by him?

"For my husband? I had three children for him."

So you must have had some kind of sexual relationship with him?

"You couldn't call it a sexual relationship as such. Eh" (she drew in her breath) "ohhh. I hated him touching me. Because ... I was sexually abused as a child and ... I don't know whether this had an effect on our relationship as a married ... I blame everything on everything. I don't know which is which at this stage but eh, I felt that if he touched me it was dirt. I just, it's like eh, if you'll excuse the expression, what colour will I paint that ceiling or, I wish he'd hurry up and get off. Or whatever. And I had three kids for him, right? There was no feelings there. There was no ... feelings there ... whatsoever."

You're telling me how you suffered, how it affected your life having been abused sexually as a child. It's something that takes a long, long time to get over.

"You never get over it."

You're not over it now?

"No. And it's all ... oh I was accused of being an alcoholic. But I know what happened because I was there. And I experienced it."

What age were you?

"Well, it first happened, right, with a man on the road and I was only nine or ten. I can't really remember what age I was. And I didn't know anything about ... and all I remember was I had navy knickers on me. That's what my mam used to put them on so it wouldn't show the dirt when you'd be sitting on the road playing, d'you know what I mean? The man he brought us over the park and he gave us chalk. For piggybeds. We were playing at this time in the park and he gave us chalk for piggybeds. And he says close your eyes and you know I was ... you're so bloody innocent you thought you were going to fairyland, that's what I thought. And he says, rub this. And I says, what is it? And I opened them. He says, close your eyes. And I thought it was his thumb to be quite honest with you. And he penetrated me but I wasn't even developed enough to have a hymen to be broke in. You know, to have your virginity broken.

"And when my father touched me the first time I was fourteen. I was in my school uniform. I remember there was talcum powder on the floor. And he says to me, you look very warm. He says to me, I'll put some talcum powder on you. And I says no, I'm not warm. I'm all right. And I remember him saying to me, open your blouse of your school uniform. And I started crying. And he says to me, what's wrong with yeh? And I says, I don't like you doing this to me. And he says to me, why? I says, cos I

84

said, it doesn't feel right. I said that doesn't feel right. And I started crying and he said to me, don't tell your mammy I touched you. And he buyed me, I won't say he bribed me, but it sounds like a bribe ... he says to me, do you want fish 'n chips out of the chipper? I says no, I says I don't want ... I was crying y'know ... I said no I don't want anything, I says. I don't want it. Anything.

"And nothing happened for a long long time but I was always aware of my father's presence and I was always afraid to be alone with him. This all came out in St. Dymphna's and it was very hard for me to talk about it but I had wrote this letter. You know, talked about what happened in the family. I still find it hard to talk about it sometimes, okay?"

Okay.

"The last thing what happened anyway was that my father was ... It was Stephens's Day. It's only going back four years. I'm thirty-two now. Me dad gave me a lift home in the car and I says to him, he had a few drinks, I knew he had a few drinks on him but he wasn't drunk, and I asked him did he want to come in and have a drink seeing it was Christmas time. I asked him if he wanted to come in and have a drink. This is only the second time it ever happened with my father, right? And he says to me eh...he ehm ... " (she was breathing hard now, as if with a pain in her chest) " ... he says to me ehm, ohhh ... I'll only come in he says, if you take me up to your bed like you do your boyfriend ... and I said to him, I says ... he told me he loved me and I said yeah, Dad, I says, I love you, I said as a daughter loves a father. And he said to me ... " (her words became incoherent here as she was crying) " ... was more than that ... he said"

You're very upset. Do you want to keep going with this?

She nodded yes and seemed to get her breath back.

"And I tried to pass it off and talk to him and y'know

and just pass it off. And I says I'll see you Da. He wouldn't come in anyway. So I says I'll see you Da. And he says, gimme a kiss. And I went to go give him a kiss. He tried to put his tongue in my mouth. And I went in my front door and I felt violently sick. And it was as simple as that."

What you're saying to me is that the abuse you suffered as a child and in later life, you still suffer from that. Do you think … do you think abusers realise the damage they do, the suffering they cause?

"I'm seeing a social worker at the moment. She knows the story and she wants me to talk to people about it but I'm finding it very hard. I find it very hard. But I want people to know that it happens and it happens in families. It happens to people you know."

You say that you sometimes drink to excess. Do you think the abuse you suffered has anything to do with that?

"Yeah. And I can't hold down a relationship with a bloke any more. I can't. Because I can't. I can't bring myself to be a normal person towards a fellah because of what happened to me."

She was fat. Many other sex abuse victims I have met over the years have been fat. One victim whom I met at a pawn shop in Queen Street was shockingly thin. She kept a diary of how many Ryvitas she ate in a day. She seemed to have near-permanent diarrhoea. I asked the woman with me now if she suffered from an eating disorder.

"When I drink I don't eat and when I stop drinking I stuff me face. And it's like as if you're eating for comfort. You just keep eating and eating and eating and at that stage you just want to eat, eat, eat all the time. I don't like being fat."

I stopped recording and she made tea. Her face had been blotched and ugly with crying but now she was much calmer. She felt good now, she told me. She joked about things.

Then we talked about something else we decided to put on the record. A week previously there had been a story from her part of Tallaght about a teenage girl who had been raped by a gang that included one woman. Politicians and newspaper editors, desperate to give some response, called for the banning of pornographic videos. Following a Garda investigation, the rape story proved to have been invented by the teenager. I turned on the tape recorder and asked my interviewee if she thought pornographic videos were responsible for encouraging sex abuse.

"No. That's a load of crap. I've often sat and watched a blue movie myself and it didn't turn me out to go and abuse somebody else or give me the right to do that."

What were you doing watching blue movies?

"That's none of your business." (She was laughing.) "I was watching it to boost my sexual life."

All right, how do you feel about banning pornographic movies?

"No. I don't think it's right. I think we have to face reality in these things. There was things were done years ago that was shoved under the carpet. There was pregnant women years ago that was shoved into convents. There was women that went for abortions years ago."

Years ago. You mean before there were pornographic videos available?

"Oh yeah. Oh yeah. There was all this went on anyway in Ireland. So why pretend that we're something we're not?"

There seemed to be a pattern about Tallaght. Each time I went there I met women whose lives had been wrecked by sex abusers. There was another woman I met on the same Thursday who told me a horrendous story about the sexual abuse of her children. I didn't broadcast it because I already had so much of that. And these are just the women on the record. Many women who have spoken to me about other subjects go on to tell me off the record about abuse they suffered as children. Up until a few years ago I would have thought the problem was exaggerated by social workers. Now I am certain there is no exaggeration. I come across it too often.

Other things came up that Thursday. An American woman who was married to some sort of Baptist Minister or something who caught her husband shagging one of his congregation. She came to Ireland where she was born but had never been back to since her infancy. Now she had taken her place in the welfare ghettoes of West Tallaght along with all the other women refugees from broken marriages. The girls in Tallaght are great, she told me. I agree with her.

There was the woman whose husband was in the circus and left her after many years for a teenage trapeze artist. When she was getting her legal separation her solicitor asked for her husband's profession. He thought she was just being bitchy when she said he was a clown.

There was one woman who was escaping the welfare ghetto. Her husband, a musician, had left her. She didn't mind all his infidelities (that's what she told me) but she wished he hadn't left her and the children to sink into welfare. During the Gulf War she watched an American programme on satellite TV which invited women to write to *Annie's Soldier Line*. She struck up a correspondence with a US soldier in the Gulf. He came to Ireland to see her and they hit it off well together. I got a letter from her since. She's in an army base in Germany.

I met a lot of women that Thursday in Tallaght. And I had made my radio programme. A damn good programme it was too.

Chapter Five

HOMELESS PEOPLE

Eastern Health Board Office, Charles St.,
Dublin; 10 July 1989

Five days a week in Dublin, around lunchtime, a crowd of
homeless people begins to gather outside the doors of the
Eastern Health Board Office at Charles Street, near the Four
Courts. They go there to get social welfare money or a
voucher for a hostel. The doors open at two-o'clock and
the crowd surges in. If you're not near the top of the
queue to see the welfare officer you're likely to be waiting
all afternoon.

I've watched the crowd grow over the years. The down-
at-heel winos have always been there. But increasingly in
that two-o'clock scramble you'll find young people of both
sexes and women with children.

As the winos came out of the health board office they
saw me standing there. At a glance they realised I wasn't
one of them. A hand came out in a reflex action. The price
of a cup of tea, sir. Tea addiction was clearly a real problem
here. My answer was always no. It had to be. I would get
into all sorts of aggravation with them if word went around
that a fellow from RTE was outside and was good for a few

bob. I had to spend a few days here after all.

A middle-aged man sat beside me on the kerb. He was high-coloured and his bald head was sweating. He had flecks of spittle around his mouth and he smelled of drink. His voice was surprising. Rather camp.

"I'm in the Iveagh. I'd 've been on the street tonight only Pat in there was good enough to give me a form for an emergency booking. I've spent twelve months walking the quays from the Nite Bite to O'Connell Bridge. Back and forth. And I have spent nights, on numerous occasions, standing to one side of the Nite Bite, which is open all night, hoping that someone will give me the price of a cup of coffee. I have slept in the buses in Conygham Road Garage and the man in charge got so used to seeing me going in there at about half-two to have a sleep at night that he came over eventually and asked me if I wanted a cup of tea and a sandwich."

He shook his jowls at me as he spoke. His voice dropped in an affected way at the end of each sentence. He was like an eccentric university lecturer.

How did you become homeless?

"When I was fourteen and a half years of age. Due to family trouble. My mother and father were always disagreeing and there was violence sometimes in the family. At the age of about fifteen I left County Longford and I went to Dublin. It was 1962. I had just enough money from a local farmer earned to pay the fare to Dublin. Well that night I ended up outside the gents. That very first night outside the gents in Stephen's Green and I wasn't two seconds there when a man came and he says, are you doing business? I didn't exactly know what he meant by business. I says, what do you mean? He says, are you looking for some money? I had to do it. I hadn't a penny. I hadn't eaten all day. All the way up on the bus I'd nothing. I had no place to sleep that night. So he took me

90

home. But it's the truth, Paddy, it's the God's honest truth. I did not spend two nights in the one bed from when I was fifteen. I was handed on from one Trinity College student to another or from one homosexual, ordinary civilian homosexual, to another. I did not spend one single night, two single nights in the one bed. That may sound impossible to believe but it's the truth."

I met a man who really *was* an eccentric academic. He was from England. He'd left his job for some reason. He told me with pride that he was very severely clinically depressed. One of the worst cases ever seen in his hospital. The Charles Street office didn't appreciate how especially ill he was.

He showed the sort of boring self-obsession that I find so common in mentally ill people. The world revolved around him. I wished he would go away. Then he was got rid of rudely by some of the rough young men who had been listening. Fook off yeh fooking English coont yeh. No business being in this country in the first place. He protested pathetically about his rights in an EC country as if his middle-class accent and middle-class values counted for anything here.

Academics and social workers get public money to investigate the will-o'the-wisp of anti-Irish feeling in British dole offices. The very real anti-English feeling I've seen at Irish offices isn't even noticed by these people. Some years later anti-English racism became Government policy when Charlie McCreevy as Welfare Minister decided to raise a drunken cheer by attacking English hippy types who claim welfare in Ireland. I'm still waiting for McCreevy's reciprocal plan to bring all the Irish welfare recipients back from Britain. Yes Minister.

A teenage girl came out of the health board office.

Bev was her name.

"I'm just turned sixteen. It was about a year ago I got

kicked ou' o' the gaff. Out o' me house cos I was causing too much trouble and tha'. I've been sleeping rough and I've been in all different hostels. Sean McDermott Street, Sherrard House, Haven House. I'm staying with me friends now."

A man aged about twenty joined us.

"I'm out of me home four and a half years. The reason I left home cos I wasn't getting on with me father. I cut me wrists. They don't let me into hostels cos I have a temper."

"I have a temper too. Just every now and again I go into hibernation up in me room in a hostel or something but they got sick of me temper. They couldn't understand it like. They sent me to doctors and all and they couldn't help me neither. I calmed down, but like him, I do cut meself up to try and control meself. Or I do go out and I get drunk."

They both showed off the scars on their arms and wrists. He lifted his jumper to show me a long, stitched wound across his belly. Then he pulled a dangerous-looking knife from inside his jacket.

"I got stabbed there. I was getting money for street fighting. Betting. It could be only four or five pounds but then it could be old fellahs who put a tenner. You're beating the hell out of each other for the lousy price of a drink."

Were you ever offered money for sex?

"Yeah. That happens all the time. Different oul' fellahs. I used to bash queers. Many a time I was standing around, that girl there will tell you, I was offered fifty pound to go back and stay the night and have a good time. Fifty pound for this, a tenner for that, come up to the ... do you want to go for a drive? And the answer was no all the time."

"It happens to me too. At night walking up O'Connell Street, I was in the same clothes that I'm in now and an oul' fellah turns around to me and he goes, I'll give you thirty pound if you gimme a good time. And I says, what do you think I am? And he goes, you're a prostitute aren't you? You're on the game. I mean to say you can't even stand against the wall now. When you're living out on the streets people think the wrong of you. It's how much are you love? But that's one thing. I go robbing and that but I won't do prostitution."

Bev told me there were people she wanted me to meet. I agreed to turn up the next day at Morning Star Avenue. Bev was a good contact. I kept in touch with her for some years after our first meeting. She always knew everything there was to know about street kids and homelessness. When other journalists were kissing social workers' backsides I would only have to call on Bev and within a day or two I could get the best and most forthright interviews. The social workers hated me for it. Bev told me how the young people in Focus Point weren't allowed to listen to the radio programme that she was on. The social workers caught them and tuned the radio back to a pop station.

I lost contact with Bev when she moved out of a dump of a flat she had in Synge Street. I hope she's doing okay today, wherever she may be.

I'll tell you now about the people Bev introduced me to the day after I first met her. A man aged twenty and a woman aged about twenty-five were waiting for me at Morning Star Avenue, just down the hill from the men's and women's hostels where they were staying. I spoke to the woman first. I thought she'd probably be more interesting. She had been in the Regina Coeli hostel for two months. Because she was judged to have made herself homeless voluntarily she knew she would not be considered a priority on the housing list.

"I've one child and I had a baby in February, died of a cot death. I couldn't go back because of the baby's death.

There was too many bad memories in the flat. I just couldn't go back. The thoughts of it. Every time I walked into the room I seen everything happening again. My little boy was the same. He went hysterical the minute you went to bring him into the room. He was there. He seen everything happening that morning. It was an awful bad effect on him."

Can your family help?

"My mother won't have anything to do with me because I've had two children outside marriage and because of the way my boyfriend was treating me, hitting me around. She's very old-fashioned in her ways. My brothers don't want to know."

At the time I was fairly new to the business of talking to homeless people but I've learned since that people often end up in hostels when they leave home suddenly due to some life crisis like the cot death we've just heard about. I've heard middle-class people describe how they couldn't bear to stay in their house after it had been violated by burglers. Fair enough. But a life crisis won't earn any transfer points for people in local authority housing. If you give up your home you will be judged to have become homeless voluntarily. You'll go to the bottom of the list and you won't be considered for rent subsidy in a private flat.

Bev had another person for me. Thomas was aged twenty. I didn't know what to expect as he sat into my car. Probably another wild, boastful young man with a story of drink, drugs and crime. I was wrong.

"There's another thing about being homeless. It's about prostitution. In Dublin. That's what it's about. You know prostitution. Men being abused. Young boys and ... it's very hard to say something like this cos I was through it all. Prostitution. But now I'm going out with a girl. It was from the age of fifteen to eighteen. Some of them were wealthy men. And they were very bad doing it."

How did it begin?

"It began when I was walking up O'Connell Street. And some man bumped into me and he asked me would I like to go for a cup of coffee. And I said yes, and we started talking, y'know? I just don't want to go near those men again because they're only using young kids. How they can get their stuff off them and then pay them. And I don't like them at all. If I ever go back on the streets again I would never go near one again."

What, in your opinion, should be done to help young people to get out of prostitution?

"We need more hostels. I was helped by Percy Place. Sister Fiona."

We drove to Burgh Quay in the city centre. There was a men's toilet there at that time. He wanted to show me where he used to work. It was late afternoon. We could see three youths waiting.

"There's young boys being picked up by older men. I was there as well. I would never do it again. I'd spend around three hours of the evening. Get two customers in them three hours. Fifteen pounds each time. I think the police should have done something. They never took any notice."

I know now that the police did take notice, at least in later years. They were doing surveillance there looking for male prostitution, child molesters, perverts, muggers and drugs. That toilet was notorious. As the broadcaster Gerry Ryan remarked of the place, it must have been a breath of fresh air when somebody came in for a crap.

To get back to Thomas and what he was telling me.

"There's another part of Burgh Quay is the amusements where old men play video games. They look out for young boys as well."

What kind of men picked you up?

"Men with money. I'd go off in their car or down to the stations. The train stations. I'd go into the toilets there."

Jesus. What would you do then with the thirty quid?

"I would get somewhere to sleep and get something to eat as well."

The next day I got a call at the office from a social worker. Somebody had told him Thomas had been speaking to me. He demanded to know how I had "accessed" Thomas. I should have consulted with him. I was putting Thomas's life in danger if I broadcast the interview. I didn't understand what was involved.

Are you saying that criminals involved in child prostitution have made threats?

He wasn't prepared to discuss it.

Fine. Thank you for your interest.

A few weeks after the programme was broadcast Thomas gave me an account he had written of aspects of his life. A folder of pages under different headings carefully written in block capitals. He thought I might want to publish some of it, some time.

Family background

My name is Thomas -----.

My dad was very good to us. Each week he would come home from work and give me sweets for me and my brothers and sister. My dad worked as a bricklayer until he got the sack for not going into work. Each Friday following, my dad would go out and get drunk and come home and hit all of us for no reason. I wished when he had me over his knee hitting me that he would die. My wish never came true. I am glad it didn't come true.

Then one night my dad came home drunk and began to hit my mum and my brothers and sister. That night my dad stayed in the house. On the second night he slept in the car. The next morning he was gone. He didn't even say goodbye to his own children. We cried for days afterwards. My mum was very depressed. She had to be put into St. Vincent's Hospital for three weeks. When my mum got out of hospital she began to argue with me a lot and eventually she told me to go. I had no money or clothes. I was about to begin my life on the streets of Dublin.

On the streets

The first night on the streets I walked around all night. The next day I was so hungry I ended up begging outside of a church. I made around five pounds. My life consisted of begging, robbing in supermarkets for food, sleeping in buses, in doorways, in bins and at the back of supermarkets.

About three weeks later I began to get used to being on the streets. It was very hard for a fourteen-year-old boy. I didn't want to go home because I was afraid of more arguments between me and my mum so I stayed on the streets for another few weeks. While on the streets I was picked up by the Gardai for robbing. I was brought to court but I got away with a warning. If it happened again I would be put away.

A few days later while on the streets I met a boy who was twelve years old. As we were getting along the boy told me he had run away from home. I told him to go back home but he said no, he couldn't because his dad was hitting him all of the time. I didn't know what to do about the young boy so I told him to come up to Hope hostel with me. He had a talk with the staff but he did not want to stay in a hostel. He wanted to stay on the streets. So the both of us walked around all night long. The next day we went down to Church Street for dinner. After dinner we went up to a church and begged for money to buy food and cigarettes. So from the streets into Hope hostel the two of us went to stay.

When I went to London

I went to London in September of 1988. I went with two friends of mine named Luke and Paul. Both Paul and Luke were drunk on the boat and the train. Eventually we got to London. There was only myself and Luke now because Paul was arrested on the train for damaging the toilets.

We got off the train and didn't know what to do next. We had nowhere to stay and no food. After a lot of looking we arrived at a bed and breakfast. It cost us the full twenty-five pounds that we had between us for the one night. We still had no money for food so I went into the subway and begged for money. I got three pounds. I bought food and brought it back to the B&B. When we finished we went to the DHSS to see if they would pay us but Luke was only seventeen so he was too young. I was nineteen but I would have to wait two and a half weeks to get paid.

When I got paid I bought two tickets to get back to Dublin. They cost twenty-five pounds each. We had forty one pounds left from the DHSS cheque. When we got home we said we would never go back to London unless we had plenty of money with us.

We still hadn't seen or heard from Paul since he had been arrested.

Hospitals

The first hospital I was ever in was St. Loman's. I was in for eight weeks suffering from depression. I was in Loman's twice.

I was also in St. Vincent's institution also suffering from depression. I was there for nine weeks.

Prostitution

When I was fifteen years old I was on the streets without any money. I needed money very badly so I went down to the toilets on O'Connell Street and sold myself to older men for fifteen pounds a go. I said to myself, what am I doing? So I ran out of the toilet crying without getting paid by one man.

A few days later I returned to try and get some more money. This is just one of the things I had to do for money. I went into one of the boxes with a man. He gave me ten pounds. This continued for three years and then I stopped.

When I stopped I was worried about getting AIDS so I went for an AIDS test but thankfully I was given the all clear.

At home for Christmas Day

Two years ago I went home to my mother's for my Christmas dinner. My social worker told me my mum had agreed to let me stay there for the day and stay overnight as well. So I went home to my mother's and had my dinner then my mother told me to go back to my flat. So my big brother took me home in the car. I asked him to bring me over to Percy Place hostel. When we arrived I walked up to the hall door. I was crying. I told the staff what had happened. They took me in for the day and gave me dinner. We watched some T.V. and videos. They asked me if I wanted to stay the night. I said yes.

Last Christmas I was working selling Christmas trees. Myself and Luke made about two hundred pounds each. I went home for the day with a sack full of presents for my family. Then I went home to my flat and went to bed.

The Percy Place Club

Each Monday night I go over to a club at Percy Place hostel. The cost each week is 30p. We go on trips to the mountains or we stay in the big hall and play games. We play football, basketball, table tennis or pool. It's a very good club for the ex-residents of the hostel.

What is a keyworker?

A keyworker is a person who works in a hostel. They will try their best to get you back home. If they can't, they put you into another hostel until they can find a flat for you. It could take one week or one year. If you didn't stay in the hostel you would not get any help. They will not run after you if you run to the streets. If you need help you ask a keyworker and they will help you as much as they can.

How I coped in 1989

It's now August the 11th., 1989. So far the year has been going well. I am now set up in a new flat with a bloke called Alan.

I have been for a few job interviews and I am starting a new job on Monday morning. I have also settled down with a lovely girl from Tallaght. Her name is Carmel.

My relationship with my mum has improved greatly over the last few months and also with the rest of my family.

This has been my life story to date. Thank you for reading this.

Thomas -----.

Chapter Six

DUBLIN'S FLATLAND

Eastern Health Board Office, Upper Rathmines Road, Dublin; 12 July 1989

I loved living in Rathmines as a flatdweller back in the seventies. The flats used to be full of young people from the countryside. Nurses, students, civil servants and office workers generally. I was a civil servant. Like most flatdwellers I paid about half my earnings in rent, lived in bad accommodation and often put up with thuggish landlords.

I wouldn't have missed my years in flatland for anything. Flatland was where men, especially, learned independence. We had to budget, cook, clean and do all the things that women would have been taught at home but which men might go through their young life without ever finding out about.

The young Dublin men I worked with had more spare money than me because they lived at home. They often had cars which would have been unthinkable in my case. But I never envied them. I had more to offer to women because in flatland all of us, men and women, met as equals. I knew all about budgeting, cooking and so on. I didn't need a surrogate mother. I think that experience of independent living went on to make better husbands of us country lads.

I was aghast when I realised that young Dublin men paid all the expenses of the pub or movies when going out on a date. Why? It wasn't fair. Dubliners wouldn't let their girlfriends go to the bar for a drink. Crazy! All that queueing and shoving at the bar. Why shouldn't a couple take turns?

I realise now that this Dublin tradition reflected a world in which men were paid more than women and men expressed this superiority by paying. Not like flatland where the sexes were equal. Flatland, as it was in the seventies, was a unique part of Irish culture and I mourn its decline.

The decline happened in the eighties. Dublin ceased to be the place to go for a job. Instead young people who were looking for work went to London or the USA. In the mid-eighties, when I started making radio programmes about emigration, I recognised the excitement that young people felt on getting their first taste of independent living. I remembered how important that independence had been to my age-group in Rathmines a decade earlier. And that's why, I think, I understood that the social workers and poverty nuns were wasting their time telling young people not to go to London or New York unless they had a job and accommodation lined up. Young people have to have their freedom, even if the price of that freedom is giving up your family home to pay half your wages on a grubby bedsit.

When young people from the countryside stopped coming to Dublin for work, flatdweller culture changed. These days the flats are full of people from Dublin and elsewhere who are on social welfare. A lot of these flatdwellers are on the housing list.

If you're in a private flat and you're on the dole, you can apply for rent allowance, although that still leaves you paying more on rent than you would be if you were in a local authority house or flat. The health board office at the Upper Rathmines Road in Dublin pays out rent allowance so it's a good place for me to meet flatdwellers who are on welfare.

The single people are here because they haven't a hope of getting anywhere on the housing list. The unmarried mothers are here because they have refused to go to Ballymun. Families are in flats for other reasons.

Lily was in her early twenties. She spoke with a strong, working-class Dublin accent. She was clearly pregnant. She had just had a row with the welfare officer and she was upset. She was refused rent allowance.

"We pay forty pounds a week rent. We left a corporation three-bedroomed house. We had terrible trouble. We had to ge' ou' o' Tallaght. Since we came here we've no rent allowance. We get sixty-six pound a week on the labour and we're living on twenty-six. And they won't give us nothing."

Why no rent allowance?

· "They said because we left the corporation house but we had police files and everything that we had to leave. I don't want to give out the reasons why but it was an emergency. We had to get out. Me husband's Arab."

Would your husband like to speak to me if I were to call to see you later?

"Oh yeah. He's very upset on it too. We're very hurt over it."

She gave me her address, not far away in Ranelagh. I called later that evening.

I was beginning to realise the two basic reasons why people were refused rent allowance. The most common reason was that the person was too young. If you are under twenty-five you are expected to live with your mother and father. The second reason was that the person was judged to have become homeless voluntarily, as in Lily's case. A lot of the homeless people I've met at the health board office at Dublin's Charles Street are people who would have fled a local authority house or flat, perhaps rashly, after some unbearable thing had happened.

Lily's husband answered the door. He was from Libya. His voice was strongly accented. They brought me in and apologised for their uncomfortable couch. Best to sit forward on the edge of the seat with the frame cutting into your bum. If you sat back it would swallow you. It was typical of the kind of furniture that landlords think is good enough for flatdwellers.

I asked Lily about how they were managing on twenty-six pounds a week but she had something else on her mind.

"Mohammed's an Arab. I'm Irish. And, a lot o' young Irish girls would want to think before they marry Arabs and a lot of Arabs would want to think before they marry Irish girls. Unless the Irish girl is Moslem. Because there's a big difference between Moslem and Catholic. Catholics are more ... they don't want to be told what to do. Like the Moslem woman is quiet. Like if she's told what to do she won't speak back. She won't answer back. She'll just sit. I've met an awful lot of Moslem women and they don't fight back.

"Like Arabs before they marry Irish girls would want to really think what they're doing. And the Irish girls would want to think what they're doing too. Like I didn't think. Mohammed didn't think. We were only fourteen weeks when we got married. We only knew each other fourteen weeks. We're not even a year married yet. And if I could turn the clock back I would never have got married."

I looked at Mohammed. He didn't seem shocked that his wife wanted rid of him. Clearly this was something they both knew.

Would you agree with your wife that an Arab man expects his wife to be more ... quiet and giving in to his will, than Irishwomen are prepared to be?

"The woman I am saying, any woman·in the world, I not speak about the men, she has to be with me, gentle with me, you know? She has to be quietly because she is a woman. She's not in the army or anything. She has to be gentle, you know? Softness, you know? To say, I mean, this person, she is really a woman. And all the women in all over the world they are the same. But somehow it's different here in Ireland."

You were married here in Ireland? Lily?

"In the registry office in Molesworth Street and in the mosque in South Circular Road. And I wanted to be married, like. This is the man I thought I loved, I wanted, I was going to be happy with, I wanted."

What was the attitude of your family when you said you were going to marry Mohammed?

"They asked me to wait. We only knew each other fourteen weeks. My mother begged and pleaded with me to wait. And Mohammed. She said it to his face. She was afraid of what *has* happened. The culture difference. She was so afraid. She said youse are from two countries. You are about to clash. You'll clash. She begged and pleaded. Of course I was head over heels infatuated with this Arab and didn't listen. And I was over twenty-one, so. They done everything they could for me to make me happy. Like they accepted him. He came to live in my home, my mother's home. And they done everything for me. But, everything just didn't work out."

Now you're married legally in Ireland. There's no divorce.

"I know there's no divorce but I can go to live in England for a year. But like in Mohammed's religion he only has to say, I divorce you in the name of Allah, God, four times and I'm ... gone."

On the word "gone" she drew her finger across her throat in a cutting action.

It seems to me that for two people about to break up you're able to talk about it very well. Without losing the head I mean.

Lily laughed. No. They were not usually as calm as this. Not by a long way. Mohammed agreed he was tired of losing the head. Loozing thee head. The slang expression sounded ludicrous in his accent. He said it was only Irish women caused all this trouble. The German women had put up with him and his ways.

I know a lot more now than I did then about Moslems. This story about an Irish-Moslem romance going sour after marriage has become familiar to me. Moslem men who were happy with Western ways during courtship seem to revert to type after marriage and then they expect their wives to know their place and abide by Moslem rules. No cosmetics. Don't even look at another man. Realise that you're unclean and untouchable when you're having your period. Be prepared for a beating if he thinks you might have transgressed any of these rules. Mohammed's German girlfriends had been just girlfriends. Lily's mistake was to have become Mohammed's wife.

A listener phoned me after hearing the radio programme. She was worried about her sister marrying a Moslem. Lily agreed to meet her. In the weeks that followed I stayed in contact with Lily and I learned a lot more about her husband. Lily told me that he got drunk and beat her. When he was a good Moslem things had been okay because he didn't drink. The trouble with the police in her house in Jobstown happened when her brother came home from England and decided to sort out Mohammed because of the beatings he had given Lily.

Mohammed ran out the back door. Lily's brother came in and beat up the wrong Arab. After this, Lily fled Jobstown. So that was how she ended up in the welfare at Rathmines, applying for rent allowance and not getting it.

I met Lily's father. He wanted me to know that his family had made Mohammed welcome. Put up with the funny cooking smells and all. But he wouldn't forgive him for the way he treated his daughter. He had welcomed Mohammed but he had welcomed the devil into his house. Lily's father had a terminal illness. He would swing for Mohammed. He wouldn't be scared. There were tears in his eyes when he spoke about Lily being beaten.

Lily's baby was born a few weeks later. I've lost contact with her since. She's no longer at the flat in Ranelagh. Some day, perhaps, I'll find out what happened to her.

Eastern Health Board Office,
Upper Rathmines Road; 26 July 1990

I've often said that drunks and social workers are the two main problems I face when I'm out working. They're the two types of people who think they can intrude on an interview without being invited. On this particular morning in Rathmines I was attacked by a drunk and a social worker in a double act.

The drunk came first. I didn't realise at first that he'd been drinking. It was mid-morning so you wouldn't expect it. He was a well-built man aged about twenty-five. Glasses. Intelligent-looking. In a middle-class drawl he asked me what I was at. Yes. He'd speak to me. He had lots of views. But of course I should really be asking about the system. Right? And the media conspiracy. And the media hype that misleads people.

His drawl was Geldof-like as he talked about the troubles of the world. (Don't get me wrong. I have nothing against Bob. Far from it.) I think he was going on about Gorbachev when I realised that he was drunk. There was a stink of alcoholic sweat when he came close.

The worst type of alcoholic must be the man who can hold his drink. Like this man. He wasn't in a pub. He was able to go about his everyday business in a stupor. Can you imagine being married to a man like that? His personality always adjusted by drink. Always close to turning nasty. Full of his own importance and convinced of his wisdom in all things. Not realising he is a bloody bore and a nuisance.

I couldn't get rid of him. I'd long since put away my microphone. Thank you very much for your views. I agree. I agree. I know what you mean. Right. It was nice meeting you. I'll think about what you have said. (Now please FUCK OFF.) He began to get nasty in the way that drunks do. He should be doing my job. I didn't have a clue how to do it. I was part of the system. The establishment. But he wouldn't be allowed on the radio because he would tell people the truth, not establishment lies. Fair enough, I said. That's your view which I have to respect. (Now please FUCK OFF you pompous idiot and let me get on with my work.) I didn't say the bit in brackets. As usual I kept my thoughts to myself because I'm in the business of making programmes, not winning arguments.

I knew his problem. He was intrigued by my job and he was jealous. Radio would be a soap-box for his self-important ramblings. I meet people like that all the time.

He left and I hadn't let out my sigh of relief when the social worker struck. She was in my face, all teeth and glasses. Full of righteous indignation.

How can you exploit that man? He has a very serious drink problem and should not be exploited by the media.

At least don't exploit *that* man.

I felt like Genghis Khan being asked to at least not slit the children's throats.

Who the fuck are you?

I'm his case worker. He has a serious alcohol problem. He's been drinking throughout the night and hasn't yet slept. He's very vulnerable and easily exploited.

(Social worker. I should have known by the halo.)

I explained that I had no intention of putting him on the airwaves. I had stopped recording him very soon after the interview started. I'd been doing my best to get rid of him without offending him.

But how did she know that I hadn't been secretly recording him?

Secret recording? Go away you bloody eejit. You don't think I want to go home and inflict all that rubbish on myself again do you? Or inflict it on the nation at large?

I was losing my cool now. Raising my voice.

She said she wasn't going to be intimidated by me. She had a duty to protect that man and would make no apology for it. Then her tone changed. She became more conciliatory. She felt that I had accepted her view that it would be wrong to exploit that man. Then, satisfied with a good deed done, she left.

Bloody social workers. How often have I had to listen to them? Looking down their noses at me. The exploiter. I'm told by my social worker sister-in-law that I use the term social worker too broadly. That's fair enough. But I hate the people, be they social workers, community leaders, poverty nuns or whatever who feel that poor people can't speak for themselves. It's what I call social worker syndrome. It's no coincidence that the clergy are among the worst offenders. Their sense of superiority over their flock transfers quite easily into the secularised arrogance of the social work profession. When a nun becomes a social worker the combined effect is horrendous. I don't like nuns.

I wasn't having a great day so far at Rathmines, was I? But I knew I was on to something good that morning at the welfare once I could get going because people were angry. Social welfare increases had been paid the previous week. That was welcome, especially as these increases had been announced, as usual, six months earlier in the January Budget. But the increase in pay from the Department of Social Welfare would be offset by a decrease in rent allowance. Today was the day that people were hearing the bad news.

This annual cut in rent allowance is one of those administrative measures generally overlooked in the media because the victims are poor people. Think of the furore that we see if there's even a suggestion of a cut in tax relief on mortgages.

A young man, like many on the welfare at Rathmines, had a middle-class accent.

"I was in and I was getting nineteen pounds a week. Last week they told me I was getting reduced by two pounds because I was getting a rise of five pounds on the dole. I'm after going in today and they're after taking eight pounds me and they're saying there's nothing they can do about it. They didn't even give me a reason. They totted up a few figures, made a weird fraction and came out with this figure. Eleven pounds they're giving me."

Breda from Castlegregory, Co.Kerry, was upset.

"I'm getting a rise of five pounds in my unmarried mother's and I'm after losing ten pounds in my rent allowance. And they wouldn't explain that to me."

I phoned the Department of Social Welfare and they told me people could lose more in rent allowance than they gain on the dole if a cut in allowance was already due. So I suppose that was the case with Breda. A few

110

months earlier she was on the dole and then she went on to unmarried mother's pay which is higher so she had been due a cut in rent allowance.

Breda was bright and articulate. She had a beautiful, clear, Kerry accent. In the afternoon I went to speak to her again at her flat off the Rathgar Road. It was a nice flat, better than most. It doesn't pay a flatdweller on welfare to take the cheapest possible place. The formula for calculating rent allowance is that the person should be left with a basic minimum disposable income after rent has been paid. So a flatdweller may as well try to get as good a place as the welfare are willing to subsidise.

Breda's cut in income turned out to be worse than she thought.

"I thought I was going to lose a fiver. It's actually going to be six pounds twenty a week. Foodwise I'm going to have to cut down for myself to be able to buy nappies, food for the baby, whatever. You're not going to be able to go down into Quinnsworth and take a box of nappies for nothing, you know?"

Now you're an unmarried mother. You strike me as a well-educated person. Probably you had a good chance of a job. And yet through becoming a single mother you've made life difficult for yourself?

"I was working. I had a good job and it just suddenly all went down the drain. I don't mope about it but in a way it did ruin my prospects for life. I went through college and then I made the mistake. I hear people saying, all these unmarried mothers they have the babies so they won't have to work. It's a stupid opinion. It's not as if having a baby is all fun. I mean you're up all night. It is a hard job. It's a lot harder than the job I was doing. And I'm not getting paid as much."

Breda was laughing at her situation here. I agreed with her that single parenthood wasn't a good economic proposition for her because she was well-educated and had other prospects. But I also said that if a woman's only prospect is a life on social welfare then that makes single parenthood a reasonable option. Breda didn't agree with me. Single parent groups don't agree with me. But I remain convinced that if there were more jobs there would be fewer unmarried mothers.

Should you have been more careful, Breda, about getting pregnant? You've heard of contraception?

Breda laughed again.

"Oh yes. I've heard of it. In my job I used to give people advice on it. But I just didn't even think. You keep thinking it can't happen to me, but it did."

You know how babies are made. Why couldn't it happen to you?

"Oh gee. Well I was going out with a guy and I mean, I must say he wasn't pushy. Nothing. But it just happened one night and neither of us thought ... and, it happened once ... and then you think then it can't happen now. It was just once. But it did. We happened to be unlucky. And I had no cause to be on contraception because we didn't have that type of relationship. And just got carried away, you know?"

Breda smiled as she remembered the night it happened. I liked Breda. I gathered she was trained as a social worker of some sort but she was a less than perfect human being which must have made her unique among her profession.

Were you drunk, Breda?

"No. I wasn't drunk. I didn't have that excuse. But I can tell you, it came as a very big shock when I found I was pregnant. I was in the middle of college exams when I found out. But I just had to pull through. I mean there was nothing I could do about it. I'm totally against abortion. I'm against adoption as well. In my work I've seen kids who were given up and it's very, very hard. So when I found out I was pregnant I said, it's my bed. I made it. I'm going to lie in it."

I met another unmarried mother at the Rathmines welfare that day. Maria was in her late twenties. Her accent was strongly rural. She was from Co. Tipperary. We spoke back at her flat on Rathgar Road. Her story was one of those ones about which the full truth couldn't be told at the time.

"I've been on the corporation list since April of '87. I just can't get where I want. It's Ballymun or Darndale. And I think it's important that I live in a nice place for the sake of my child."

But this place is much more expensive than Ballymun would be?

"A lot more. It's thirty-eight pounds a week. I get twenty-two pounds allowance, so that's sixteen pounds out of my money. I worked for the first year after my baby was born and then the company closed. That's three years ago. I would like to work full-time and be independent. My daughter will be in school in September and I'll be just sitting here. But when I enquire about salaries ... by the time I pay a child-minder ... I'd be better off staying on the unmarried mother's allowance."

Was your baby planned?

"No. And then the father didn't want to know and he was gone as soon as he found out."

That must have hurt?

"It did. It makes you very wary of men. I just don't want to be hurt again."

Two years ago the status of illegitamacy was abolished and that's made it easier for a mother to chase a deserting father for maintenance. Have you thought of going after him for money?

"Well I've enquired into it but it involves blood tests. It's not easy."

I argued this with Maria. When the law on illegitimacy changed in 1988 it also became permissable for a court to draw inferences if a man should refuse a blood sample. I remember interviewing a woman about the bad old days of proving paternity when the man could refuse a blood sample with impunity. In court, under cross-examination, that woman had to give evidence about conceiving the baby in a car in the Phoenix Park. That woman's mother and father were in court. So was her deserting boyfriend's mother. That woman eventually won her case and the father of her child ended up with a weekly attachment to earnings order on his pay cheque from Arigna Collieries. If she had proved paternity then so could Maria.

"Well the father of my child has since gotten married. I don't know if his wife knows anything about the baby and I think I want to leave the past alone in case I create trouble there or anything."

Maria asked me to turn off the tape-recorder. The father of her child was, in fact, married with children when she conceived the baby. He was a policeman in her Tipperary home town. She didn't want anybody who might recognise her voice to know this.

I agreed to stay off the subject of the father and she agreed to let me tape her again.

Should you have been more careful about getting pregnant?

"It wasn't wise but we were both in love, I suppose, at the time and it just happened and I wouldn't be without my daughter now."

You're not from Dublin. Why did you choose to come here to live?

"Well, at this stage it doesn't bother me, but at the time when I did have the baby I felt everybody was talking about me and a lot of people snubbed me and wouldn't salute me. I think there's an awful lot more single parents in the town now but at the time I had the baby I felt everybody was talking about me."

So this was Maria's story. Her reason for being in flatland. The father keeps his job, his family, his money and his standing in the local community and she gets a lonely flat in Rathmines and her weekly welfare cheque. No doubt the same people who snubbed Maria are still talking to the father, a pillar of the community.

Chapter Seven

FAMILY COURT

Dolphin House, Exchequer Street, Dublin; 6 November 1989

There are several court rooms in Dolphin House. The family cases are heard upstairs. These are held *in camera*. So you can't go in but you can get an idea of what the atmosphere of the court must be like if you sit in the waiting area outside. There are couples who are in for barring order hearings against the man. Other couples, long since separated, find themselves in the same waiting room before they go into court to dispute maintenance money.

I waited on the street outside. I tried to guess who were the family cases. The court on the ground-floor seemed to be for driving offences.

A couple in their mid-twenties came out. He was a big, strong-looking man. She was small and slight. They smiled as they talked to each other. Not a family case, surely? Perhaps they had just got off lightly on parking fines or something like that.

I approached them and they said they would talk. They had strong Dublin accents. The man answered first.

"It was for a barring order."

Against you?

"Against me, yeah. The judge gave her the barring order. I've to stay away from the house or I'll be locked up."

Was there evidence given against you?

"The wife gave evidence, yeah."

What did you say about him?

"I said he was violent towards me all the time."

Was your word enough?

"Yeah."

Did you have to show bruises or anything?

"No."

Did you admit to doing it?

"I admitted it in a way, but then, you know women. They ask for it."

What do you mean?

"Well you tell them to do something, and she'd tell you to get up and do it yourself. She's a daring one. She never does a thing I ask her."

Have you often hit your wife?

"No, not very often … How long is it now since I last hit you?"

"Six months. He'd hit you for no reason though."

"You don't do things I tell you."

You have to stay out of the house now, do you?

"Yeah, I've to stay out. Stay away from the house altogether."

Have you somewhere to live?

"I'll stay with me ma."

How long does the barring order last?

"Six months."

What will you do in six months time?

"Go for another one."

Even if he hasn't touched you in between?

"Yes. I'll still go for it."

Why is that?

"Because he'll never change. He'd come back for two or three weeks and then he'd be back to his old self."

Is it drink?

"No, I don't touch drink."

It doesn't seem very ... manly to be hitting a woman?

"I know. Sure I hate meself for it. Anytime I hit her ... what did I say to you? When I hit you, what do I say?"

"You said you hated yourself for hitting me. But at the same time, you still hit me."

"But didn't I say, hit me back?"

"Then I'd know all about it. I'd never hit you again."

The two of you seem friendly enough still?

"I'm married to her amn't I?"

"It's no use holding grudges."

Have you children?

"Two sons."

Will you get to see them?

"Ah yeah. I'll get to see them at the weekends."

What do the children make of this?

"They don't really notice it."

Can you forgive him for thumping you?

"No."

In what way are you still friends now?

"I talk to him. I won't pass him by, but that's it."

They moved on. I'm sure if I had just been barred from my home for hitting my wife I would be so ashamed that I would never speak to anybody about it, let alone speak to some wally from RTE. But it was routine for that man to hit his wife. Wouldn't we all do it? Sure you know what women are like?

Three women came out. Two were well-dressed. The other was tatty. I explained that I was interested in barring orders, protection orders and the like. One of the well-dressed women answered me sharply. There are books available in which you can find out everything you need to know about barring orders. I disagreed. But I was wasting my time. The tatty-looking woman was in the company of professional, middle-class people (social workers or solicitors, I expect) so she wasn't going to get a chance to speak.

A woman told me how she got a protection order the month before.

"Well I had to go in and state me case why I wanted a protection order. Just to state that he assaulted me and they wrote out a statement. And it was put before a judge and the judge read back the statement to me and it was given to me. And then I just had to bring it up to the police station in the district where I live. And then I had to tell my husband that I have the protection order out against him otherwise it's not valid, unless you tell them. And tell him that I've brought it up to the police station. That was in case, if he hits me like, I can just ring up the police and they come down and take him out of the house."

She agreed with me that the value of a protection order was greatly enhanced if the recipient had a telephone with which to ring the police.

You make it sound very straightforward, getting the protection order?

"I was surprised. I got it fairly quick. I thought there would be a lot of eh ... you know, you'd have to give proof, and things like that, but you don't. You just state your case. I just told the truth and they believed me all right, you know?"

How did your husband react when you served the order on him?

"He couldn't understand it. He got angry and then he packed and left. It's something that you don't like to do to your husband but you just can't sit back and keep taking the beatings."

He can still come in and out of the house. He's not barred yet?

"Oh no. He's up with the children now. The only thing that can keep him out is a barring order."

Her husband, she told me, was getting legal aid, as she was, for the barring order hearing the next month.

A middle-aged travelling woman spoke with me.

"I was in for a 'tection order. The law will serve it on him. There's a copy of it. That'll be for the time being. My husband's very bad. He's an alcoholic. And I'm putting up with this for the last twenty-nine year. And no more. I've had enough of it. I'm in a caravan. I reared a family on my own the last twenty-nine year. I've given him all the chances. I've forgiven. You know? I've hidden ... I'm a travelling woman and I'm after hiding murder on him, you know? And I'm not doing it no more. Honest to God. Never again."

Will you stay in the caravan?

"I'm applying for a house. If they get me a house on my own I'll take it with the kids."

Well good luck to you, I thought. Travelling women hardly ever stand up for themselves against violent husbands. But this woman had taken enough. I hoped other travelling women might hear her on the radio and follow her example. I would also like to have been a fly on the wall of that particular caravan when the protection order was served that evening.

A young couple came out. They had a priest with them. It was Michael Cleary, a well-known media pundit whose working-class accent and folksy manner gave him an aura of radicalism that was, to my mind, entirely without substance. I told them I was working for the *Pat Kenny Show*. Is that right?, said Cleary. So Pat has you out working on the difficult jobs?

Cleary told me he thought it was too easy for women to

get barring and protection orders. I agreed with him that it was far easier to get these orders than the text books would have you believe. There was no need for medical evidence of violence. The courts took the woman's word for it.

The young woman said she would talk. I don't remember what she said because I was too conscious of Cleary behind my back signalling to her to shut up. At that time Michael Cleary was hosting his own radio show. A phone-in programme on the Dublin station 98FM. And now he was using his cloth to make life hard for me, a rival broadcaster. Thanks a bunch, Michael. The young couple obeyed their priest and they all moved on.

Dolphin House Court, 26 June 1990

He stripped me naked out on the street. I will of course talk to you. Naked I was.

She was laughing about it. She was tough and good-humoured. I suppose she had to be both of those things to live with a man like that.

I still meet people from the Neilstown area of Dublin who remember the night when the woman with the long red hair was out on the road in only her knickers. It was the evening the Republic of Ireland beat Romania in a penalty shoot-out. But whatever the result of the match, this woman could expect a beating when her man came home. The next morning she came to the family court with her friend to see if she could get help.

"I was in for a protection order. I couldn't get nothing against him because I'm not married to him."

A protection order is the temporary order until a barring order hearing is arranged.

"That's right. And there's nothing. Is there?"

"I went with her to the police station, and they told her to come straight down here. That there's nothing they can do about it unless she got a barring order, even a protection order for yourself."

"But because I'm not married there's nothing. I'd have to get a High Court ... an injunction against him. I mean I'd be waiting months for that. I could be dead. He broke me nose there a couple of months ago."

She was laughing again.

"He gives me hidings and that when he comes in with drink on him. I mean he ran out on the road last night, didn't he?"

"She ran out to get away from him. And he ran after her. And he caught her trousers ... "

"He reefed the trousers off me. If they hear that they'll know. The neighbours'll know it's me. He reefed the trousers, jumper, bra and all off me on the road last night. He had me naked out on the street. I was running around the gardens and that. I ran in to her house. There hasn't been any trouble in a couple of weeks, but I think now the football has a lot got to do with it. When they're out drinking. That's all they want. Drink."

He goes to the pub to watch the matches?

"Yeah, then he falls in the door, causes killings."

Is he a big man?

"Stocky bloke all right. But I'd give him a bang of something now in a minute. Bang of a kettle ... and leg it then."

Do you have children?

"I've four children for him. But he never wanted the responsibility of the children. He never grew up."

It crossed my mind to suggest that she should marry this man. Then she could bar him. But I kept my thoughts to myself.

One of the staff at the court told me that there was

always an increase in violence against women during major sporting events like the world cup finals which were on at that time. The morning after a match there's an increase in barring order applications.

I asked the Department of Justice if I could see the court records for barring orders and protection orders applied for. The answer was no. No reason given. At that time the Department, under Ray Burke, wouldn't even talk to journalists. All enquiries had to go through the Government Information Service.

A woman of about forty came out of the court building. She had a West of Ireland accent.

"I come every week for my cheque. Sometimes the cheque isn't paid and I have to wait till the following week. The following week then, the cheque would come in, there'd be only money for the one week, thirty pounds."

Would you be better off on Deserted Wife's pay from the social welfare?

"I won't get it because he can afford to pay me. I got advice on this. But I would be better off. It would cut out the hassle of going to courts and all that."

A Dublin woman was applying for increased maintenance.

"I'm only getting eighty pounds for myself and four kids. I'd get a hundred and ten on Deserted Wife's. I'm after being in twice about it."

What broke your marriage up?

"Gambling. He wasn't bringing home a wage to me one way or the other. Then the rest went on drink."

Every woman, it seemed, would prefer to be on social welfare rather than on maintenance. I realised that unmarried mothers get a better deal than deserted wives. That remains true today even though both payments are now called Lone Parents Allowance. The ummarried lone parent gets her money without question. The deserted wife has to chase her husband for maintenance whenever he can afford it.

A Dublin woman of about forty had a doleful voice.

"I went in to collect maintenance. I'd prefer to be paid by social welfare, if I had a choice. Because your security would be there. Every week when you go in there you don't know whether you'd be paid, or what's going to happen in your life. He didn't pay me at all the first four months, until I took him to court. I was living in Women's Aid."

So you had to rely on the community welfare office for the first four months?

"Yeah. And then they put pressure on you to get payment off the husband."

Isn't it reasonable, though, that he should have to pay maintenance?

"Oh, it is. You can't bring children into the world and then forget about them, expecting somebody else to pay. And if you have extra-marital affairs you have to pay for them."

Why were you in Women's Aid? Was he beating you?

"I was driven from my home with the three kids. He was beating me up. He was bringing women home. One girl from the road, she was mentally handicapped, and I found them in the kitchen."

What do you mean, you found them?

"Like they were in the kitchen. I disturbed them. She was all exposed."

I heard a similar story two months later in Buncrana, Co. Donegal. A woman told me her husband, who had since fled to Derry, had a sexual relationship with a mentally handicapped teenage girl. The story was unbroadcastable because the people concerned would have been too easily identified.

A couple in their mid-thirties were swearing at each other. Here we go, Paddy. This looks like one for you.

Damn right he'd talk to me. She would talk too.

"Maintenance order. She wanted more money."

And did you agree to give it to her?

"Well the judge agreed. A hundred pound for her and three children. And I'm left with thirty to live on. I was paying eighty-five. That's not fair."

Do you think your husband has a point? He'd be getting more on the dole.

"No. Because he earns more than he says he does when he goes in to court."

"That's only if I do overtime. Why should I have to do overtime?"

Does he always pay the money on time?

"He didn't in the beginning. But lately, yeah. I have a court order that the maintenance comes out of his money. Which should have been done in the beginning. They should give you an attachment on earnings order the day the maintenance is granted, instead of waiting to see if the man is honest enough to pay it."

Why did the two of you break up?

"He went off with somebody else. That was his decision. Not mine."

"No, no. She threw me out and then I met up with somebody else."

How do you get on with each other now when you meet?

"She does lose her head after about fifteen minutes. Listen, I have to run. Good luck."

"He has to go to work."

Your husband's girlfriend, is she an attractive woman?

"No. She's an awful looking bucket. I don't know what he sees in her. And then I've been told, the girls in the job is the worst thing that ever happened. My husband's a busman. There used not be girls in the job at one time."

I realised, from talking to that woman and others, that maintenance orders were routinely ignored. A marriage often breaks up because of drink or gambling. After that, I think the courts make a stupid act of faith when they expect a man who was never reliable with money to suddenly start providing a weekly maintenance cheque.

Sometimes maintenance cheques were paid on a Friday afternoon. Those cheques were useless to a woman and her children until they had been cleared through a bank account, which takes several days. No local shopkeeper will cash those cheques. They know the reputation of the man who has signed them.

I realised as well that people on maintenance pay were the poorest people in Ireland. They were on less than social welfare money. And men on an average wage who were paying maintenance might also be left on less than social welfare money. Marriage break-up is fine for those who can afford it but for most people, marriage break-up is a short cut to poverty.

Chapter Eight

REFUGEES: THE IRISH IN BRITAIN

Social Security Office, Cricklewood, London
14-16 June, 1990

The waiting rooms of welfare offices always look the same. Queueing for a living. In London the faces are predominantly black. In New York they are exclusively black. (Unwanted Irish people are not wanted in America either. They can only go to England.) But the mood, a mixture of tension and boredom, is the same in London, Belfast, Dublin, Cork or New York. Take your ticket and wait.

Some people look as if they've gone beyond boredom and have become inured to queueing as a way of life. Others sweat with anxiety as they wonder what will happen to them when they reach the top of the queue. They rehearse what they're going to say in order to explain whatever life crisis it is that has brought them here. You can smell tension along with the cigarette smoke. (No Smoking signs are never observed.) And there's the general dirty smell of the alcoholics and the homeless. Children become fractious. Every now and again there's an outburst of anger from the top of the queue. Somebody has waited all morning to be told they need to get a form signed in some different office across town. If you hurry you might get there before it closes at three-thirty. No, it's not possible to pay anything here.

I was sitting outside the Cricklewood office when I heard the anguished and angry shouting of one Londoner. Perhaps he was one of the psychotics, perhaps not. Clearly this place had pushed him over the edge. I went to the door to see a very big man being overpowered by security. Fark this farking place, you farking ... and so on. He was lashing out physically and verbally. The only way an otherwise powerless man can respond when all else has failed. A security man promptly blocked me from coming in even though I had put my tape-recorder away. He must have noticed me earlier doing interviews outside.

There was the usual group of middle-aged, Irish winos on the steps. They were passing a bottle of sherry around. The accents were Donegal. They were cursing incoherently and growling in the way that drunks do, challenging anybody to disagree with them and making it clear they will listen to no argument on whatever it is they're worked up about. They were giving a particularly hard time to the young black women who had to walk their gauntlet.

I sat on a plinth a bit away from the drunks. I enjoy the hot sunshine. My broad-rimmed hat, which keeps me warm in the winter, serves, in the summer, to keep me from getting sunburned on my bald head. It was a beautiful day. I knew I would meet Irish people who would talk to me. It was only a matter of waiting and waiting is something I'm good at.

A young man with a strong Waterford accent was in good form. He took his recent troubles calmly. He was working in a butcher's shop at home but had been laid off six weeks ago. Because of the strike in the glass factory people aren't spending. The strikers should go back to work. They were earning more than he had ever got.

His argument was familiar. Two months previously I had been at the dole office at Ballybricken in the city of Waterford to see what unemployed people made of the strike. Some were sympathetic to the strikers but more were not. There was resentment against the glass men as a labour elite. I was in Waterford's huge welfare ghetto of Ballybeg. A place stuck outside the city like some modern-day Bogside. People there told me the glass factory strikers were able to get cheap pints of beer from publicans who wanted to keep their custom when the strike was over. Jobless people in Waterford weren't worth that kind of concession and they knew it. So Ballybeg regarded the glass men's troubles with satisfaction. Something like the satisfaction among Cork's unemployed which had shocked me when the men of Ford and Dunlop had lost their jobs in 1984 and even better, had had to face the humiliation of the social welfare means test fifteen months later and account for what they had done with their redundancy money. Poor people don't conform to the image you would get from the pronouncements of trade unionists or the pages of militant socialist publications.

Then came a man whom I would never forget. He was thirty-two, from Kilkenny, accompanied by his much younger girlfriend.

"Well I've been working for the Queen for a while."

What do you mean?

"I was in prison."

The black-haired girl with him turned out to be exactly half his age. She was clearly pregnant so I asked him if he was married or single.

"Well I've a girlfriend here and she's due our baby in two months and I have a wife and three children back in Ireland, you know what I mean?."

And are you supporting your wife back in Ireland?

"No. The government over there is doing that. I deserted, you see. So at least she's getting money over there. It's for the best anyhow. I used to drink the money. I was a fecker for it."

So I asked his girlfriend what her parents made of this Irishman. Her accent was working-class London.

"Well they think 'e's mad but they like 'im now. They think 'e's great fun to go drinking with. And me friends like 'im too cos 'e's about the same mental age as they are. About sixteen."

And after the baby is born, do you think he'll stay with you or might he desert you like he deserted his wife in Ireland?

"Well if 'e stays 'e stays and if 'e goes 'e goes."

Of course she was only being sensible. Some day I would get used to the set of values that has evolved among people who never expect to do anything but live on welfare. It didn't really matter if her Irishman stuck around or not. He could never support her anyway, nor did she expect him to. A man who had fond notions of marriage would only be a liability who would cause her a reduction in income and independence. So a wild Irishman would do fine as a father and a lover. That he might be a rotten husband was irrelevant.

I asked the Irishman what he had been in prison for. He told me he had smashed a shop window one night and stolen electronic equipment. He was very drunk at the time and had been arrested almost immediately.

"Prison was interesting though. It was like when I was in the army back in Ireland. The Thirteenth Infantry. You're just locked up the same. I was in the F-wing. We called it the Fraggle wing because it was where they kept all the mad people. There was a Corkman on the same landing. Corky was his name."

Anything you'd like to say to your wife or children in

case they might hear you on the radio?

"No. Nothing."

Terry was thirty-four. He was from Finglas in Dublin.

"I reckon I had to leave Ireland. I wouldn't have got anywhere where I was. I'm getting myself sorted out now but it's taken me six years. I was the first four years on the streets. Mainly sleeping down the ramps in Euston Station. You can't leave anything anywhere. You have to bring everything with you. You're carrying your home on your back."

You have a scar over your eye. It looks recent.

"Yeah, a dog chain. Just there going by Marylebone Station these two Scottish guys asked me had I any odds and I said no, I'm in the same boat as you, I'm not paid till next Tuesday. And I just don't know what happened. It was blood everywhere. I couldn't see nothing. I couldn't do nothing. It was me girlfriend who said it was a dog chain."

Have you worked in your six years here?

"I haven't managed to get work because I have a problem with reading and writing and I've got a drug problem. Which is two really bad problems that I have. I started on drugs in Dublin. I want to get a course to learn to read and write. You can't beg off people. I've tried that and I feel really guilty doing it. People don't want to know you."

Are you getting treated for drugs?

"I'm on methadone at the moment. I've done two ten week courses in UCH but I've ended up getting a private doctor."

Terry made me turn off the tape-recorder. A private doctor was expensive but he didn't want anything more to do with the drug clinics because he wanted to stay out of the company of junkies. He was using his brother's birth certificate to claim money at the Lisson Grove DSS. His brother had died from drug abuse. And a Dublin man he shared a squat with died when he fell through the roof of a warehouse he was trying to rob. I recognised this story. That was Vinnie from Drimnagh. Vinnie's brother, Thomas, was a man I knew well in Dublin. Thomas died of AIDS in 1991.

Terry pointed to the growling Donegal men on the steps.

"I don't want to end up like those fellahs. I've got a good family at home. A big family. I want to go home. I'm getting treatment for drugs. The main thing now is to stay away from old friends. Just ignore them. Like I done a course in Coolmine in Dublin and it's true what they say. You have to dissociate yourself from everybody. Like they're not friends. They're just associates. Like they'd rob you if they were sick, you know?"

(By "sick" he meant if they badly needed a fix.)

Do you still take heroin?

"I won't now cos I've got my scrip for methadone. But I know what it's like to wake up sick. You don't know cos you're not a junkie. It's not just all the little aches and pains. It's mental as well. Like any argument at home you say, feck it, straight away heroin will get you to forget about everything. Like I started on heroin twelve years ago. I started off in Dublin, drinking down the fields. Then it turned to hash. Then heroin. When my dad died my mam was getting too much pressure from the police and that was because of me. I came over here and just toughed it out by myself."

Have you been in trouble with the law here?

"Yeah. Cos heroin gives you more courage to do things. Like, we'll say for a kid robbing an orchard, getting caught by somebody is like a life sentence. But for me, a junkie, I'd break into a car without thinking. I even went as far as robbing me own mam. Here in London I've sold [drugs] to keep me habit going."

Are you worried about AIDS?

"Here you can go into a chemist and buy a packet of needles. That's another thing stupid at home. You can't get clean needles."

You can now. There's a needle exchange in Baggot Street.

"Six years ago you couldn't. And like, if you want a hit you're that sick you don't care about the works. You'll clean it out. Take a chance. But to answer your question, I don't have AIDS. I want to live a long life. Like I've had enough of drugs, of waking up sick, running around looking for money for drugs. That's not living. That's torture. I'd sooner do prison rather than that."

I wished Terry the best of luck in kicking his drugs habit. I've never met him since.

I waited to see who else I would meet at the Cricklewood welfare office. A young travelling woman with thirteen children had come here two years ago. She had been put up by the homeless persons service in Hammersmith. Then she had a row there and had gone to live in a caravan. (A "CAARavan" she said, as only a traveller can.) Now they were in two B&Bs paid for by social security. She left Ireland because her husband beat her and the children. She was getting on well here. The children's allowance was much better. It is, in fact, more than double the Irish rate, so I could see her point that it paid her to be in Britain, even though unemployment pay is only roughly the same as in Ireland.

There were two single mothers from Kerry. Both had come to Britain when they learned they were pregnant.

"They'll get a land back home if I go back with a baby at Christmas."

But surely you can tell them? The days of throwing out single mothers have gone.

"Not where we come from they haven't."

The ugliest man I have ever met was a youth from Roscommon. He wasn't just ugly. He was mean and he looked it. He and his followers frightened off the nervous young Irishman I had been interviewing who was, I think, a homosexual. It might have turned into an interesting interview but these aggressive louts made him move when they demanded to know what I was doing with the microphone.

I wish I could have moved on as well. The ugly man kept spitting. There was nothing he didn't know about. He was signing and working. Screw every English bastard you can for everything you can get. A priest told me that. He repeated, a priest told me that. He looked at me to be sure I was suitably awed by the high authority he had for his actions. There had been trouble at Quex Road hostel the previous week involving English thugs after the World Cup match in which Ireland held England to a draw. Of course, the ugly man had beaten shit out of the English.

I really disliked this Roscommon man but he was a boastful fool and I thought he could be of use to me. I asked him about drugs and he showed me his hashish and his LSD tablets. I asked him about squats. They brought me down one of Kilburn's roads of big, old, red-brick houses where he thought we would meet some Irish. There was nobody at the house we went to so he walked around to the back garden and smashed one of the windows. That put me into a sweat so, trying to hide my panic, I suggested we should all go for a pint. I wanted to get the hell away from there before the police arrived.

We walked for a mile along a path by the railway track to a pub at Willesden Green. They sat outside in the hot sunshine and I went in to order four pints of lager. Are you sure you want four pints? The barman was looking past me over my shoulder. The police were outside. The Irishmen were turning out their pockets. The police were collecting pills and little tinfoil packets. Then they led them into the van. I explained to the barman that I was a journalist and that I had been interviewing those men. The barman seemed entertained by the whole thing. That's one pint of lager then, is it?

Jesus Christ. Jesus Christ. This is London and I've learned so much about Ireland from being here. I had an overwhelming sense of relief as I sat there sipping cold lager beer. Relief that I wasn't in the back of that van. Relief that I had a well-paid job and that I wasn't part of the levels of Irish society that I had seen over the last few days. The refugees. All these people were in Britain because Ireland had no place for them. Criminals. Travellers. Wife-beaters and beaten women. Deserting husbands and deserted wives. Drug addicts. Drunkards. Single mothers. Psychotics and depressives. The poor. The unemployed. They were in Britain because Britain is a country where sinners and imperfect people have their place too.

It was another two years before this dependence on Britain would be given formal, constitutional recognition in Ireland. That was when we dealt with an Irish problem, abortion, by guaranteeing the right to travel. We have always relied on English solutions to Irish problems. That keeps Ireland a morally superior place.

And those who don't measure up can go to England.

Social Security Office, Dyne Rd., Kilburn, London; 21 October 1992

"I've had all me giros stolen. I've gone in for an emergency payment."

There was a faint chance Michael was telling the truth,

but that was all. He was the third Irishman that morning to tell me the same story. That was just the Irish. The other people from Liverpool were the same. As Michael relaxed he explained a commonsense approach to emigration for somebody in his position. Michael came from Dublin. He had no skills and no place to live. So he was signing on here and claiming for the hotel he was living in.

"Hotel would give you the wrong idea. Really they're just big old houses around Kilburn that have been divided up into as many rat-holes as possible. Some of the bedrooms are like going into cupboards."

I understood. I lived in flats in Rathmines once.

"I couldn't afford to take a job. So I get what I can from the social and then I work on top of that. But that's getting very hard now. You wait for hours outside The Crown in the morning in the hope you'd be picked up and then the most you'd earn is twenty five pounds for the day."

So why did Michael come back to London just recently when he knew from previous experience that housing was bad and that work was bad now as well?

"Do you want the truth?"

Yes please.

"I have a load of warrants for tax and insurance and that. In Ireland, I'm looking at two years if I go back. Like I'm driving again now with no tax and insurance but I can get away with it here for a while."

Why was it so important to have a car?

"Because I have a wife and a couple of kids. They're around the corner now if you want to say hello."

Michael and Sandra gave me a lift to their flat in West Harrow. Sandra and the children have a good flat from the Social Security. No, Michael doesn't live in the hotel. He just claims for it.

"I just survive a lot better here. The opportunities are better. A few of us from Dublin are here. None of us are working but everybody I know is doing well."

You mean you rob, Michael, is that it?

"Well, sometimes, but I haven't been caught for it."

And in Ireland?

"When I was younger. I was in St. Patrick's in Dublin and I was at a borstal in Manchester before that."

I asked Sandra if she was glad she'd moved to England.

"Well we had to. Tell him Michael."

"Harassment."

What do you mean? Sandra?

"Well it was harassment by the neighbours in Tallaght. Concerned Parents."

And were you using drugs?

"Yeah. Well no. Michael was. Well he was accused of it. You tell him, Michael."

"The neighbours saw us bringing stuff into the house. I mean gear that was robbed and then they said I was dealing in cocaine and heroin. And then the Sinn Fein were in me home. I had nothing at the time when they were in the house. But then they had a march on the road, the neighbours did. They said the house was a shooting gallery."

There was a chance he was telling me the whole truth. The shooting gallery accusation, meaning that the house was being used by heroin addicts, had a familiar ring to it. It's routine now in parts of Dublin to accuse undesirable neighbours of drug abuse when people want to get rid of them. So I couldn't make a judgement on that. But I had no doubt he was telling the truth about the accusation and the action by Concerned Parents in the Fettercairn estate of Tallaght. So Michael was in London now. Another person not wanted in Ireland. A refugee.

How do you feel about raising a child in London? Michael?

"There's too many scumbags. Like, fellahs who wouldn't

be allowed anywhere else in England. They all come to London."

At the time it struck me as a laughable comment, coming from the source it did. But he had a point. London is a place where unwanted people from everywhere else can hide. It is hard to hide in Dublin. Dublin is small and has a close family and neighbourhood structure, which makes organisations like Concerned Parents Against Drugs a viable proposition. (The flats of Ballymun are probably the only exception because the extended family structure has been largely dissolved in single-mother land.) It's even more difficult to hide in Belfast where the paramilitary groups of both communities regularly force their unwanted people to leave for Britain under the threat of death or kneecapping. Unwanted Irish people, like unwanted British people, end up in London.

Michael gave me a lift back to Kilburn. He was going there anyway, he told me, to score some dope.

Kilburn Social Security Office. The next day

Meeting the Irish isn't too difficult. Most people here are black or Asian so I simply restrict myself to the whites who, quite likely, will be Irish.

I met more drug users. One Dublin man was gaunt, scruffy and unwell, but he didn't at first choose to admit to being a drug taker. I asked him about his appearance.

"It's because I'm only just out of prison and I'm looking for a crisis loan to get things for the flat. And I've had me giro stolen."

What were you in prison for?

"Petty crime". (In his working-class, Dublin accent it came out as "pe-ee crime"). "I mean with homelessness and joblessness and all I ended up mixing with people I

138

shouldn't have and ended up getting done for stolen goods. But getting back to the social, the most they're willing to give me is five hundred and sixty pounds for a bed, cooker, basic stuff for the flat. I mean it's hard enough living in a house with a cooker and all. That way you can buy cheap food and live. But when you're going to cafes and eating out your money goes in half the time."

He was holding back on me. No mention of drugs. But he was clearly a good talker and worth taking time with. I turned off the tape-recorder. I guessed that he would know other drug users in Kilburn. He had been here for nine years. Perhaps he used to know two friends of mine from Cork, Tommy and Niamh. They had lived in a council house off Shoot Up Hill. Niamh died in 1986 as a result of heroin abuse.

He knew them very well. Tommy was a hippy fellah. He died last year taking drugs. He was found dead in the toilet of a pub here.

So that's what happened to Tommy. It didn't surprise me. I had met Tommy again by chance in Kilburn in 1988, two years after Niamh's death. Tommy and I both loved Niamh once. I bought Tommy a pint in Biddy Mulligan's and we talked about Niamh.

Tommy told me that the night before Niamh died the two of them decided to get married. They celebrated by doing some smack. The next morning Niamh turned on again on her own. She was planning to get a flight to Ireland in the afternoon for an interview with AnCo. She wouldn't get a chance to take heroin again for some time. Tommy came back to the house later that morning and was surprised to see Niamh's little girl still there in her night clothes. Mummy had gone blue in the bath. Tommy explained to me that she must have been using the hot bath to get her collapsed veins to swell and so make them injectable. The heart attack had happened, he thought, because she was using her usual quantity of heroin despite the fact that she had been clean for about a year.

I remember Niamh in Kilburn in December 1984 assuring me that I would not, some day, be going to her funeral. She was dead less than two years later. And now Tommy was dead too. Many of Niamh's friends had blamed him because Niamh went back on drugs. I knew this was rubbish. Tommy was simply a drug addict. So was Niamh.

It was nice to meet somebody who knew Niamh. I've cried all my tears for her now but I still like to meet anybody who can help me to understand how a good-humoured, good-natured and very brilliant young woman gave up everything else for the sake of heroin. And eventually died at the age of twenty-eight. I asked the Dubliner, why? He told me he was also a heroin addict with a very heavy habit. A quarter a day he was using which, I took his word for, is a heavy habit. He was intrigued to discover how many of his old acquaintances from the drug scene in Dublin I had interviewed over the years. He seemed to want to talk but, as happens so often with drug addicts, he had to see somebody that evening. We arranged to meet the next day at the Black Cafe across the road. I guessed that his evening meeting was either to get drugs or to do something to get money for drugs, the only two real imperatives in a drug addict's life. The next day at the Black Cafe he never turned up.

Social Security Office, Moseley Road, Birmingham;
21 December 1992

I was surprised when Maria told me she was from a traveller background. She didn't have the rough, prematurely aged look of a travelling woman. She was still

140

very good-looking in her middle age. Her West of Ireland accent was clear and beautiful and it made me think of the nuns who educated me in my London childhood.

Maria was at the welfare with her daughter, a young adult whose accent was pure Birmingham. I introduced myself and said I was interested in meeting Irish people who were unemployed in Britain. Maria invited me to join her in the Moseley Arms pub, next door to the welfare office. There would be people there I could meet. Normally I loathe working in pubs because I know I'll be bothered by drunks who react to the sight of my microphone and tape recorder but that day I wanted to get in from the freezing cold of the British winter. I made an exception.

The pub was full of middle-aged Irish people. Mainly travellers. They looked tough and weather-beaten. A lot of them were drunk and some were talking aggressively to each other. I thought about British caricatures of Irishmen and how true they are.

In the pub Maria introduced me to her friend, Patrick. Again I was surprised when he told me he was a traveller. It turned out that neither of them had had a traveller's upbringing but had been brought up in care. When I took out my microphone Maria and Patrick spoke to me intently. They had a lot they wanted to say.

Patrick had lost contact with his sister Anne when his family had been broken up. He had been taken into care. He went to Glin Industrial School in Limerick. I don't have fond memories of Ireland, he said. At Glin, beatings on the hands and bare buttocks were routine. Patrick laughed about the fact that he was beaten with leathers which he himself had to make in the workshop. He was apprenticed to a butcher in Tarbert, Co. Kerry. The butcher had recruited deliberately from Glin and he could send Patrick back there again if he wanted. At seventeen Patrick took the mail boat and got a job in Scunthorpe at a steel mill. Five years later he moved to Birmingham. He hadn't been back in Ireland for forty-one years.

Patrick and his brother Desmond, a bus driver in Coventry, wanted to find their sister again. They had another brother as well but he was killed in a car chase with the police in London some years ago. Patrick told me what he could about his sister and I'm pleased to tell you now that the following February I got a letter from Patrick and Maria to say that Anne had got in contact again after their appeal had been broadcast on radio.

Maria was, I think, a person more wounded by her childhood than Patrick was. She was born in Clifden, Co.Galway.

"I too have very bad memories of Ireland but I was better off in care than I was as a nomad. The nuns taught you how to live the settled life. As a traveller you would just brush off the hay from your clothes and you were ready to face the day."

She had no regrets that she had brought up her own children away from traveller culture. She was in care from the age of seven to sixteen and went to England at nineteen. I asked her what she didn't like about the nuns.

"They were too fond of the cane. For losing a lace, for having dirty socks, runny nose, we got the cane. And, oh yes, one thing we did get badly caned for was bedwetting. We were made get up, take our sheets off, take them down to the laundry. Then you would have to lift your nightdress and you would get caned on the, eh, buttocks."

I was blazing with anger. I remember a woman, originally from Drogheda, whom I met at a welfare office in Ballyfermot, Dublin, in 1986. As she queued to see the welfare officer she made frequent visits to the toilet. She explained she had a bowel and bladder disorder since childhood. She had been raised by nuns whose cure for bedwetting was to strip her and beat her with their rosary beads. She had gone from one institution to another. Her crime was that she was abandoned as a baby. Now in her thirties, she was a mental wreck. She was living with a man whom the health board had told her to stay away from because they believed he was molesting her children. Michael, who was with her, said he was not guilty. She didn't know what the truth was for sure but Michael was "all she had". (After this was broadcast Michael's mother phoned me to say that she had no doubt about her son's guilt. He had molested his young sister throughout her teenage years.)

Maria had spent time in mental institutions in Ireland and in Britain. Her teenage behaviour was unruly. She had been greatly helped in Ireland by Dr. Noel Browne, who was an MP as well as a doctor. Had I ever heard of him? Her problems continued in Britain but she was less wild now. It had been some years since she was last in a British police cell for being drunk and disorderly.

I asked Maria if she thought her mental illness was caused by her upbringing in care.

"No. It doesn't go back to the nuns. It goes back to the time I was a traveller. It was more horrific things happened to me in the caravan than in the convent."

You're telling me you were sexually abused. Is that it Maria?

She waved her hand to tell me to stop recording her. She didn't want to talk about that because the men concerned were still alive.

Maria called Johnny Casey over from the pool table to talk to me. Another traveller. He had lost contact with his family thirty-seven years ago. He named a list of brothers and sisters whom he remembered but hadn't seen since he was taken into care in Artane in Dublin. He was sent to Monaghan to work on a farm for a man called Markey. He moved to England when he was eleven. I was aghast. Why Johnny?

"Because I was running away from the Christian Brothers."

I realised that this place was full of refugees. Then I was shoved roughly from behind. He was middle-aged, loud and drunk. Patrick Ryan is my name, from Clonmel, and what fucking about it? Go away and go to hell, you stupid drunk, I thought. Go and bully your wife or whoever it is you bully. But I had to stay calm. I drew on experience. I held out my hand and introduced myself, ignoring his aggression. It had worked for me many times in the Irish pubs of New York where drunken men came looking for a fight with the radio interviewer.

Ryan kept shouting, proving what a big man he was. He felt he had triumphed over me as he squeezed my hand and realised I wasn't going to challenge him. A stout woman with a leathery face spoke to me hopefully, saying she would love to speak on the radio. I was sorry I had to leave before I knew what she wanted to say. I hate working in pubs.

It was a relief to get out of the pub and back into the freezing fresh air. I like working the street. The streets are mine. I don't have to be nice to drunks or worry about being a focus of trouble. I don't have to kiss social workers' backsides as so many journalists do when they are looking for "case histories". It was nice out here in the cold, crunching the ice under my boots. It was already getting dark in the mid-afternoon of this, the shortest day of the year.

A mile away across the valley of Digbeth, the tall buildings of Birmingham city centre were turning into silhouettes against the sky. The temperature was set to drop to nine below freezing that night as the West Midlands remained the coldest part of Britain. I stamped my

144

feet and walked up and down the road outside the social security office. There were lots of drunken Irish in the Moseley Arms and the other pubs of Digbeth and Balsall Heath but I wouldn't get trapped into that again. Better to stay on the street and wait. I like working the street.

More travellers. And more middle-aged Irishmen who looked toughened by a lifetime of working and most likely drinking as well. They were cautious of me when I approached them. We're saying nothing. We know nothing about it. I've been told many times by other people that this is country cuteness, the tell-him-nothing syndrome. I don't believe that. I think their reticence is due to an upbringing in a totalitarian Catholic culture which never encouraged people to speak for themselves or to even think for themselves. There was no *Late Late Show* or radio chat shows when they were growing up. So now they couldn't believe that this stranger from Ireland with a tape-recorder could possibly be standing out in the cold for hours to hear what they had to say. Why should their opinion count for anything? We know nothing about it. You'd better ask the priest.

From the homeless persons section, just next to the main doors of the social security office, there was a steady procession of psychotics and alcoholics. Many of them had, no doubt, been "discharged into the community" from psychiatric institutions. Now they were in danger of freezing to death. One ragged old man with a ludicrous, shaggy beard was talking excitedly to himself or perhaps to some imaginary companion. I could hear his Brum accent as he passed. Then I saw a woman in her mid-thirties with a teenage child. I guessed she was Irish.

Geraldine was pleased to talk. She left Nenagh, Co.Tipperary in 1988 and had not been back since.

"Well I had a still-born birth there and I have too many memories."

I know that people often rashly give up a home after a bad experience. They want to run away, I suppose. But Geraldine was so adamant that she would never go back to Ireland again that I felt there had to be something more.

Geraldine told me that after she had arrived in England with the children and Declan, their father, she had promptly barred Declan from the home because of violence. This was something she could never do in Ireland because of the peculiarity of Irish law which allows barring orders only against a husband.

I remembered the Irish women I'd met who were stuck with common-law husbands they have no way of getting rid of. The Family Court at Dolphin House, Dublin, 1990. He stripped me naked in the street. Reefed the trousers off me. She gathered up the courage to apply for a barring order. And the court clerk explained to her that she couldn't get a barring order because she wasn't married to her attacker. The only alternative was a lengthy and cumbersome injunction against him entering the home that she was, of course, free to discuss with her solicitor.

Geraldine from Nenagh had no regrets about coming to Birmingham.

"The police here do much more for you. Fair dues."

To my Irish ears, it was strange to hear the West Midlands Police spoken of in this way. Geraldine's perspective was different from that of the Birmingham Six.

When you were coming here, why didn't you just leave Declan behind and not tell him where you were going?

"To tell you the truth, I was afraid of him. And he said it would all be different when we'd get to England. He'd stop drinking and get a job. He knew nobody in Nenagh would give him a job."

Like a rhinestone cowboy ... Another bloody Irish drunk. Geraldine was still speaking but I knew the drunk

146

wouldn't go away so long as the microphone was on view. At least this one wasn't aggressive. Eventually he grew bored and moved on. Geraldine told me about the domestic violence she had suffered.

"Batterings ... and things you wouldn't believe. I'd never go back to Ireland. Not after what I went through. Too many memories. I'd never go back, ever."

Our noses were running in the cold and we decided to go to the cafe just down the hill. It was then that I realised the man who was standing near us was with Geraldine and her child. He was about ten years younger than she was and of Pakistani or Indian appearance. His voice was Brum. He told me it was lucky that Geraldine's Irishman was a small man like himself. Declan still visits her sometimes and Geraldine goes off with him for the day. He said she's scared of him.

The cafe was one of those working men's places where you get a big mug of tea for 20p. The staff were friendly and full of Christmas cheer. I noticed that a lot of the homeless men I had seen earlier were in here. The man with the shaggy beard was at a table by himself, still talking to his invisible friend. I think they were discussing the weather. Looking at him closely I realised he was a good deal younger than I had first thought. Probably only about forty but aged by a cruel life.

Geraldine's dark-skinned friend told me he was homeless after his divorce and Geraldine was putting him up for the while. He seemed a good-natured man but I wondered to myself what sort of legal separation would put him out of the house with nowhere to go. Perhaps he had been barred by his wife. I wondered if Geraldine was the sort of woman who always ended up with a man who would mistreat her.

I asked Geraldine what advice she would give to somebody who was thinking of moving to Britain, perhaps to Birmingham. She said that work was not good here but if you wanted to get away from Ireland for other reasons it might be the right thing to do. It was the right thing for her. After the beatings and "what he had done". What do you mean Geraldine? What did he do?

"Well, put it this way, I mean my child was three days dead, and he come in one night with drink down him. And he says the child is not dead and all this. So I just told him to leave me alone. And I had my back to the back door and he walked out the door and he come back about a half an hour after and he dug the child up and he threw it in my lap and he says, there's your son."

Her daughter, aged fifteen, joined in.

"And there's proof that he dug it up because I buried a little teddy bear with it and the teddy bear was up."

Had Geraldine's daughter seen this dead baby?

"No. I was in bed but I heard everything that went on. I used to stay in bed because it was me he hated because he's not my dad you see. When he used to beat her up he used to say it was my fault. He was an alcoholic you see. He used to say the baby wasn't dead and he could hear him crying and crawling around. Mum was going mad."

Geraldine said the stillborn baby had been buried by his father in her grandmother's grave. Nobody else had seen what he did three days later. She would never go back again.

That evening I called to the Castle and Falcon pub. A man I met at the dole earlier told me there would be a music session there. I felt very good now as I knew I had a good day's work behind me. As I listened to the musicians here, I realised why my favourite Irish music band, The Pogues, had come out of the British tradition of Irish music. The music here is played with real enjoyment and passion and is part of popular culture. That makes it much better than the sterile instrumental performances which are laid on in West of Ireland pubs for respectful and hushed European visitors in the summer. I hate that diddle-eye shite.

I played a song by Phillip Chevron of the Pogues. It includes lines that seemed appropriate to the day I'd had.

> *"Where'er we go, we celebrate the land that makes us refugees*
> *Through fear of priests with empty plates and guilt and weeping effigies."*

The Brums were interested to meet me, especially after I had played a few songs with them. They told me about their love of Ireland and Irish music, their visits to Ireland and their Irish ancestry.

They are strange Englishmen. In truth, they understand little of Ireland and the Catholic, un-British aspects of Irishness. I remember the Irish soccer captain Mick McCarthy declaring himself, in his Yorkshire accent, to be a hundred and ten percent Irish. McCarthy is English-born, of Irish background, as I am. But I have been beaten about the ears by Christian Brothers. That makes me Irish. People who claim to be Irish on the basis of mere ancestry don't know what they're talking about. As in this Birmingham pub. They don't realise that they are not Irish. In Ireland they would be just as English as I was when my family moved from Britain to Ireland when I was a child.

Everybody was cheerful and friendly. Not for the first time I found my mind wandering to what happened in two Birmingham pubs on a night like this in 1974. The Birmingham Twenty-One.

There were lots of Irish here but all of them were travellers. That's bad news for me. Travellers are secretive people at the best of times. At the welfare they're particularly secretive. No, you'll get no information from me. The word "information" is spat out. It's a dirty word among travellers.

The Hiace vans came and went. I settled in for a long wait. It was Monday morning. I would spend all week here if I had to.

The young English people were interesting and friendly. A lot of them were homeless. Some were drug addicts. But I felt I couldn't base my programme on them.

I talked with the security guard at the DSS. He brought me in for a cup of tea. He told me about his son's heroin addiction. His son had robbed their home to pay for his habit. As a father he had done everything he could for his son but now he felt helpless. There were tears in the man's eyes. I could only sit and listen, just as I have sat and listened to the parents of heroin addicts in Dublin.

I talked a while with an out-of-work builder. I told him how difficult it was to get Irish travellers to talk on tape. Is "travellers" the word you call them by here? No. We call them TGBs. Thieving gypsy bastards.

It was four o'clock when my luck changed. Two traveller women I had been watching all day finally came out of the DSS. They were both in their late twenties.

"I went in and asked for me giro, and cos I only got released from prison, they didn't want to give it to me. They told me to go home to Ireland where I came from."

Did you get the giro?

"I did. She got eighteen pounds and I got fifty-one. She'll get the rest of hers on Thursday. They tried to tell us we weren't entitled to an emergency payment."

"They said we got enough of the social."

"But we told them we'd come to whatever country we want and claim whatever we want."

"We're entitled to our money."

Are you just out of prison too?

"Yeah. It was bad. We were in Risley. Because you're Irish they're against you. After the Warrington bomb they were all against us."

Why did you come to Britain?

"To fraud the Government."

"My ex-boyfriend was very violent and was only out of prison and he *did* stab me and he was looking for me again so I just left. Know what I mean?"

Could you not have hidden from him in Ireland?

"I didn't want to be a burden on any of me family."

Why were you in prison?

"Your life leads to crime in England cos they won't give us our social. You go out shoplifting. You go in, you do social books. You do fraud. Just to get money to live."

So why were you in prison?

"Fraud."

"Social books. We used all different names in our claims. You could do seven or eight in a week if you're clever enough."

Do you need a lot of birth certs for that?

"You can take a birth certificate and you can just keep cleaning it and putting in different people's names. If you tell them the birth cert is all you have, they'll accept it."

How were you caught?

"We were squealed on by me sister-in-law and me cousin."

"They grassed us up."

"We have to go. We've to get to the post office to cash these."

Kathleen jumped at the chance to talk. I hadn't finished explaining what I was doing but she was in no doubt. She had done an interview for radio once before, she told me.

Kathleen was about twenty-three. Her brother and his wife stood with her as she spoke.

"I'm only a single parent and they wouldn't give me no money to do me house up. I only got two hundred pounds there two months ago and I got me washing machine with that. When I come to Manchester first, two years ago, they wouldn't give me no money cos me birth certi ... certic ... they weren't happy with me birth certicates. And I was homeless. I was sleeping in Picadilly."

Picadilly is the central square of Manchester. Homeless people sleep in the green there or in the bus depot.

Kathleen told me she used to live at a halting site in Dundalk. That's when I remembered that I had interviewed her once before. In March, 1990, outside the gate of Mountjoy Prison in Dublin. A prisoner, Sharon Gregg, had hanged herself in her cell the night before and I went to the prison gate for the *Pat Kenny Show*. I met a number of women prisoners who had got early release that morning in advance of a visit by women politicians due in the afternoon. I interviewed Kathleen and a woman from Clonmel.

Kathleen said she didn't recognise me to begin with. Must be the hat, she said. I asked Kathleen if she had stayed out of trouble in Manchester.

"I'm three years out of prison. I was in prison for stealing stuff out of shops. Clothes and ... Mickey Mouse things. I come to Manchester and I've kept out of trouble here. I've a baby now and I've kept myself clear."

Kathleen's brother began to laugh. He said she was in

more trouble now than she had ever been. Then he asked me not to let his voice be heard on the radio.

I asked Kathleen again if she had broken the law in Manchester.

"I'm up in court on Thursday. For robbing."

From where? Was it a shop?

"I can't tell you that. It was a street robbery. I'll get off cos it's a first offence. And they won't send me to prison with the baby."

Why were you robbing?

"Cos I was drinking. And I needed money to get by."

After the DSS closed I walked over to Picadilly. I had heard a lot about this place from the homeless people. There was a soup kitchen at night. I eavesdropped for Irish accents but I found none.

The place is full of beggars. A lot of the young people who are begging don't look particularly poor. It's like a job to them. There's no other work, I suppose.

Others looked ill. These were the drug addicts and the alcoholics.

I went to use the public toilet and a young man came in behind me. He was pasty-faced and sweaty. He was drinking a can of beer which I thought was an unhygienic thing to do in here. He stood at the urinal next to mine, leaned towards me and peered down over my shoulder.

It's strange how, with shock, my mind reacted against the obvious. Was he trying to read my watch? Then I realised there was no urinal next to mine. He was standing there to watch me take a pee.

I felt sick. Do you mind?

He walked over to the toilet cubicles, pushed each door until he found one that was occupied, knelt on the floor and looked up under the door. An angry Mancunian voice erupted from inside. Getting an eyeful then are you?

The youth ran. A burly man burst out of the cubicle. I'll fucking kill him. I don't know if the man ever caught that revolting young pervert.

I went back to my hotel. There was a friendly atmosphere in the bar where I could sit and chat with the other men who, like myself, were working away from home. I was glad to leave Picadilly behind.

Chapter Nine

GHOSTS: DUBLIN'S DRUG USERS

*Pearse St., Dublin. Outside the drug treatment
unit at Trinity Court; 1 August, 1990*

It was the younger, slighter and more feminine looking of
the two women who spoke to me first.

"I'm trying to give up drugs. I was sent to Pearse Street
by my probation officer to give up drugs because when we
take drugs we have to go out and rob. One of the rules of
the court is that I must come here. I hate having to rob
people. Sometimes I have to do cheques and things like
that. I do them for fifty pounds or else maybe in
restaurants I go in for a meal and write the cheque for a
hundred pounds and I'd get the change because when you
write a cheque in a restaurant, you're not robbing the
person who owns the chequebook. But you run out of
restaurants, don't you?"

She looked respectable enough to be able to get away
with cashing bad cheques. No visible tattoos. Her accent
was slightly midlands rather than the strong Dublin accent
usual among drug addicts.

As she offered me a cigarette and then the first drink
from her can of Coke I could see how her wrists and arms

had been crisscrossed with countless scars. I asked her how she began taking drugs.

"Curiosity was enough to make me snort it, never inject it. I said I'd never put a needle to my arm. But eventually snorting it, snorting it, I was getting less and less from doing this, right? So I said I'd just try a little skin-pop into my arm. I done that and it creeped up on me and it was like something else. It was like, God, that's great. But when I actually mainlined into my vein that's when I thought, wow, this is it. I've never ever felt like this in my life. It took me three months taking it and taking it because, aaah, I loved the buzz."

Her voice quivered and her face had the expression you would expect if she had been recalling a deeply pleasurable sexual experience. I asked her how she was coping without drugs. How would she cope today?

"I'm going now to get stoned out of my head. And eh, I've five hundred pounds on me now and I'll spend the whole bleedin' lot of it today."

She pulled a thick, blue wad of twenty pounds notes from inside the front of her pants. It certainly looked like it could be five hundred pounds. The belly she exposed was slim, flat and shapely but once again I could see scars. I asked her how she had earned the money.

"Well I've done everything to make money. Everything."

She fell silent.

Do you mean prostitution?

She nodded.

Was that a yes?

"That is a yes. I have my own clientele. Not a street thing. It's a whatdoyacallit, it's a massage parlour. Blessington Street. Condoms I use. They have to be hidden in case of raids from the police, right? It's up to you what you want to do. You don't have to do sex. You can do topless massage, you can do reverse massage. You can do ehm ... shit, you can make up a load of things. You can do discipline. Usually I get a hundred pounds for discipline."

She was laughing now. Even as I blurted out my surprise at how much she charged I realised I should have shut up. But she didn't seem to take offence.

"Well, see, discipline is a thing where guys who want discipline, and I don't know why it is, they're all moneyed men. Whatever it is they just want to be domineered. Maybe it's because they're a boss themselves and maybe they feel they want someone else to boss them for a change."

I realise now why she could charge so much. Over the next few days I met a lot of prostitutes but these were middle-aged and often beer-bellied. The woman I was talking to here was in her early twenties, blonde and sexy.

Her companion spoke next. She was a bit older and definitely bigger in every way. She had a deeper voice. She was butch.

"We're all gay. We're mostly all lesbians. All the prostitutes. There's only about ten of us are straight and there is a lot of us. The rest of us are all lesbians. Like we're girlfriends, you know? The two of us are living together and I'm five months pregnant. We planned it. We got this guy."

"Like we want a family."

"So we got this guy, like he was clean. The two of us took our tests so I asked him. It took him three years to say yeah, and eventually he said yeah."

"I was in the room while they done it. There was nothing sexual. It was just he done it. They had to try and try and try but they done it eventually."

And now that she was pregnant, had she stopped taking drugs?

"I knew I was pregnant when I was a week over me periods, right? And I gave up drugs then. And we don't use other people's works. I use her's and she uses mine."

Clearly she was still using drugs. For the baby's sake isn't it very important that you stop taking drugs?

Her voice was plaintive in reply.

"But I can't and I'm trying. I never looked for help until a while ago and I'm still waiting. I'm in there every day giving urines and I'm begging them for help and they said Tuesday and I don't know whether they're going to put me on it Tuesday. If they don't I'm finished and me baby will be ruined."

I've never met those two lesbian women since, which is unusual for Dublin. I hope that they no longer take drugs, that they have remained free of the AIDS virus and that their baby was born healthy. Too many of the other voices I have on tape from the drug clinics are the voices of ghosts. I'm listening to them now.

I liked Ellen Dixon. She was in her late thirties. She was older and calmer than most of the people attending the Pearse Street clinic. She was in an advanced stage of the AIDS virus but could still walk and talk and she still had the use of her mind. When she told me she had attended St. Martha's Therapeutic Community near Johnstown, Co. Meath, I asked her if she had known my friend Niamh. She had known her very well. She and Niamh had been involved in drama together and she had loved Niamh's sense of humour. Then she asked me how Niamh was getting on now? I told her Niamh died nearly four years previously. Ellen looked saddened but not shocked. Her reaction was like that of a soldier in wartime who hears of the death of a comrade. Ellen was used to death. She expected it. Ellen Dixon died in 1991.

I was talking to Ellen when we were joined by Frances Flynn who said she would like to talk to me. This was the start of a friendship between Frances and I that would last for the remaining two-and-a-half years of her life. Frances was thirty-nine years old when I met her and, like Ellen, she was calm enough to accept that the regime in the drug clinic was there for her own good. When I told Frances about the two lesbian women and their anger at not getting an immediate dose of methadone she told me to never mind those two, sure they're both on the game, which was pretty damned unfair of her considering what she went on to tell me about her own life.

Frances was tall with fair, bobbed hair. She wouldn't have looked out of place as an air hostess. People tell me now that she was especially beautiful when she was younger. When I first met her she had a lovely complexion. AIDS had yet to ravage and torment her skin.

I gave Frances a lift to Ballymun where she was staying with her niece. They gave me dinner. Frances had a lot she wanted to tell me.

"I started on drugs late in life. I was married and had me children and all. I was offered a turn-on and I took it and I liked it. I liked the feeling it gave me, that you forget everything. But you never get that feeling again. You always try to reach for that feeling but that only comes once when you get your first hit. And after that you keep taking extra. More and more and more, trying to get that hit.

"But anybody who is out there I'd advise them to stay away from drugs. The only thing it really does is it brings heartaches to homes. You wreck your mother and father's lives. At the time I know we don't listen and it's too late when we do. But this advertising on AIDS, it's no good. They should let kids see the AIDS ward in St. James's and let them see how people die from it and it might just frighten them."

I asked her how long she had had the virus.

"I've known now about six year. That's good going. I

think I'm getting a fair innings really."

This was 1990. I was still influenced by the wisdom of the time that to be HIV positive was not necessarily a death-sentence. It had been thought that perhaps one in twenty would go on to get AIDS. As the years went by that prediction turned out to be far too optimistic. I asked Frances Flynn if she thought she would develop the full-blown AIDS virus.

"Well the last time I was told that things had changed."

But are you developing AIDS?

Her voice was almost a whisper but her reply was definite.

"Yeah. Ah yeah."

And how does that affect you?

"Like I say, nobody knows how long it will take. Maybe I might get a bit lucky and have another couple of years. I'd like to see me kids get a bit older. Specially the younger ones. It's hard at times but I know I can't blame anybody for it. We put our hand out. We put the needle in and we have only ourselves to blame. Nobody knew about AIDS but we done it ourselves. And the people that's going around now blaming everybody bloody else, why don't they just start saying no? I mean this business of blaming the clinic. They're only trying to help. And you need help. I mean I'm going to try to come down off the fie. I don't want to be on it. I want to go out and when I do I want to go out clean. So people can say, at least she came off the fie."

("Fie" is physeptone, the drug used to wean addicts off heroin.)

Frances began to describe her own eventful thirty-nine years of life. Her voice sounded weary, like that of an old woman. I didn't interrupt her. At times she would go quiet as she gathered her thoughts. During those silences I became conscious of the sounds coming from beyond the balcony. The children of Ballymun were playing, their happy voices floating up from below as the summer evening turned to twilight. I think that people who are faced with an unbearable life crisis sometimes long for their childhood and the certainties that it held. Frances recalled the day, six years before, when she had been diagnosed as HIV positive.

"I remember I walked for miles. Miles. And I walked all up ... me mother lived in Drimnagh one time but before that when we were kids we lived on the Naas Road. I remember walking up to the old house and ... the woman must have thought I was mad. I was staring in. And she said, are you lost love? And I said no, I used to live in that house. And I just started crying and she said, what's up with you? And I said, ah, nothing, I'm sorry for troubling you. And she said, ah, no, you're not troubling me. Are you in any kind of trouble? And I said no, I just heard that me health wasn't so good. I didn't go into full detail with her.

"But I walked on then and I walked for miles and I sat down in the grass. Miles up again from the Naas Road. And I was just sitting there thinking, and saying to meself, what in the name of God am I going to do? Y'know, how am I going to tell me sisters? How am I going to tell them that I'm going to die? Like I had a brother died there in October and we knew that for a good while Jimmy was going to die and I was saying to meself, now they're going to have to face all that with me. And we are very close too. I could just imagine her face. A social worker broke the news to her. I couldn't. She came home, the cries of her and all. She kept saying you're not looking ill, there's not a bother on you. And I said to her, Breda, it's not like that. And now I just carry on all day. But at night when I go to bed I'm lying there thinking. Thinking about the kids. Thinking that I'll never see them get married. I'll never see ... "

Frances told me that her children, now teenagers, were

in England with one of her sisters. She wouldn't ask them to come home.

"To what? To nothing. They're getting better chances. It would be very greedy of me to take them home now. For what?"

But Frances, in London especially, there's plenty of drugs.

Her voice changed in tone as she answered. She was far away, dreamy, wistful. She was talking now about a different world.

"Ah no. My children live out in the moors in Yorkshire. It's miles out. A farmhouse. It's a lovely place. My daughter's going with a lad around the corner. They all marry within one another. Everyone knows one another. And one day, even if I'm not around I just hope she marries someone from around there."

I asked Frances to tell me about the onset of AIDS.

"Pains in the legs. Under the arms. It's gland trouble. An awful lot of cramps. I often woke up out of sleep with pains in me legs. I often cried with pains in me legs. Then I often find I go sideways, lose balance. I was told like that is all part of it. Like it comes slowly. But other than that, thank God, I've been lucky."

And in the case of your brother there were other stages?

"Oh yeah. Oh yeah. My brother died a hard death. He lingered for a long time. He went through an awful lot. And eh ... it wasn't great for him, to tell you the truth. There was times he thought he was in Vietnam and he'd pick up something and say, duck, quick, I'm throwing this grenade. It would be a big statue or something. It got to the brain. He really got bad. He was in a wheelchair and all."

So you've seen your brother die of AIDS. Frances, are you frightened?

Frances thought for a moment.

"I won't actually say I'm frightened. I'll just never let my kids, I'll put it this way to you, see me the way my brother let himself go so far. I'll never bring that upon me family and upon me kids. I don't think they deserve to see all that."

Her voice was dropping now. The room had grown dark. She spoke quietly but passionately.

"There's other ways out. I don't think your family deserves that. It's bad enough them knowing. But I think there's ways of getting out without going through all that."

You'll take your own life? Is that what you're telling me?

"I said I'd never touch gear again. That'll be the last day I'll ever touch it."

I stayed in contact with Frances Flynn over the next weeks and months. She moved into a flat in St. Michael's Estate, Inchicore. Frances had a telephone there, which made her almost unique in that estate. She told me she was born Frances Henaghan. She was separated from her husband, also a drug addict. He was in Mountjoy. Her first child was born when she was a teenager and had been fostered. And she told me that she had given her brother a fatal dose of heroin to end his suffering in the final stage of AIDS. I never asked her about that again, although it was a story she would repeat to my wife in greater detail another time.

She told me about her evenings as a prostitute on Benburb Street. She was on the game to pay for her drink and drugs habit. She said making money that way was too bloody easy. She could always blow all her money on drugs because she knew she could make it up again in a few hours standing at the wall. The strangest man she ever picked up drove her to a lane off Arbour Hill and parked the car with the passenger door against the wall so that she couldn't get out. Then he opened his coat and made her pray to the holy pictures he had pinned all over the coat's

163

lining. But most of the men she met on Benburb Street were "all right". She only had to say the right things to some of her regulars as they masturbated in the car.

Four months after I first met Frances, Mick, her boyfriend of the last few years, answered the phone one day and told me that Frances had been taken to St. James's with a bad haemorrhage. She had been losing her balance and the use of her legs but this had been her worst setback yet.

I called to Hospital Five in St. James's, which is where the AIDS cases are usually treated. They directed me to Hospital Seven. Frances wasn't in her room when I arrived but one of the staff told me she had gone to the toilet. She would be back in a moment. I sat on a seat in the corridor and waited. From around the corner at the far end of the building a frail, stooped woman was approaching. She was wheeling one of those things that holds a plastic container high up with a drip from it that entered her arm via a tube. Her hair was thin and lank. As she came close I could see her face was ruddy and inflamed. Jesus Christ. It was Frances.

I helped her into bed. There was so little of her there beneath her nightdress. Her smile was skeletal, her skin taut against her skull. She told me that nearly every day some different part of her body would begin to fail. Her chest, her bowels, her skin, her legs. If God wants me so much I wish he'd fucking take me instead of carrying on with me like this. She was aggressive towards the hospital staff, a side of her character I hadn't seen before. She resented the nurses and cleaners who wore surgical gloves to change her bed linen. I held her hand against her chest as she lay on her back and eventually fell asleep. Her breath was rasping. I stayed for some time holding her hand. Then I kissed her forehead and left.

I don't like a lot of men but I liked Mick, Frances Flynn's lover. Most husbands or boyfriends tend to be very protective of their women where I am concerned. It's as if I should ask the husband's permission before I interview the wife. When I approach a couple at a welfare queue, or wherever, I always aim my words mainly at the man. This flatters male pride and is likely to lead to the best results for me from both interviewees. If I address myself to the woman the man is likely to get possessive about the woman and is likely to turn me down on behalf of both of them. Most men feel it is their right to answer for their wives.

Mick was different. If Frances liked talking to me that was fine by Mick. He was aged about fifty, ten years older than Frances. Mick was a calm and easy-going man who had seen a lot of life. He had been in prison in three jurisdictions: Ireland, Britain and the USA. He had wrecked his marriage a long time ago. He was now making his money as a roofing contractor. Mick seemed to have worked all over and we always had stories to swap. He had been doing less travelling recently. He couldn't leave Frances alone in the flat. He told me he was only going to stay in his native Dublin while Frances was alive. After that he would like to go back to Cork City which had been his favourite place. Maybe he's living there now. I lost contact with Mick after Frances died.

Mick told me he met Frances a few years before in a house in Dublin. He had been sleeping on the floor and so was Frances. He told her he couldn't sleep because he had a horn on him. That night they became lovers. Mick told me it was a long time before the thought of AIDS crossed his mind. He wasn't from a drug-taking background and there wasn't the same talk about AIDS when he met Frances first. But I must surely have the fucking thing by now, Pa'. But at least I enjoyed meself getting it. I said to

Mick not to be so sure. I think there's been a lot of misleading information about how AIDS is spread. There's every chance he didn't catch the disease from Frances.

Once I gave Mick and Frances a lift to the Pearse Street clinic. We nearly had to carry her in, her legs were so bad. He had been nursing her at home and he was showing the strain of watching her suffer. Mick and I went for a pint. A lot of people, Pa', think I stay with her because I feel sorry for her. But that's not it. It's because I love her. On the way back to Inchicore Frances got me to pull in outside Frawley's of Thomas Street. A few minutes later she came out, sat in to the car, pulled a pair of men's socks from under her jumper and dropped them in my lap. That's for you Paddy. Thanks for all your help.

Oh my God. I sucked in my breath and drove off, fully expecting to see a security man chasing us or at least noting the car number. For Frances and Mick this was just routine.

Mick told me a lot about Frances. He told me not to always believe what she said. I think back on that now when I tell you about an interview she asked me to do for radio in July of 1991, a year after I first met her.

What happened was this. I told Frances one day that a listener had sent me five pounds to give to her friend Ellen Dixon. Ellen spoke movingly about how she wished she could have money for a holiday with her children before she died. I think this gave Frances an idea and that's why she asked to do another interview with me. I said okay. I decided that listeners would be interested to know how she had been getting on in the year since I first met her. I told Frances she would have to be sober. She had been drunk a lot recently and I didn't like Frances when she was drunk. She was rambly and boring. Frances agreed to stay sober and she was as good as her word.

We recorded the interview in her flat in St. Michael's

Estate, Inchicore on Thursday afternoon, 25 July, 1991. It was broadcast the next day.

Well Frances, it's a year ago since I met you outside the drug clinic. You had begun to develop full-blown AIDS at that stage. How is your health now?

"Well me health is very bad and it's getting worse. It's not really going to get better as everybody knows. I feel time is running out on me fast. I've got myself in a lot of debt through drinking. I took to the drink and I just made a bit of a mess there for a while. But I'm getting back on me feet ...

"The AIDS has progressed. I go down to Fiona Mulcahy to the clinic in James's. And she says she's not God, she couldn't put a time on it, but she says I'd see Christmas this year but not by next year or by then I'd really be getting sick. So all I can do is hope that I get a bit of extra time to see me kids."

I can see your skin has changed since last year.

"It comes with the AIDS. They did try to help me a lot with it but they still don't know what it is."

You say you've been drinking a bit. You're in debt. Tell me about that.

"Well I got involved with a loan shark and eh ... over the last twenty-five pounds he's coming up today. He said he'd take me unit out or whatever. I can't give his name cos I know I'd be blown to bits or it wouldn't be me. It'd be one of me children would be picked on. And I have a son here and I'm more worried about him because it'd probably be him that'd get it."

How much did you borrow?

"I borreyed first of all, he gave me one hundred pounds and I paid him one hundred and forty back, righ'? Then he lent me another two hundred. All in, I got three hundred off him and I'm after paying him back three hundred and eighty, nearly four hundred back for the three and the

167

twenty-five I owe him and eh ... that's it."

So he wants his last twenty-five pounds. You say he's going to take the unit here in the room. Now this is a big bookcase and its worth a lot more than that.

"The mother-in-law gave it to me and I said, over me dead body. I said I'd go out on the game first. God forgive me I had to do it when I was on drugs and if I have to collapse on that beat today I'll have to get that money no matter what happens."

You're a frail person at this stage with your illness. You're telling me this man has been coming in and threatening you here?

"Yeah they don't care less. Everybody knows they're from Ballyfermot and eh ... they don't care less."

Is this a stupid question, but could you go to the guards and say look, you're in trouble with a loan shark and he's threatening to take your furniture?

"You could all right but you'd end up with one of your kids in hospital with their leg broke. I known someone that tried it before and that child was hurled up into the air. Grant it he didn't die but it was no accident and she knew it was no accident. She couldn't do anything about it."

You say you'll go back out on the game, but you're hardly fit for that kind of work, now are you?

"I know Paddy. I'm not fit. I mean I'm ready to collapse as it is but I'll have to get it no matter what happens."

You've done a lot of that in the past when you had your drug habit which gladly you're over now. Tell me about that life. About working there.

"It's terrible Paddy, you know? You get into a car and you don't know how you're going to get out of it. You get some blokes that are alrigh' but you get some that get smart and treat you as if you're scum, you know? And it's really like you never get over it when you live a life like that and you never forget. I mean it turns your whole life, especially your sex life, upside down. You think everybody just wants to use you, you know? Well I did when I was younger and eh ... I used to hate going out, I used to dread it."

Tell me about the first time you went out to work as a prostitute.

"I was brought out. Two friends of me husband was home from England. A girl and a bloke. She was out working and he says to me one night, you better go out working with her. He says we've nothing for the kids for Christmas so I says to him I'll just do it for the Christmas. After that it used to kill me. In the end I got away from him through the police. I got a legal separation on the grounds of mental cruelty. I got away from him then with the children and then I started getting sick and I got to the stage where I really couldn't look after the kids. I was giving them food and dressing them but I wasn't giving enough time to them. I was out all the time trying to get money so I got me sister to take the three girls over there, you know?"

Yes, your children are in England. I'll ask you about them in a moment. When you were on the game what was the most frightening thing that ever happened to you?

"I got bet up one time. I went off to do business with him. He took out a knife to me. He said, give me every penny you have. So I said to him, I haven't any money and I had. Thank God it was down me shirt and in me bag. So he gave me a dig, a couple of digs and I got out of the car, he let me out now and he says, you prostitute you. That was the only bad experience I had, thank God. I was lucky that way cos I wouldn't just go with anyone. I had regular people at the time, you know? But like since I got sick, it's no good, you know, standing around. You know you're standing around for hours. There's only young ones down there now you know? You're left standing for hours."

It was the Collins's Barracks, Benburb, Smithfield area that you worked?

"Yeah and sometimes I used to go over to Baggot Street. But in the daytime that was the only place you might get a few bob and then you mightn't. Sometimes you'd be standing there for five hours and get nothing."

Along that stretch outside Collins's Barracks it looks to me that there are mainly women of your own age. Women in their forties. And you're telling me you're prepared to go out there this evening and stand up against that wall?

"Yeah. Yeah."

And how much will you charge?

"Well I'll ask for fifteen pounds, twenty pounds. If I get it I'll just be blessed. Sometimes you're lucky. You'll get someone who'll feel kinda sorry for ye knowing that you're so sick you know? And it's come to the point when you are too sick and I know I'm too sick."

And I'm looking at you, you're frail, you're sick. What are you going to have to do to get that twenty pounds?

"I'll have to go out on the town."

Yes I know but what exactly are you going to have to do to a man in a car? Might a man ask you to have full sex with him today or what's going to happen?

"I couldn't have full sex Paddy. Not even with a … a whatdoyacallit? All I could do is use me hands. I couldn't condemn anyone else to death. A Durex could burst, you know? Anything could happen so I wouldn't do that to anybody, you know?"

Your children are in England, apart from your son who lives with you here. How are they now? Have you seen them in the last year?

"I haven't seen them in a while, Paddy. I've been trying to get a few bob here and there but it's not working out to go over and see them. I can't do it on the money I'm on. And my sister and her husband are only ordinary living

170

people. They're rearing them. I can't ask them. My sister often said to me come over, all you'll need is your fare. But you just can't go over like that to see your kids cos I know this time is the last time I'm going to see them, the last time I'll be travelling and ... that it's just saying goodbye to your kids and knowing you'll never see them again."

How many have you there?

"Three daughters. Me sister looks after them. She's very good to them. She's a very good girl. The three of them are doing very well in school and I think that's the only good thing I ever done in my life even though I had to part with the kids."

But you will get to England in the next few weeks and you'll see your children then?

"Please God I will."

As I listen to the tape now I can hear the quiver in my voice. Frances shook me. After I left and made my way down the steps of that block of flats I had to lean against the wall and I wept. I don't think I was ever so moved by an interview before. I think part of it was that Frances was so damn nice. She told me again that she blamed nobody but herself for her problems. What she wanted now was that her death would be as painless as possible. She didn't want to suffer as her brother did. And no, for Frances there was no God in heaven. No afterlife. How could there be a God when innocent babies were born with the AIDS virus because of the behaviour of their parents?

I broadcast the interview with Frances the next day and there was a huge response. I was sent eight hundred and ninety pounds in all to help Frances to see her children in England one more time before her death. An unemployed woman in Sandymount got together with some of her friends to buy Frances the plane ticket. Frances didn't take up this offer, partly because she was barely ever well enough to travel. But also because she had no real intention of going to England. Frances eventually asked me if the Sandymount women would give her the money instead. I didn't pass on this request.

Mick helped me separate fact from fiction in the story Frances had told me. There was no loan shark. She worked the quays for money for vodka, same as she had always done. It was much easier for her children in Yorkshire to visit her than it was for her to visit them in her condition. The dying wish to see the kids had been carefully thought out by Frances to get sympathy, and therefore money, from the listening public.

And didn't she do well! Eight hundred and ninety pounds wasn't at all bad for an interview on radio. And do I feel cheated and used by Frances? Well I don't and I hope those listeners who were fooled along with me don't feel too bad either. Enough elements in the story were true. I don't begrudge Frances her little scheme to make money when the opportunity presented itself in the form of a gullible reporter from RTE. That money helped to keep Frances in vodka and Mick in pints in O'Donoghue's of Inchicore. Why shouldn't Frances look for a little pleasure and comfort in the short time left to her in her life? She had always lived by her wits. She was true to herself until the end.

Bernard Curtis Flats, Bluebell, Dublin;
30 June 1992

Rose Waldron was dying and she wanted to talk. When I phoned my wife from Berlin she told me Frances Flynn had been looking for me because her friend, Rose Waldron, wanted to meet me.

Surely it was Rose Weldon, I said to Jacinta. You remember we met her in Hospital Five several times, across

172

the ward from Frances? Jacinta and I had been in St. James's Hospital a lot recently to visit a friend who turned out to have Hodgkins disease. Rose Weldon was a mild-mannered woman in her early thirties. She was in a lot of pain but liked to talk when she could. She didn't like Frances Flynn and I couldn't blame her for this. Frances was drunk and truculent any time we had met her recently in Hospital Five. She was difficult to talk to. I think this character change was as much a result of the virus affecting her brain as it was a result of the vodka that someone, probably Mick, was smuggling in to her. Rose believed that Frances was stealing her underwear and other things in the hospital. She got me to contact one of her relatives to get her replacement clothing.

Rose Weldon's husband had died the previous year. She believes she caught the virus from him and for once I was inclined to believe this story. I've heard distraught Dublin mothers fool themselves about their children. My daughter never took more than an aspirin. It was that fellah she was going with that gave her the virus. But Rose seemed very straight so I decided to believe her when she said she never took drugs. I was delighted that Rose wanted to talk now. I had never asked her to do an interview. But she had seemed interested in the fact that I made radio programmes and it had crossed my mind that she would be a good interviewee. She had a case coming up against a man who had driven her into the Phoenix Park and allegedly raped her. Her ill health had prevented her from testifying so far. (A year later I met two women at the welfare in Rusholme in Manchester who turned out to be sisters of Rose and they told me she had caught the virus through this rape but my own very clear recollection was that Rose told me she caught it from her husband.)

I had it all worked out by the time my plane landed in Dublin Airport. I would go with Rose to court and speak to her at the end of each day. Then when the case was over, presuming the man was found guilty, I could broadcast the result. Rose was the sort of person that people would listen to.

It turned out to be all fantasy on my part. I rang Frances. Rose Weldon was dead. When I saw Rose over the previous weeks I hadn't realised how close to death she was. She had breathing difficulties and continuous muscular aches. I remember how the pain would show in her eyes. She had been haemorrhaging and had a high temperature at times due to a cervical infection. One day in the hospital I bathed her forehead to help cool her down. She had gone through the familiar torture of AIDS and now she was dead. The fact that a rape case trial was aborted by her death earned her a small mention in the newspapers.

So now I was following the arrangements Frances Flynn had made for me to meet her friend Rose Waldron. A different Rose. The address was on the fourth floor of a block of the Bernard Curtis flats in Bluebell.

Rose's husband answered the door. He was her second husband and he had been separated from her for some years. He had come back into her life to nurse her now that she was dying. He had been expecting me and was welcoming. He explained that the curtains were kept closed in Rose's bedroom because she had developed a sensitivity to light. Then he led me into that gloomy room to meet Rose. Before I recount our conversation I'll try to describe what she looked like.

Rose Waldron looked about thirty years older than her forty years. She was frail and shrunken-looking. Her nightdress gave the impression of being on a coat-hanger instead of on a woman's body. Most of the hair on her head had fallen out. Her eyes were bloodshot and agitated. You could tell she had difficulty seeing you. She was obviously blind in one eye although it turned out that this had been due to a car accident years before. Her fingertips were swollen and bloody. Some of her fingernails had been removed in St. James's because of infection. Her teeth were gapped and her gums showed signs of bleeding. Her lips were a mess of cracks and blood. Her tongue was blistered with the fungal infection that goes with AIDS. She was extremely pale. She looked the way a victim of radiation sickness is meant to look according to the various movies that have been made about nuclear war. When she spoke her voice was weak and very hoarse. At first I thought this might be a problem for radio listeners. I needn't have worried. Nobody could have *not* listened to Rose Waldron.

Rose's husband brought us tea. After he had gone back out I asked Rose about the care she was getting from him.

"I'd be lost without him. Now like we've had our rows and decided to separate. But I'd be lost without him. Like on the stairs outside it's a bloody nuisance on the fourth floor. I have to take them one at a time. It's like starting to learn to walk again. It takes us half an hour to get up here. I've a twenty-year-old daughter who comes up on a Saturday. But the little fellah, the four-year-old, I can't manage any more. That's why my husband comes here as well."

Rose told me she was fourteen when she started on drugs. It surprised me that there were drugs in Dublin in 1966.

"It was coming in from England. There used to be little tiny pills and they were pure heroin. They used to call them jacks. I don't know if you'd remember them at all. Anybody who was going over to England would bring them back. There was only a handful of us in Dublin and we seldom went through withdrawals because we looked after one another, like y'know?

175

"Then I got married when I was sixteen and I stopped [taking drugs] and eh, he was nasty. Like he used to beat me up a lot and he put me out on the game. But he came in one night and he was stoned and he told me he'd had a fix and the whole lot and I said damn you, I want a fix as well. Like he was using only about four months and he died. He O.D.ed. He was a very greedy junkie. Like he was forever chasing his first hit, y'know?"

I did know. Frances described something similar.

You mean he was always trying to make it as good as the first time?

"Exactly. So off he went. He died and I don't mean to sound so ... " (Glad about his death is what she meant, I think.) "Well, like the guy that I met after him was lovely. I lived with Gary for ten years then he got into a bit of trouble with drugs in England and I'd love to see him again. But ehm ... it's gone, Jees, what was I saying?"

Okay Rose. Tell me how did your first husband put you out on the game? How could that happen?

"I was afeared of him. I was absolutely terrified of him. Cos up to this, like I'd gotten a few beatings. He came in one night and I was up on the bed. I was asleep and he started kicking. Kicking me in the head. Just, for no reason. When he did die, to tell you the truth, I was over the moon. You know I really was. It was like getting out of this prison, you know? Then I picked up with Gary and he lived for ten years with me and the daughter.

"Then I was with my husband there who you've met and it was when I was having the last baby that I was diagnosed as positive. It was the pregnancy that brought it kind of alive. My son was born with the virus. With me I've only gone full-blown the last two years."

Your son is four now. How is he?

"He's marvellous. He doesn't have the virus. It's left him now."

That made sense. Children born with the virus are the only people who can recover from AIDS.

"But I don't think I'll be here myself to see him grow much more. But thank God he's healthy. But I've gone downhill. Like I used to be size twenty-two and now I've lost an awful lot of weight. I'd get into a ten size now."

She showed me a photograph of herself at a wedding some years previously. A fat woman with a big bosom straining against her dress. She'd had thick black hair. Apart from her one blind eye, she was completely unrecognisable from that photograph.

I helped her to drink some of the tea. Rose excused herself frequently for dribbling and spitting as she was speaking. I told her not to worry.

"And I have the thrush, the fungal infection in my throat and it's very hard to swallow. And the pains in my chest. I mean if people only knew they would never take risks with their health. If people only knew how hard and how heartbreaking this disease is. You suffer every day. It's something different every day. Every time you open your eyes you know, well Jesus, what's it going to be today? I mean I'm bleeding from ... I don't know, some part of me underneath ... and underneath me tongue and all around inside me."

Why is your hair falling out Rose? What's causing that?

"The virus. The AIDS. It's all part of it. And me teeth. I'm losing me sight as well. I'm depending on the one eye. And I don't know whether the eye will go first or I'll go first."

She was laughing a bit at this.

Rose told me what she did to pay for drink and drugs.

"I was a kiter. I used to do cheques. Like I didn't look then like I do now. I was a lot heavier and I had my teeth and me sight and that then, y'know? I was abusing drugs but I was able to cope. But not now. I can't even have a drink now. Apart from going to hospital I was last out of this flat last Christmas. I've been in here and I've asked for help.

"See I'm going to die here. I'm not dying in hospital. They're arranging it like for a nurse and the whole lot when my time comes. And eh ... it's just the room. I'm beginning to see things that's not there. You know I'm beginning to hallucinate. I needed wallpaper for in here because it's going to be my last place I'd say, isn't it?"

I propped her forward to help her drink more of the tea. She talked more about hallucinations.

"It's the brain. It's because of the infection on the brain. Like I'm lying here and I'm seeing things in the room and I have to sit up to see that it's not there. With me sight like failing as well. I'm seeing things that aren't there at all. But with me sight I can't sit in the light. It's too painful. So I'm sitting in here every day. I mean every night and every day. And I don't really have too many visitors. It's just the odd neighbour drops in. Now only for my husband I'd be lost. Last year I went to Lourdes but now I can't even get to Holyhead to see my bloke. I mean Gary. I'll always look upon him as my best friend."

Is Gary a drug addict?

"He's on maintenance. I am too since they discovered I had the virus."

Have you enjoyed your life, Rose? Did you enjoy your years as a drug addict?

"The freedom was great. I ran amok. I wish I had those years back again. I was healthy. I had to hustle. I was supporting two habits. I was supporting Gary's habit as well. I'm talking ten years ago, three hundred and sixty quid a day. We had a car then and I changed cheques all over the country. You'd go into a pub to buy drink and ask would they change a cheque and they'd ask did you have a card and the answer was yes. You'd have a stolen cheque card and we used to clean the cards, the owner's signature off it with brake fluid. I forged a lot as well.

"When I look back on those ten years, they were the best ten years of my life. Although I was strung out they were the happiest. They were. With Gary we were great friends. We worked together. We were a great couple. I only got a letter from him the other day. He's very broke up about me and the way I am. He's in London but he can't come home. He's getting plenty of help. He's maintained on one hundred and twenty mils a day. That's a lot. The withdrawals from that would kill him."

But Rose it was a rough life. Tell me about being on the game.

"Well I had to. I remember being down on the quays one time for a Christmas Eve night so that the young one could go to Funderland. And then I had to make sure that we had our supply in for the Christmas. They were hard times like the bad weather. It is horrible. Like when I was out on the game twenty years ago it was different. Different kind of punter. Like the punters now are different. They're looking for more kinky sex. They're nasty. But a lot of punters I had a friendship with. If I was healthy I'd be still seeing them.

"When I started I used to work around Fitzwilliam, Baggot Street. But I ended up, retired more or less down the quays at Benburb Street. Meself and Frances. Through me twenties and then me thirties."

Was it ever frightening getting into a man's car?

"Terrifying. I was always drunk on those quays. I could never get into a man's car sober. No way. It's the same with Frances. That's what destroys us. It's the same with Fran and a lot more that I'm sure you know. The drink. They have to get involved with alcohol to do this job."

Would I be right, Rose, in saying that drink or drugs always seems to be a reason for prostitution?

"Everybody has their reason. But there's also girls down there out to keep their family. I mean there's one girl, she's a lovely person. She doesn't even drink but her husband is a habitual gambler. So she has to hustle or the kids go hungry. Everybody down there in Baggot Street or the quays or wherever they choose to work has their reason. They're out through their husbands gambling or whatever and then it just becomes a habit. Every day you get ready at five, six o'clock, and then you're off. A few drinks and then work.

"I mean my finger was nearly chopped off a couple of years ago. It was a hatchback and there was a guy hiding in the boot of the car with an open razor. And they came at me. It was down a lane. There was nowhere to roar for help. Fuck it, I got a beating. I got an awful beating. He was putting the razor up to me face and I put me hand up to stop him and he cut my finger. See the scar there? They were only young fellahs. The fellah that was driving the car was laughing. When he pulled up first he said twenty quid. I said right. I got in. And then down the laneway this other fellah got out the boot. You take your life into your hands doing work like that. It's very dangerous. I reported it. The guard did his best. He really did. He came up to see me a few times. They never caught anyone.

"But I wish I had it back, my life. I wish I could just get up and do the normal things. But I can't on account of this bloody sickness. I'm lucky to have my husband."

What was it broke you and your husband up?

"Drinking. And going down the quays. Mostly from drinking. Only one night a week but I'd really hit the booze. It got to the stage his nerves were gone. You know. Me coming in drunk and starting rows. But since we split up, since we separated, we're better friends. We were only married a couple of years. I done all the right things. I got off the drugs and then married a bloke who doesn't even drink. Then to be knocked back with the AIDS virus. And the hardest thing about the whole lot was the baby. It wasn't explained to me. I was pregnant and I said I was already after being checked for AIDS and this nurse says, ah no, its a rule now, you have to be checked. And I was discharged and I come back the following week and I had to go to the doctor's office and ask him and he just bluntly opened up the chart and he said, HIV positive.

"That was the start of the marriage break-up. Because I started hitting the drink. See I've always had a habit on something. If it wasn't the drink it was the heroin. Because I gave up the heroin I thought I was a marvellous person but I was drinking like a fish. And I was worse when I was drinking and my daughter she was running off to my brother. She didn't like me when I was drinking."

I asked Rose about her own upbringing.

"I was spoiled. I got too much. The father was very fond of his pint. My mother never drank. She smoked Woodbines. But my father, he used to go off and get pissed and he'd come back and there'd be murder in the house. I kind of take after me father, you know what I mean?" (She was laughing again here.)

You're very frank about everything Rose so I'll ask you, have you any idea how much longer you're going to live?

"Not long, I wouldn't say. I'm failing, going downhill a lot quicker than I was a couple of months ago. I don't think it'll be long. The only comment, the only thing I can say about that is, I asked down at the hospital if it will be long and they said they couldn't give me a positive answer but they said it would be soon and I won't be in any pain."

Rose Waldron died at home in Bluebell, 10 September 1992.

Frances Flynn died in Cherry Orchard Hospital, 20 January 1993.

Chapter Ten

CORK

City Hall; 25 June 1991

The housing queue for Cork City can be found in a corridor of City Hall five afternoons a week. I was going in and out of the building, memorizing faces from the queue then waiting outside on Anglesea Street.

Housing is an easy one for me in Cork, Dublin or anywhere else. People who have been on the housing list for years are fed up and they're glad that somebody from the radio is taking notice.

A young couple said they would talk. As always, I spoke to the man first.

You two have just been in applying for a house, how did you get on today?

"Eh ... you do the talking, Helen."

"We got the same answer and there's nothing there for us. And we're down for the past eight months. And we had one baby and she died. And I'm expecting my second baby. We're paying forty pounds on a flat and there's moss and everything growing from the walls and we still can't get out of there."

Helen and Peter invited me to see their flat. I called

later to the address on Wellington Road. It was in one of the terraces of what were once fine old houses on the steep hills of the north side of Cork. Now, in disrepair, some of these houses are let out in flats. In all my years as a flatdweller in Cork and then in Dublin, in all my years since, interviewing people in flats, I have never seen such an awful flat as the one that Helen and Peter lived in.

It was on the ground floor at the back. I suppose it was once the living quarters of some domestic servant, or perhaps just a store room. The dampness was visible, as Helen had said. Worse than that was the breathtaking smell of damp. You could taste the smell. It gave me a twinge in my teeth.

The flat was dark. When Cork's bourgeois classes in the last century built their houses against the steep hills of the city they accepted that the backs of the houses would be dark. It's fallen to flatdwellers of this century to live in that darkness, against the cliffs that were quarried out by workmen long ago.

The flat was the smallest I've ever been in. That's because an extra room had been jammed in as a kitchen. This kitchen was a windowless corridor with a cooker at one end of it.

Forty pounds a week. The Irish taxpayer was paying thirty-six of that through rent allowance. I wondered what sort of brave entrepreneur the landlord was, who made his money through letting out rubbish like this to families stuck on the housing list.

Helen showed me a little *in memoriam* card on her wall with their daughter's picture. I gives her a kiss each day when I wake up and then again going to bed. Peter does the same now cos I told him it would help.

But this flat is so bloody awful, dark and smelly. It would depress anyone living here. Did you do the right thing moving here? Peter?

"I was having problems at home, myself and Helen was having problems at home, so we decided it was best that we start out together and start a new life after what happened our daughter. She died at six weeks old and we decided it would be best if we could get together and seek a future for ourselves, like. We were between houses all the time but after the baby went we got more stronger for each other."

"When she did die we made a vow for ourselves, meself and Peter, that we'd try and do what we could for one another and be strong for one another. But the flat like, what we're living in, we do have our arguments."

Do you mind me noticing, Helen, the marks on your arms and wrists?

"They're scars. I cut myself. I was locked up. In '88. I got fifteen months in Mountjoy prison for ABH and assault. Mostly on guards cos I kind of had a drink problem at the time. I admit that. So, when I was brought to court I got sentenced. But I didn't really believe I was going to Mountjoy. I'd just seen photos of Mountjoy on the television and that. So I thought it would be rough now and all that. So when I got to Mountjoy there was a prison officer. She brought me in. I was terrified. I wouldn't come out of my cell or nothing."

What age were you?

"Three years ago. I was twenty."

You're a Cork woman. How did you like ... Dublin?

"I hated it. Most of the girls that were in Mountjoy, they were all from Dublin. The travellers were nice people. But as for the Dublin people I didn't like most of them. I stayed with a traveller for most of me time. But I used to cut my wrists and that because my mam never came up to visit me and my dad was in London at the time working. So when my dad came home he used to see me for half hour visits and then every time he went away I just cut my hands."

What did you cut your hands with?

"Cups or bowls. Put 'em into a tea towel and lash 'em off the ... there's kind of bars, they're heaters, d'you know, to heat the cells for you. And I'd lash it off that. And it'd all break into the tea towel and I'd just get the sharpest bit. I didn't know how to do it. I never knew how to cut my arms cos I never did until I went into prison."

You were in for ABH? Why did you beat up the guards?

"For the ABH charge it was two girls that I bate up. But I did have a drink problem at the time because even before I went to prison I was seeing a psychiatrist. But I was inclined to get worse. On the drink all the time."

One of the things about Mountjoy that women tell me is that the place is full of lesbians. Did that bother you?

"Yeah. I'm not a holy person but when I was inside for the eleven months I used go to Church every Sunday and I used read at the Mass and you'd see the carry-on. We'd say two girls and they'd be kissing one another and mauling one another, d'you know? Even people that came in like meself and they were straight, d'you know, but they're from the country, the lesbians that are already in there would try and make the straight people be like them. So there's a lot of girls terrified in there because at one stage I was. I used go to the school all the time. I was going to sit for my Leaving Cert and I enjoyed going to school because it took me out of the misery that I was in. And there was one girl in particular she was a lesbian and she used try and make passes at me and that. It got reported."

Who reported it?

"There was another woman there was very good to me. She was doing three years for manslaughter. I told her cos I used be crying over it and I didn't know what to expect in Mountjoy when I went up. She told the teachers and they warned your one off. I had no trouble then."

Did you ever do solitary in prison?

"Yeah. I was in the solitary confinement. It's known as the Black Hole in Mountjoy. I was there for three days and three nights. And it was horrible. You're just in your nightdress. Your underwear and that is taken off you. You've a matress. You've no blankets or nothing. You get your food the last and you have to use plastic knives and forks and that. You can't go out on recreation in the mornings with the other girls. You have to go out by yourself.

"The reason I did go in to the Black Hole was I was in school and I used do photography and typing by night and I just got fed up one night and I seen Tippex. So I started sniffing the Tippex and I brought it in to the cell with me. And I didn't get caught the first time but they gave me the warning cos they knew what I was up to. So the second time I done it again and they walked in on top of me while I was doing it. So I was put in to the Black Hole."

I called to see Helen and Peter again a few months later. I met the landlord. He was a creep. He had that mincing, camp manner of Cork's middle-class. Ooh, noo. Those two don't live here any more. He looked down his nose at me because I was someone who knew Helen and Peter. He was full of his own sense of virtue. The type who would have told tales to teacher when he was a kid at school. I said I was glad Helen and Peter had gone because the flat was a disgrace and I hoped that landlords like him would soon be put out of business. And who did I think I was? Paddy O'Gorman is my name. I'm a journalist with RTE. Ooh, I see. Well if oar tee ee will excyoose me now some of us have work to do.

Ireland isn't that big and Cork isn't big at all. I knew I would find Helen and Peter again sooner or later.

In November of 1992 I was standing outside Cork's

Court House on Washington Street interviewing the joyriders and drug takers. I met Helen on her way out. She was in good form. She had a son now. She'd been in to see Peter who was remanded in custody. She didn't think he would ever grow up.

They had a local authority flat in Mayfield. Mount Erne. Helen said the area was a dump. I would go further and say that Mount Erne has the worst housing in Ireland, along with Castle Park in Moyross in Limerick and St. Michael's Estate in Inchicore in Dublin. There are rats and rubbish. Decaying buildings and a smell of rot and dampness.

Helen was living on the first floor in one of the blocks in Mount Erne. There were not many inhabited flats left in that block. They've been surrendered to the vandals. "Hoodies" are what the young criminals in Mayfield are called. They wear their anorak hoods turned up to make it hard to identify them. At night the flats are used by drug-takers. You would have to be tough to live there and to raise children in Mount Erne. Helen was tough.

I called to Helen again a year later in November of 1993. Peter was with her now. Out of prison. Peter's sister, who had done time in Mountjoy, was there too.

I first met the two of you two and a half years ago outside City Hall when you were on the housing list. Your baby died soon before that. How are you now?

"At the start things were very bad for me and Helen. We were only fighting and crying and taking pills and killing each other. Luckily in one sense she was pregnant again so that was a consolation."

I asked Peter what he meant by killing each other? As he answered, Helen's jaw began to drop. She said nothing to begin with.

"It has a lot to do with society as well. If I'd an argument with her now, right? I'd say, era, I'm going away off now to a pub, maybe have a few pints. Grant it I'm not a saint or anything. I could be gone missing for a few hours and I'd come back, before closing time now like, and she'd snap at me like and say, oh where were you? Things like that."

"Can I say something here, Paddy? Peter went out one night on a Friday. I asked him to be in by one at the latest with a cheeseburger and chips. Left me here with a child, Paddy, and didn't arrive back till Monday. Now what would you make out of that, honestly? When he came back in the door I was saying who were you with, who were you with? Cos that's what would be going through your head. I was left with the child ... "

"Tell the man why ... "

"While he went away for the whole weekend ... "

"Because the same week, the same week leading up to that weekend, I was given mental torture off you ... "

"Mental torture? MENTAL TORTURE!!! I got some beatings. Didn't I truthfully? I bate him. He bate me. Last week we had an argument ... I'm going saying it ... "

"Say it."

"He went out. Had his bellyful of drink of course. Which is usual. Came back to the door. Started booting in the door. I was afraid to open the door below. Looked out the window. I knew it was him. He bounced off the door. He was on the floor he was so drunk. The boy upstairs let him in. He came up the stairs. He said, I'll blow the door in if she don't open it. I had to open the door cos I was shitting. I opened it. He came in. Bate me around that hall and bate me in to the bedroom, Paddy, and opened my kids' bedroom door as if to say, boys, look at me bating your mother. Took my oldest son out of the cot ... "

"Tis a lie."

"Excuse me. IT'S NO LIE. Took my son out of the cot. And was waving a knife out there in the hall. Right or wrong?"

"You're right."

"Thanks."

Peter was rocking back and forth. He was gasping in shock. His eyes were wide with amazement. It seemed as if he had forgotten this episode of the previous week until Helen started telling me about it.

"Excuse me now, Helen. Would you be able to say to the man the reason I actually done that?"

"But there was no reason to come to the door that night. You could have said it in the morning."

"But would you explain why?"

"Because I gave the child a clatter that Sunday."

"And it drove me mad."

Now Peter, I don't want to upset you ...

"There's no upsetting, Paddy. The reason why I'm saying this now, back on my behalf, is because when I was young, I got enough of clatters meself when I was growing up. And when I seen her clattering the child, I just went blank and I didn't say nothing but it reflected on me mind. And I admit, I stormed out the door that day. And it must have been what happened to me through childhood that I retaliated and I did hit her. And I apologised to her afterwards. And the reason why I done it was because she hit my child."

Peter's sister spoke up now. So far she'd been quietly nodding in agreement with Helen. But she said Peter was right about the childhood he had. She had a shy, quiet voice and she didn't want to talk on tape but she wanted me to know that she had looked after her brother when she was a child even though she was only a year older than he was. The two of them were often taken in to care. When they weren't in care they were neglected. Her shoplifting, which led her to Mountjoy, had started in childhood through necessity.

Mahon was turning into a disappointment. I thought I would do well there but the health board office wasn't busy. I hung on to see who I might meet.

Mahon is one of the newer suburbs of Cork City. Council houses and people on welfare. Lots of one-parent families. A Cork version of Tallaght. It's in a beautiful spot on the south bank of the River Lee but people don't want to live there because it's so far from the city. One advantage of Cork City is that it's compact enough so that young, poor people don't have to live too far away from their families when they get a house. But Mahon is definitely a long way out.

I met only one person at Mahon who turned out to be exceptional. Unfortunately, I'm no longer welcome at her door.

Margaret I'll call her. Age early twenties. Yes. She'd like to talk to me. She often thought she'd like to talk to Gerry Ryan, if only she had a phone. She had a story to tell. Did I have the time? Yes. I've got time. I called to her home that evening.

"I was only married two years altogether when I decided that my marriage had to end. The reason it had to end is that my husband was a very violent man. People say even now that I was very young and he was extremely young. I wasn't in my twenties at that stage and neither was he. We entered marriage with a child. She was only six weeks old when we got married. It was very pressurising as he wasn't working and I wasn't working and then he hit the drink and it turned out violently. I didn't drink at the time which I do now unfortunately but he hit it very bad which made matters worse. Because I didn't drink I couldn't understand why he reacted the way he did in drink.

"If I questioned him at all it ended up in a beating. If my daughter woke when we were arguing or fighting he would go up and would punch her one. At two years of age like. And I never realised that was going on until one night I followed him when he went up to her and he hit her and he had a towel on her mouth, and like she was hysterical and I kind of flipped, myself, violently over that when I saw my daughter in the bed after being woken out of her sleep. It was then that I had to start thinking seriously about ending the marriage.

"Now if I had my choice like I wouldn't have. If I thought it could be rectified in any way I would have hung on but two years, on and off, it wasn't getting any better. It was only getting worse. I didn't want to leave. My son come up in the same environment as my daughter did. It actually took me two weeks to the day practically to sit up and think, on my own, what I was going to do. I got up one morning, and I woke, and I said this is it. I asked my friend to mind the children and I walked in the rain into town and I waited for a judge to come out of his chambers for three hours. So I dried out in the three hours. 'Twas then I realized I had to swear. I didn't know anything legally or anything about the law. I had to swear blind that I was telling the truth. He swore me in and they set a court date for a barring order. He told me all the ins and outs about how I had to be telling the truth and did I realize what I was doing, that there was no going back once I swear in and like I was nervous cos I was never inside in a courthouse. I did it and I came and I notified my husband and he thought I was bluffing."

Did you get a protection order in the meantime?

"Yes. It was a letter saying it was pending on a barring order. He didn't believe me. He thought I was bluffing. He always said I'd bluff like. Actually he must have read it in the meantime as I had left it on the table. He left then once he realized I was serious. I got the letter on a Thursday and he was gone by the Saturday.

"About four days after, my daughter started asking where he was gone. I told her that he was gone. Even to this day she is very close to me. Like if she sees me crying even over a stupid television programme she worries like that someone hit me because she seen it so often. She asked if her granda could be her daddy and I said yes. My father and my brothers, I have three brothers, they all stood by her. She was very nervous of men. She actually opened up to one of my brothers then one day that her own father hurted her. He thought and I thought automatically that it was through the belting and the roaring and the shouting that he hurt her but as time went on, day after day trying to listen to her, I really didn't want to think the worst. We then found out that it really was a lot worse than the belting and the whole shouting and the whole lot."

She was sexually abused. Is that what you're telling me?

"Yes. She was only two years old. Two and two months actually. My friend said to me that I should listen to what she was saying. I said no, I don't want to hear. I even fought with my friend at the suggestion that something like that would have happened. She was saying, just leave her finish what she is saying. Don't cut her short, which I was, cutting the child short. I was saying she was silly. One day I did, in front of my own father, left her carry on what she wanted to say. She described horrific details like of how she was ... hurted. I rang the doctor thinking that maybe he could shed a bit of light on, maybe was it her imagination, maybe it was me over-reacting. He came out and he panicked me altogether. He was there at eight o'clock the following morning cos I wouldn't sleep like. We went to the hospital anyway and they counselled the child before they do anything."

What did the hospital find out?

"Well they found out that he was using her with his own private parts, obviously to get some kind of kick out of it. I don't know how he could be so sick, even thinking of it. He is a good-looking man and had everything going for him, you know? It's not as if he had to turn to his own daughter. Most people were looking at me in disbelief like, because he looked the part of the ideal man."

How's your daughter now?

"She's great. Thankfully she is great. You don't mention the hospital to her like, where she went to be interviewed. The examination is probably still in her mind. She hasn't spoken about it but as time goes on she might come out with an outburst. Like for example we were doing a massive clean-out of the house last week and she found her father's watch. I didn't know who owned it. It's a broken old watch, and she mentioned his name and she said ... I hate him. She's five now like and it's two and a half years on. I said, he's gone and you don't have to worry about it. We don't even see him. She was saying don't ... ever ... leave me go see him again and I said I won't.

"She started on about how he used to use her, like. I don't know if you will understand this now but it took me ages to understand it. She used to say she was all shampoo. I used to say to myself, what does she mean by shampoo? It's kind of embarrassing now but you can understand what shampoo was referred to."

Margaret clarified that Daddy putting his shampoo on meant masturbating on top of the little girl. He particularly liked to do this when his daughter was sitting on her potty.

"When I found it out first I couldn't believe it. I even said it to him myself. I actually built up the courage and said, how could you? I sympathised with him more than anything else like. He is sick. What really turned my stomach was that I was in bed with him. When you think of it, I gave him what he went to get off his own daughter. It's sick. It turned my stomach that I could be in bed with someone that could molest a little girl."

I called to Margaret six months later, over Christmas. She was pleased to see me. Her dad had been worried at her speaking on radio but she had no regrets. She was glad she did it. It might help anyone else in the same position to gather the courage to do something about it. She was in good form and her little girl was very well.

I called to Margaret again six months later. The summer of 1992. She looked shocked when she opened the door. Then she coloured. Hello, she said. How are you? She kept me standing there. It was clear she wasn't going to ask me in.

Is everything okay, Margaret?

Yes. Everything's fine. But I'd appreciate it if you'd leave. My husband is living with me again. We said we'd give it another go. Goodbye.

Cork Prison; 20 December 1991

The prison is high on the brow of a hill on Cork's northside. I was warm from climbing the hill but it was a freezing cold day. Icy wind and rain. That's the worst part about not having the car with you. I much prefer to take the train, as I did from Dublin early that morning, but it means you're left with no shelter from the elements.

I walked up and down stamping my feet. No luck so far. All travellers. Travellers nearly always keep their business to themselves.

Two plain-clothes policemen arrived. One approached me and the other stood back behind the car. They had a report of a man outside the prison carrying a gun. I explained I had a microphone in my pocket. I pulled it out carefully, dangling it between my fingers like a fellow on television handing over his weapon. They were amused. Could you not find an easier job for yourself, Paddy? You'll freeze to death here.

Some young men came out the gates. Good. Young men are rarely as interesting as people with a bit more life experience but young men hardly ever turn down an interview.

"I'm out two months. I'm just signing now. It's good to be out for Christmas. I was in D-block for punishment. You're down there just on a mattress. No fags. No radio. Just for stupid things. Fighting with another prisoner."

"Once you're locked up then you've only an ole pisspot to go the toilet. You'd ring the bell at night and say, officer, can I go to the toilet? He might say yes or sometimes he might tell you fuck off."

What were you in for?

"Malicious damage. Tell you straight I was drunk one night and I bursted a window, like. I've two brothers in there too. It's very hard on our mam, like."

"I was in there six times and I think that's just about enough like. Joyriding, larceny."

"We're both going to England after Christmas. No one will give us a job here."

They were right. England. The forever refuge of failed Irish people.

The rain turned to sleet. My fingers had gone white. I thought about calling to some people in the flats in Comeragh Park, just down the hill from the prison. Seamus and Patricia were a young couple with two children. I met Seamus in the summer when he and another man told me that they were supplementing their dole with money from a drug-testing clinic in Shandon Street. Human guinea pig stuff. Seamus and Patricia were both intelligent and articulate. Patricia had a beautiful speaking voice. A clear and precise working-class Cork accent that let you hear her smiling as she talked. I'd kept a note of their address. Seamus told me he missed getting a job as a caretaker in a school when they found out about his prison record. Maybe Seamus and Patricia would talk to me about prison.

Patricia answered the door. Come in. Seamus, we have a visitor.

They were happy to talk about prison. Seamus had spent years there.

"Well there was two or three twelve monthses, then three years and I'm after finishing seven years. I did five. So I'd say I've done about eleven years. I'm twenty-eight."

Why so much time in prison?

"I started fairly young. My family just didn't care what I did. I was put into a school for backward children because I am a bit backward. That school were the only people who ever looked out for me."

Do you still get into trouble?

"This is my second Christmas out. Now I haven't been very good. I've made two mistakes. And I'm getting on with my life. I've two children and a good wife. I still get the urge to go out and do these things and if it hadn't been for my wife I'd be back in prison."

What were the mistakes?

"Petty theft. When I was very young I was doing things and I was actually getting away with it because there was no borstal would take me. I got worse and eventually they sent me up to St. Laurence's school in Finglas in Dublin. I quietened down a lot but when I got out I mixed with the wrong people and I was back in trouble every day. When I look back on it I'd change things if I could because I stole

196

from people like myself."

I was doing a mental calculation about the age of the older child. How could Seamus have been the father? I wasn't going to ask. Not yet anyway.

The last five years you did, your wife suffered as well. And your children?

"Everybody makes mistakes. I got five years. The relationship between myself and my wife just dropped. There were times when I just wanted to end it all in prison. Then the visits from her like cheered me up, you know?"

"When Seamus got the seven years in the courts I was completely dumbfounded. It was like I was after losing my husband forever. I was shocked. And then there was the fact of going home and coping on my own. As the years went on I got more lonelier. Sometimes myself I felt like giving up. I suppose love made me keep going. We had our hard times as well. Seamus was getting told this and that above in the prison about me. That I was with this fellah and with that fellah. And he said if he got a penny for every time he heard it he'd be a rich man now. There was other blokes in the prison going through the same thing as well."

"Like Patricia says, there is an awful lot of rumours in prison. You see, inside in prison, it is the only weapon they have to fire each other up. They say look, your ole doll was with this fellah last night, your ole doll was with that fellah. And then marriage breaks up then. Tis wrong like because he has to stay there. He can't just say, come on we go and talk about it. He has to go back to his cell and she has to leave the prison. Nobody understands the hurt you go through. Your man goes in to the cell and he's thinking all different things. It mightn't be true. Eventually like, he is going to think of suicide cos I've often thought of it. Fellahs say, your wife was with this fellah last night and I'd go in to the cell and say, it's not true. Then after a while you'd come back and you'd say, is it true?"

"Meself and Seamus, we didn't see each other for six months because of these rumours. I didn't go to visit."

And did you ever have another man?

"Well ... "

"You might as well tell the truth like. Everybody makes mistakes. My wife made one mistake. I made a mistake going to prison for five years. That was my fault. I left her. When you get married like you're there to protect your wife and everything. Everybody makes mistakes like. Even I made a mistake going to prison. My wife went out for a few drinks one night and she made one mistake. I don't hold it against her. I blame myself for that because if I had not been in the prison, it wouldn't have happened."

"I'll answer that question now. Seamus got three years. We were going out with each other eight months and I knew Seamus had a charge up against him. It was only a small thing and he got three years for it and I said I'd wait for him. But Seamus only done a year of that and when he came out we got married. And we were only married a year and Seamus got seven years. So when Seamus got the seven years then, I sat down one day, this was about two years after he was in, and I was so fed up with myself I didn't know if I wanted to stay with Seamus or what to do. I was confused. Ehmm ... I did, I went out one night and I went away with a fellah and I'm still paying for it because I still feel guilty over it. I only slept with him the once but I still get very depressed about it. Maybe people wouldn't understand that but Seamus even knows himself I get very depressed at times."

A lot of men wouldn't treat that the way you're treating it Seamus?

"Oh, I still want my marriage. My wife went away with somebody. My first words were, I still love her."

"I want to say too, I moved here to be near to Seamus

when he was in prison. I gave up a three-bedroomed house in Mahon to take this two-bedrooomed flat. People might think this is funny now but, when Seamus was in prison he used give me his clothes to wash and I wouldn't wash them until the next day. At night-time I'd hold his clothes and I'd actually smell his clothes and I'd hold them and I'd have a cry thinking that I'm close to him. Pretending that he's there."

It was when I finished taping that Seamus and Patricia told me that Seamus wasn't the father of their oldest child. They didn't mind saying this because everybody knew anyway. But I noticed they hadn't said it on tape. I didn't push the point.

I still see Seamus and Patricia. The marriage is stormy. The last time I called Seamus had left home for some weeks. Then I heard from a Cork woman I met visiting Limerick prison that he was back. I suppose his years in prison have meant that he never has really got used to being married. In ways I think they're very suited to each other. Both bright, interesting and candid about themselves and their feelings. But unless he changes, I'd guess Patricia must some day grow tired of having only a part-time husband.

Chapter Eleven

BELFAST

Department of Social Security, Great Victoria Street, Belfast; 6 July 1992

I knew by the look of her that Rose wasn't a student. It wasn't just the toddler with her. I'd met lots of students here who were signing on for the summer. Likeable young people for the most part but not terribly interesting. Rose was small, stout and tough-looking. The students were often glamorous young people. I think men with money tend to marry good-looking women and their children inherit those looks. Rose looked like somebody from generations of poverty.

"I was in for my giro. I have to run down every week with the child cos I'm on my own with her. And she keeps losing my book and they won't give me a new book."

"Losing" was her word.

I had been hearing a lot about delays and lost documents. The IRA had blown up the nearby social security office in Shaftesbury Square a few months before. Now the Great Victoria Street office was overburdened. I asked Rose how she felt about living on welfare money.

"Oh it gets me down all right. You couldn't live on what

you get from themens. I'll go up to Westside Stores nigh and when I get back tay m'hice that's me skint."

We talked about a lot of things. She wouldn't marry the father of her child because he was an unstable person. She was tired of the religious division in Belfast. Her child had been injured as a baby when glass showered in on her cot after a bomb blast. She was planning to move to Scotland. From the way she talked about the war it wasn't obvious to me what her loyalties might be. And then I asked her about her tattoos. These were the reason I have called her Rose in my mind. Colourful and elaborate red roses on her forearms.

"All cover-ups."

This was familiar ground, I thought. The name of an old boyfriend?

"No. Ulster and UVF. All different things just."

And you didn't want those things showing on your arms any more?

"No. I don't like them now. I hate them. Especially going out anywhere people look at you. I've UVF on m'leg too."

She hitched up her pleated skirt and showed me the inside of her thigh. The tattoo was one of those self-inflicted jobs done with a needle and blue ink.

Do you think that people put on tattoos like this when they're young and then they're sorry later?

"I hate them. I regret them now. So I do. You get into a lot of arguments when somebody sees tattoos on your arm. You get into a fight right away."

And when you're with a man, your boyfriend I mean, what does he make of it when he sees UVF written on that part of you?

She pointed to the toddler with her.

"Well her daddy, her daddy cracks up because I've got Peter at the top of my arm and that's not his name. So every time we have an argument he brings that up."

I noticed a lot more tattoos in Belfast. Months later a tattoo artist named Pert, who worked from a premises at Smithfield in Belfast city centre, told me that about sixty percent of his business was cover-ups of paramilitary slogans which people had put on themselves when they were young and foolish. He showed me how he made flowers and leaves sprout out of the letters UVF or IRA. A black panther also served to cover a multitude.

A man I met outside Great Victoria Street dole office was trying to make it as an actor. He had been an extra in a comedy that had been on TV a few weeks earlier. I forget what it was called but I remembered I had seen it. It starred Warren Mitchell of Alf Garnett fame as an Englishman in Belfast. Now this young actor was signing on again. He was from the Shankill Road. I told him I was thinking of going up to the dole office there but he thought that would be a bad idea. Especially with the Twelfth approaching and with what he called my brogue. You could end up on a bonfire.

Fair enough. I had to be careful here in Belfast. I couldn't work as I do in the Republic, introducing myself with abandon around welfare offices and housing estates wearing my broad-rimmed hat which makes it easy for people to identify me and find me. But I wasn't going to use so-called community leaders here either. I was going to find my own people my own way. I wouldn't be guided by established pressure groups. The best tactic available to me for the moment seemed to be to stick to city centre welfare offices.

Two young men who came out of the dole office seemed to be in good form. They joined me sitting on the low wall. They told me being unemployed was better than doing boring, low-paid work.

"It's just a pain in the ass getting up out of bed. We

spend our days boozing. We're only out of bed a half-an-hour ago. I was out raving all weekend so I was only home now."

Raving. That word again. A few days earlier in Dublin I'd spoken to young criminals outside the courts at the Bridewell. I'd heard a lot about raving and the drugs, especially ecstasy, that the ravers like to take. I asked the Belfast men to tell me about raving.

"Go to night clubs or beaches or whatever. Take loads of drugs and go crazy. Take everything. E's. Acid. Speed. There's bucket-loads of drugs in Belfast. E's are the main one."

I noticed that they didn't mention heroin. Bucket-loads of everything else in Belfast but not heroin. That's something to be deeply thankful for. You can't catch AIDS by smoking dope or popping pills. You can catch AIDS by sharing a needle as heroin addicts do. At the Bridewell probably half the young offenders I'd met were drug addicts using heroin and half again of these had AIDS. But it's only in Dublin that heroin and other injectable drugs are used widely and that's why it's only in Dublin that AIDS is endemic among drug addicts. So Belfast is more like Cork than Dublin in this respect. In Cork, despite widespread drug use, AIDS is a disease of homosexual men rather than of drug addicts.

I told the Belfast men about the interviews I had done in Dublin. They thought it was very bad that an ecstasy tablet in Dublin cost twenty-five pounds.

"Ah you'd never pay that for it here, no way. You'd pay fifteen pounds for an E and it'll last you a few hours. It'll keep you going all night but the main buzz of it only lasts a few hours."

And do you like living in Belfast?

There were no doubts here from either of them.

"Love it. Love it. It's fucking great. Specially the last few years the buzz has got so good."

I told them that sounded surprising to a Southerner like me. A third man, also in his twenties, who had come out of the social security office, was listening. He answered me.

"You only hear the bad bits. You hear the news. If you avoid certain parts of the town you're okay."

The other two agreed. Then they said goodbye to me. I asked the man who had joined us which areas he avoids.

"West Belfast."

But that includes both Catholic and Protestant areas.

"I avoid both. Like if I went drinking in loyalist West Belfast I'm a stranger as far as they're concerned. Like there's two boys there and I don't know what they are. I'm a Protestant and I wouldn't drink in loyalist West Belfast. I wouldn't drink in republican West Belfast either. But you come into town. Meet. Have a drink. Have a laugh. See the ordinary boy in the street here? We don't want troubles. We don't like paramilitaries. Like them boys you were talking to there are probably Roman Catholics. If I meet them boys down the town they don't ask am I a Protestant and I don't ask are they Catholics. But as soon as we go back to our estates, our own domain, the old crap starts again."

How do you know those men were Catholics?

"How do I know they were Catholics? The clothes they were wearing. We've got our own ways of dressing and that. The old green jumper with a stripe down it and all that."

And he named a pub in town where he had seen them drinking. I know that pub and hadn't noticed it as having a particular denominational leaning but I suppose he knew what he was talking about.

He got on to Articles Two and Three of the Republic's constitution. Your government is wrong to have those articles. I dropped most of this from the interview as broadcast as there had been, and would be, other public platforms for these arguments. Then he talked about paramilitaries.

"Paramilitaries. We don't like them. We have to live with them. Paramilitaries are ... ninety percent of the people in this country respect the paramilitaries."

Do you respect the paramilitaries?

"It's not that I respect them ... In some places paramilitaries are the only people who keep law and order. Law and order would be a lot worse if it wasn't for paramilitaries. They do good things. They do bad things but they do good things as well. I live in loyalist South Belfast. All Protestants. Ninety-nine percent Protestants. There's boys where I live breaking into people's houses. The only thing that they fear is the paramilitaries. They don't fear the police. They don't fear the establishment. The police are getting boys there for breaking into old women's houses and they're going in and they're getting fifty pound fines. It's no deterrent for them. I don't believe in gun law but ... "

I noticed how he said "fear" when another person might have said "be afraid of". There is sometimes, I think, a biblical sound to Belfast speech.

You say you don't believe in gun law but that's what you're talking about. There's people in Dublin, too, who want to keep out drug addicts by threatening them with the IRA. But the alternative to the police is kneecappings and beatings and all that. Is that what we want?

"I was kneecapped myself. I don't agree with gun law but I think the authorities should take a hold."

Why were you kneecapped?

"Why was I kneecapped? For ... crimes against the loyalist cause."

What does that mean?

"It means ... if we do something where we live and we bring the establishment, namely the RUC, into the estate, you get punished for that. It was a fight between our estate and a neighbouring estate. Two loyalist estates. It's been going on a long time."

Tell me about being kneecapped.

"It was ... sore. I got pulled out of my house. Took down an entry. Shot in the leg. At the time it's just like a punch in the leg. What happened I was meant to turn up and I didn't turn up. Shooting by appointment. You must have heard of that? This is when they come and tell you to be at a certain place at a certain time but I wouldn't go for that. The next thing they came to the door. Knocked at the door. My elderly mother and father were in the house. I just went with them down the back of an alleyway. Got it done. They phoned the ambulance."

Where exactly did they put the gun?

He rolled up the leg of his pants. The entry and exit wounds of the bullet could be seen on either side of the calf.

"There. They said, that'll stop you from fighting. When it happens it's like a kick in the shin. The next day in hospital when you move your leg, that's when you feel the pain. The police say to you, could you identify those men? Like the police know. I know who they were. My whole family know who they were. But to stand up in court to identify them? Your whole family would have to leave Northern Ireland."

Department of Social Security, Corporation Street, North Belfast; two days later

The door staff at the social security office told me to be careful of a particular group of young men who were always hanging around. They're bad boys. They'll take your tape-recorder. They'll take your hat.

But I wasn't too worried. I've handled bad boys before. What you have to do is pretend you haven't noticed their aggression and then win them over to your side by asking their opinion on things. It works for me with bad boys everywhere. Besides, for a lot of the time I had nobody else to interview. The bad boys were forever applying for a crisis loan of some sort and when they were hanging around most other people wouldn't dally to talk with me. What's the crisis, I asked one of the bad boys?

"I'm going on my holidays."

You didn't tell them that, surely?

"No. You wouldn't say that to themens. I told them I needed a cooker for my flat."

He didn't get the loan when their records showed he had already got a loan for a cooker the previous year.

Another of the bad boys was homeless.

"I'm still waiting on my giro. I got no clothes to wear. I had to steal these off clothes lines. I just skipper about from house to house, you know what I mean?"

How did you become homeless?

"Peelers put me out of my house."

Why?

"Fighting with my wife."

He had a beer can in his hand. Was drink part of the problem?

"No it was the caps."

What are the caps?

"Fucking RUC bastards. They just don't like me."

Of course. The cops. That's what he was saying to me. The rest of the bad boys were laughing because he had battered his wife. Was he to be charged?

"For fighting with my wife I'm barred from the house. Plus I'm up on five assaults for assaulting RUC men."

Is that something you're ashamed of, fighting with your wife? It doesn't seem a very manly thing to do.

"No. She thumped me too."

More laughter from his pals. Then they got bored with me and left.

Two rough-looking, middle-aged men were upset that their giros hadn't come. How would they celebrate the Twelfth?

A man told me he was getting out of Belfast and going South for the weekend. Was this to avoid the Twelfth? His wife tried not to laugh. No. He was going motorbiking. Most years he takes part in the parade with his local Orange Lodge. I told myself to stop making assumptions.

A disabled man in his car had been listening with the window rolled down. He heard me introduce myself over and over to people who wouldn't speak to me. He told me he was waiting for a friend who would have a story he could tell me. The friend came out walking with the aid of a stick. Both men were in their early forties. I sat into the car.

The man with the stick had just spent the last fifteen days in Crumlin Road prison for non-payment of a three hundred and fifty pounds fine. The PSV disk on his taxi had run out. They also took his licence so now he was out of work.

You're walking with the help of a stick. What happened?

"Got attacked in the prison. Paramilitaries. Just different religion. They sprained my leg and tore the ligaments in it."

"They jumped on his leg."

I know the Northern Ireland Office resists segregation of Catholics and Protestants in the prison. But I was surprised that he had mixed with paramilitaries.

"I was an orderly cleaning the landings. I don't believe that you should have to work with paramilitaries but the problem is, if you don't work with them, your sentence gets longer and longer. What can you do?"

They suggested to me that I should make a programme

talking to people visiting Crumlin Road jail. I said I would, soon.

The driver told me his disability was progressive. Cancer of the spine. Then he talked about politics.

"The thing is the police are very biased against Catholics. This man is a Catholic and I'm a Protestant and we're firm friends and have been for a long time. I didn't realise it until I was driving him about doing bits and pieces and whenever I showed my licence I never had a problem. Never. But whenever he showed his licence, his ID, he got the hassle. He got searched."

I told them it had been put to me that paramilitaries help to prevent street crime. They would have none of it. The Protestant man's car had been stolen and destroyed by joyriders only recently. It was obvious that he was now driving a true rust-bucket. The fact that it was a disabled driver's car made no difference to the thieves. Stealing a cripple's wheels, he said.

The Catholic man spoke next.

"I go with a Protestant girl and we find it very difficult to live either in a Protestant area or a Catholic area. They'll put you out. I've been forced to leave my homes. What can we do like? We've decided now we would be best going across to England or to Scotland."

"He's a Catholic living with a Protestant girl in a Protestant area. And because I know about him if he's found out I'll have to move as well. It's just a case of we're all going to have to move across the water. Why should we have to move out of a country that we like and that we've lived in all our lives for the sake of a few thugs?"

Social Security Office, Corporation Street,
Belfast; the next day

The bad boys turned up early. They were drunk. I'd been

talking with a young couple pushing a pram. He was from Belfast and she was from Cobh, Co.Cork. That was my home town too. But the bad boys put a stop to our talk about old times. The couple sensed the aggression instantly and moved on. I wish I could have left too.

I didn't record most of what passed as I was trying not to encourage them.

They all had relatives, friends and acquaintances shot, imprisoned and maimed by security forces. There are very few good men in the South. Only those who have joined the IRA. You men from the South don't understand what it's like to be a Catholic in Belfast. You're here talking to people about jobs. They'll never get jobs because they're Catholics. Here at the dole you haven't met any Protestants unemployed, have you?

They were like youths you could meet in welfare ghettoes in any city. Rough-looking with those inevitable, ugly, self-inflicted tattoos. They had criminal records practically from childhood. Today was pay day. So today they were clutching beer cans as they would be every pay day. No employer would touch them, ever. I agreed with them that the worst unemployment ghettoes in Belfast were nearly all Catholic.

That's why they support the IRA. One man worried me. He shouted into my face, spraying me with beer, snot and spittle. He wished he had joined the IRA years ago instead of wasting his time drinking and stealing cars. His friends were gathered around him in support. They had to fight the British Army, the RUC, the UDR, the UVF. Men from the South won't help because the media tells them lies.

I thought about a million pub brawls that must have taken place in this city over the centuries. I put out my hand to him in a gesture of friendship. I told him I was soon heading back south and I would think about what he had said. This seemed to confuse his emotions as it was designed to. It made him more maudlin and less aggressive. He started to cry.

Come on, his friends said. It's a waste of time. You'll never get him to understand. He's from the South. Don't bother coming to Belfast again, mister.

And then they got tired of me and left me alone.

Outside Crumlin Road Prison, Belfast;
25 August 1992

Crumlin Road Court House with its barbed wire defenses is a familiar sight to anybody who watches television. I stood across the road outside the prison gates opposite. Under the road, I'm told, there's a tunnel for bringing prisoners between the two buildings.

I was conscious of the man outside the court who had been hanging around all morning. He had the initials of loyalist paramilitary groups on his neck and hands. No doubt plenty more of the alphabet was hidden under his red, white and blue track suit. He had a can of beer. I tried to speak to him earlier but he didn't seem to understand me or what I was doing. He may have been sub-normal.

Each time I heard the gate to the prison visitors' area rasp open that was a sign for me to stand up, put the crossword away and get ready to make my pitch. They were three athletic-looking young men. Their Belfast accents were sharp and clear.

"It's a Victorian jail with Victorian attitudes. Very poor facilities. I think it's disgraceful. Compared to the Maze Prison and Magharberry and Magilligan it's a long way behind."

Do you have experience of those prisons?

"I have indeed. I have served time in two of the three prisons that I have mentioned and also in here, Crumlin

Road. Conditions in here are getting worse."

But once again recently all the toilets and washing facilities were destroyed in a riot. What do you expect if this is the way prisoners carry on?

"I would blame the attitudes of the prison authorities and the Northern Ireland Office for causing the frustration that comes from being locked up twenty three hours a day."

Were your convictions for paramilitary-type offences?

"They were indeed. I want to say that we didn't set about wrecking the prison but that we were forced into a situation where two loyalist prisoners was blew up in the canteen. And if you can't get segregation for that, what can you get segregation for?"

I hope you're not a member of the UDA. I'm forbidden by law to interview paramilitaries.

"I'm not a member."

Were you in the past?

"I was indeed. I come from a community where the UDA was the only safeguard that we seen of counteracting republican terrorism. So that was the reason that myself and numerous other young men joined the UDA at that time."

He had left, he said, because he'd done his time in prison and now it was up to politicians to find a way forward.

A few minutes later he and his friends came back with the card I had given them with my name on it. Your name is Paddy. This seemed to be remarkable.

The three loyalists called across the road to the man with the track suit. There was something they wanted me to see. To describe the man as monosyllabic would be to exaggerate. He gave only very faint grunts. His eyes never met mine. Eventually he did what they asked and pulled down the front of his track suit and got me to peer into his underpants. The name Paddy was tattooed in blue ink on his prick.

Nurses from the City Hospital have told me since that Belfast men often do this to themselves. Snakes are popular and girlfriends' names not uncommon.

Why do you have Paddy on your penis? No answer. He was bored in prison, said one of the others. He must have been very bored. That kind of tattoo involves scraping open the skin with a needle and then infusing the wound with ink, usually with the help of a darning needle and a piece of thread. Did it hurt? No answer. What was he in prison for? I feared the worst. He struck me as the sort of man who could be manipulated into doing anything. They told me his most recent offence was stealing goods from a car roof-rack. His previous crimes were all in the same petty vein involving drink.

Everybody thought it was very funny. I laughed too. It seemed like a good idea.

I met more paramilitaries and their relatives. A lot of the visitors display tattoos that leave you in no doubt about which religion they are, especially in summer. One middle-aged man was wearing a string vest, showing off garish murals of IRA gunmen and tricolours across his arms, chest and shoulders. Catholic women might wear holy medals showing the Virgin Mary. The two sides distinguish themselves by their words. Protestants talked about the two loyalists killed by the bomb in the prison. Catholics talked about the republican inmate whose ear had been bitten off and eaten by a loyalist the previous week.

Remorse is rare. Everybody has been framed. The prison is full of innocent men. But as I explored their stories I often found that I was speaking to paramilitary members. The argument would become circular. We suffer harassment from security forces. And are you a member of a paramilitary group? Yes. Due to harassment. I think listeners should know if the person being interviewed is a member of a paramilitary organisation. It's relevant information. But because of the law I had to drop these interviews altogether.

Since that time Section 31 has been lifted and paramilitaries have responded by refusing to answer questions about paramilitary activities. ("You should address your questions to the British Government.") I can now speak to Sinn Fein members about their concern for their friends and relatives in prison but I cannot ask them about how planting a bomb in the prison can be reconciled with a concern for prisoners' rights. I can now ask paramilitary members attending dole offices about their grave concerns about unemployment, something they like to talk about, but I cannot ask them about the role of extortion rackets in the destruction of the economic life of Northern Ireland. I can speak to grieving paramilitary bosses whose sons have been killed but I cannot ask them about the grief that they have inflicted on countless other fathers in Northern Ireland and beyond. I can now interview terrorists about everything except what they should be interviewed about.

I say remorse is rare. It is not absent. A woman talked about bad and unhygienic visiting conditions, exhausting daily waits, and the fact that she, like other relatives, had to wait many agonising hours before she knew the identity of the two men who had been blown up in the prison some months previously. That meant she was Protestant. Then she talked about who she was visiting.

"My son. He has to be punished. What he did was very wrong. I'll not say what, okay?"

He was involved in some kind of loyalist violence?

"Yes. It was. It happened a year ago yesterday and it nearly killed me because he wasn't brought up to be in any organisations, so he wasn't. He has two other brothers and he definitely wasn't brought up to be like that."

Why did he turn out like that?

"Drink and bad company. And it was the company that

he was in got him into this. My son was brought up in a good area, went to good schools and that. I don't know why. Just bad company and drink."

It's taken a lot out of you.

"Oh it has indeed. He's been in a year now and it has really killed me. When this happened I wrote to the boy's mother and I told her that I was a Protestant and she was a Catholic and that my son had done wrong and I couldn't understand it, that he wasn't brought up to be like that. And I sympathised with her. I just couldn't believe it that he would do ... now there was more than him in it. There was three other ones. I even went to the parish priest at Lisburn Chapel and I asked then what I could do. It really killed me. It did. Killed the whole family. But just by luck a new grandson come into the family, the first one and that has brought us a bit of happiness."

What do you say to him now when you visit?

"I tell him he has to take and behave and if he gets a light sentence, when he comes out he's to stay away from those boys and not be in any organisations."

And what does he say to that?

"He says he'll disappear out of the country. So."

And is that the right thing for him to do?

"Well I know he could never go back to the place where he was living."

And then we talked about the predominantly Catholic small town in County Down where she was from. It was a town I was familiar with. Her husband drove a lorry with a man I know well. We talked about people we knew in the village of Seaforde and the town of Newcastle. Then she got worried and asked me not to talk about her to those people. They didn't know what her son had done and she didn't want them to. I assured her I would not. I agreed not to mention the name of the town when broadcasting her words. She thanked me for my time and left.

215

Outside Crumlin Road Prison; the next day

I don't know how many times I gave my name and stated my business to the RUC. Nothing unusual in policemen asking me for ID. That often happens in the South, too. And because this was a high security zone I had explained in advance to the Northern Ireland Office who I was and what I would be doing. They would know me by the hat. No problem. The NIO man warned me that it might be tense there and he wondered if anybody would want to talk to me. I'll be fine, thank you.

But the arrangement I made only seemed to have been communicated to the first shift of security. After that I met a lot of policemen. Some made an effort to be pleasant. Some didn't. Why are you here? And what exactly is it you're asking about? A soldier at a machine-gun post overhead really annoyed me. 'Ere. 'Ave you got a loighcence for doing that? Yes I have. His bossy manner made me seethe inside. I don't know what he meant by a licence but I had already been interviewed too many times by policemen and I didn't see why I should put up with soldiers suffering from boredom as well.

I asked a tall young man who he had been visiting in prison.

"I actually served time in Crumlin Road."

Was it any way politically-related?

"No."

Was it in any way drink-related?

"Myself, it was drink. Just fighting. GBH. But the mate he's in for ABH."

Aggravated bodily harm. Is that worse than grievous?

"Yes. It was his fiance's ... he only got engaged last Monday ... it was his fiance's birthday party. Somebody else started trying to touch her up. A fight broke out and he ended up arrested and put into Crumlin Road."

How was prison for you?

"It was frightening going into it. But I had family. My cousin was in the paramilitary wing. I got looked after. That helped me out."

Was your cousin a republican or loyalist paramilitary?

"Loyalist. I'm loyalist but I've no ... I'm going out with a Catholic girl. I've nothing against Catholics. That's me personally but cousins ... I couldn't bring her onto the Shankill Road. I've been on Lower Ormeau Road with her but I have to keep me arms covered up cos tattoos. Ulster. UVF. UDA. No surrender. I've got a coat on now. I've a T-shirt under it. If I'm walking the wrong area like Lower Ormeau Road, Springfield Road, I'll get done. I'll get jumped."

Could you see yourself and your girlfriend settling together?

"Yes. We are settled. We've got our own wee flat. Botanic. University area. It's all mixed."

You say it's not a good idea for your Catholic girlfriend to come up to the Shankill?

"She can come up to the Shankill. Meet my family. But I wouldn't say she's a Catholic. I wouldn't say where she's from."

To whom?

"To anybody. Even to me own family."

Your own family don't know she's a Catholic?

"No."

Bloody hell.

"It's just me. She's my girl. I don't care. Me own father he's not paramilitary connected or nothing. He'll meet a Catholic girl. A Protestant girl. It doesn't matter."

Would it matter to your dad that your girlfriend's a Catholic?

"No."

So why don't you tell him?

"I'd take me own time to tell him."

Petty Sessions Court, Chichester Street, Belfast;
11, 12 and 13 January 1993

I was standing at the bottom of the court house steps. It's behind security barriers, back from the main road. The court takes much longer over cases than its equivalent in the Republic, the District Court. About every fifteen minutes somebody emerged from one of the three court rooms and then came down the steps outside where they did or did not agree to talk to me. Royal Irish Regiment soldiers, formerly known as the UDR, were patrolling back and forth. One of the soldiers noticed my microphone and asked me if there was somebody famous up in court. No. Nobody famous. I'm interested in anybody in there who will talk to me.

A young man told me he had got a deferred sentence for taking and driving. Taking and driving was the single most common offence I heard about in my days outside the court. It's commonly called joyriding. Was it your first offence?

"No."

And will you keep on joyriding?

"If I can stop I'll stop but I usually get a wee tempt just to go out for a drive."

You know that joyriders in this city have been shot by security forces and have been victims of punishment shootings by paramilitaries?

"I got my arms done and my legs and I was meant to go down but I never went so they just came and done me arms and me legs."

218

"Baseball bats", his friend joined in.

"They baseball-batted me and hurley-batted me. Then they shot me through the arm and the leg."

Both legs?

"No. Just one arm and one leg."

I've seen the result of a kneecapping before. Usually it's a shot through the fleshy part of the calf.

"No it's the back of it."

"That's the Prods. Provies do you right through a joint."

You're right. He was a Protestant.

"It's done different. Cos we're Catholics."

"The Provies are more severe than the Prods."

A while later I met another young man who was up for joyriding.

"Taking and driving. I'll probably get time. I've got time twelve months ago for stealing a case of whiskey."

Are you worried by paramilitary punishment squads?

"Before my court case well, I was up for a few cases there, couple of months back. They let me out on bail. I cleared off to Manchester. Stayed there for about a month and a half cos there was a couple of boys around me area, there was fellahs looking for me, you know, for stealing cars and stuff. And they says, you know, they let people know they were looking for me to give me a hammering or a punishment. So I got off scene so I did."

Republican or loyalist paramilitaries?

"Loyalist."

And what's happened since?

"I got that sorted out. I went to see them. Just says look I'm not going lose the head not do it no more like. They gave me a by-ball you know. A by-ball that's like a second chance."

So you won't go joyriding any more?

"Nah. Go in do my whack this time then once I get out try and get a job or something."

A tall, middle-aged couple came out. Travellers. They were dressed the way gypsies are supposed to dress. She had long hair, a long dress and lots of jewellery. He had his long black hair tied back and had a pointed beard and moustache. He wore a colourful waistcoat and an earring. She looked like Dolores Keane, the singer. He looked like Robert de Niro.

I introduced myself and immediately her words came gushing out. It was disgraceful what her husband was let get away with by the court. She'd tell me everything. She didn't care who knew. She was sobbing. Not for the first time I noticed how travellers seem to speak in their characteristic, sort of West of Ireland accent no matter what part of the country you might meet them in. How could the courts have treated her this way? And after what she had been through? I tried to interrupt her, to say that I wanted to record her, if she was willing, for possible broadcast.

Then the man spoke. There would be no interview. Perhaps if you let me explain? There will be no explaining. She's giving no interview. I withdrew. I couldn't afford to be the cause of a disturbance. Besides, he was a big bastard and I'm not. I don't know if he was her husband but he was a man in authority over her. She did what she was told and left with him.

There were a lot of cases of assault which usually meant fighting in pubs. This was a man in his forties.

"A hundred pound fine. ABH."

Could that be an imprisonable offence?

"I've received a month prison sentence suspended for a year. I've a month to pay the fine."

Aggravated bodily harm. Did you badly injure someone?

"It was mostly bruises. One of them received two or three stitches in his jaw."

How did you manage to get into that kind of trouble?

"It was just a fight started in a club, in a night-club. We

were sort of defending ourselves, know? They started the fight sort of thing. I fell for it. But one of them was left marked and we weren't."

("Marked" meant injured.)

What was the fight about?

"Religion. Crack made about religion, know?"

Who made the remark?

"He made the remark, know? Started to sing a song about the Ormeau Road, know the bookmakers?"

This was the five Catholic men killed. So you hit him?

"Yeh."

A song gloating about five men killed. That must really get to you?

"Five fellahs murdered just going out doing a bet. I think anybody would be sick now to sing a song about it, know? So I think he deserved the dig in the jaw. It was worth the hundred pounds."

Another man had been fined fifty five pounds because his dog strayed. This was the third time it had happened. He was living in an area which was seventy per cent Protestant and he was a Catholic living by himself. He would keep the dog.

A young man was fined two hundred and thirty pounds for criminal damage to a window in McDonald's fast food restaurant. It was an anti-meat protest and it was what Jesus had wanted.

A fat, middle-aged policeman came out of the court and asked me what I was doing. I told him and said that I had already cleared all of this with the NIO, which is routine inside a security zone. But he should have been consulted. The NIO should have had the decency to consult with him. Had I any idea that this was a security zone? Did the Northern Ireland Office not understand what was involved? I just nodded in the hope that he would go away. You know the type. A petty bureaucrat who couldn't resist the opportunity to show how important he was. He couldn't get me to argue but he still continued to drone on at my expense. Was it five minutes? Ten minutes? He was still there. I hit the wall with fellows like this. I'm told that after a while my eyes glaze over and my face muscles sag when I am cornered by some bore who isn't interested in conversation but simply wants to tell me how the country should be run or why Gay Byrne is a prick. Two really interesting-looking young women came out of the court but I could hardly ask them what they were up for when there was an RUC man with me. And he would be taking it up with the Northern Ireland Office who clearly don't understand procedures that are to be followed. Will this guy please go away? I figured he'd been passed over for promotion many times and now he was embittered, taking refuge in rules and regulations in the way that petty people do. I meet them all the time. Eventually the cloud lifted. He went.

You were just in the Petty Sessions Court. How did you get on please?

She was in her late thirties and tough-looking. Her only visible tattoo was the letters A C A B across the fingers. That's familiar from Dublin. It means all coppers are bastards. She had children with her, including a teenage boy.

"We were up in the juvenile court with my son for shop-lifting in Virgin Records. He stole a wrestling tape. At twelve ninety-nine. This was his second offence and the judge wasn't too lenient with him. He gave him two years probation. That means there'll be a probation officer comes out every week and they'll well-manner him. See that he's plenty to do."

What do you think the judge should have done?

"He should've been put away. Keep his hands to himself."

You wanted your son put in prison?

"Oh, no. But you can't go into other people's property and lift things. He shouldn't have stole at all, so he shouldn't."

Does your son want to talk to me?

"Do you want to say anything?"

No. He doesn't.

"Before a juvenile goes up in the court there's a probation officer comes out and sees you. To see what kind of a family life there is. She came out to the house three times and she has it all in the report to see what kind of home background he came from and did he attend school, which he doesn't."

What does your husband make of it?

"Haven't got one. Divorced."

Do you think that the fact that you and your husband separated had anything to do with the difficulties your son has had?

"No. If his daddy had've been here he might've been worse because his father's an alcoholic."

You know we're considering legalising divorce in the Irish Republic. Do you think it should be allowed?

"Yes cos, why should women get beat about and not get their money every week for a man to be able to go out and sit in a bar and give all his friends money to drink ... "

This is your own husband you're talking about?

"This is my own husband I'm talking about. And then coming in every night and getting beat about the head for absolutely nathin'. Lookin' after the children. Not going out over the door, so ... "

So you barred him?

"Barred him first and then divorced him."

Did you want to marry again? Is that why you divorced?

"No. I wanted a divorce just to get rid of him."

That was the answer I expected. But I still wanted to

satisfy myself that this Belfast woman had the same wish for divorce, not just separation, that abused and deserted women have in the South.

Are you worried about raising your son here in Belfast where so many of the young people go joyriding?

"No. He's not a joyrider. He's a thief but he's not a joyrider. The area that I'm from, thank God, we have no joyriders and our area is supposed to be one of the most deprived in Belfast. That's Duncairn Gardens. We're on a peace line and all."

I was curious now about her religion. The anti-police tattoo had made me think Catholic. I said to her that I knew Duncairn Gardens. It's all painted red, white and blue.

"The right-hand side is Protestant and the left-hand side is Catholic. One side's red, white and blooy and the other side's green, white and gold."

And which side are you?

"I'm the red, white and blooy."

With hindsight, as I listen to my tapes of her now, I think I should have spotted what I have come to believe is a Protestant trait, based on my experiences outside the prison five months previously – that is, that Protestants hold that people must be punished for their crimes.

I asked her about her tattoo and she told the familiar story of teenage foolishness which she regretted. She had been a tomboy. Part of a gang arrested at that peace line twenty years earlier for trying to riot against Catholics. They were bundled into the back of the van and brought to the station where their heavy jackets and boots were forcibly removed. Before being taken to the cells they were all strip-searched for weapons. She began to scream that she was a woman, a fact that had been overlooked in the confusion. Even twenty years on I could see how that mistake could have been made. A policewoman was called and she was taken to another part of the station. She described her experience as torture. I didn't bother to argue, but I know I would far rather be strip-searched than be a victim of any of the more generally recognized forms of torture.

Department of Social Security, Corporation Street, Belfast; 24 January 1994

He was aged about twenty-five. Scruffy-looking. He had just come out of the DSS to use his mobile phone. When he finished his call I explained what I was at. He was friendly and good-humoured.

"I'm just come back from London. I was in there trying to sort out my brew. I just want to get back out of the country again. There's nothing here for me. I think I've a better chance across the water."

Is it because of the lack of work that you want to leave Belfast, or are there other reasons too?

"It's the troubles too. I don't think there'll ever be peace here. There's too much money in it."

Have you, personally, been affected by the troubles?

"Oh, aye. I've been kneecapped twice. Both legs."

The form of the kneecapping, was that through the back of the knees?

"Aye. Through the back of the knees."

You're a Catholic?

"No. I'm a Protestant."

I thought you Protestants get it through the calf of the leg?

"Oh, no. We can get a six-pack too, the same as the Catholics."

What's a six-pack?

"A six-pack? That there's the hands, the knees, the ankles."

That scar I can see on your wrist, what happened?

"That there's different. I fell through a skylight."

I made a mental note to ask him how he came to fall through a skylight. I knew of a Dublin man who died when he fell through the skylight of a warehouse in London. He was trying to rob the place.

And did you get a six-pack?

"Well I didn't get a six-pack. I only got done through the knees twice. They accused me of selling drugs."

And were you selling drugs?

"No. I'm not into anything like that. I just like a drink now and again."

Was it the UDA or the UVF?

"The UVF. The UVF is more or less over this whole territory. North Belfast. They run the show. The UDA is nothing."

Was it a shooting by appointment?

"They just called down to my house. They pull you out. Take you in a car. Hood you. Take you down into an entry. You're spreadeagled. Just put the two in. Whatever they want to do, you know?"

Did the police interview you in hospital?

"Oh, aye. I was questioned because they tried to say I knew the people what done it. But there was no way I was giving any names, cos they would have ended up getting lifted and probably charged, and I would have ended up getting one through the nut."

How are your knees?

"Dead on. Not too bad."

Two years ago I interviewed a man kneecapped by loyalists and he got it through the calf of one leg, but you got it through the knees.

"Oh, aye. I heard that there is sore. Most of them [men about to be kneecapped] take a drink whereas I never. I just rather take it there and then, sober. Because in the hospital they won't give you any pain-killers or anything while you've got a load of drink in you."

It has been said to me that paramilitary punishment squads help to keep law and order in parts of Northern Ireland. Do you agree with that?

"Oh, aye. Cos there's not, that there, much raping and that going on over here. You see over in London, there's all rape and perverts running about there."

He was right there. Unwanted Irish people, whether from the North or the South, always flee to Britain.

May I ask you again, please, about the scar on your wrist. You say you fell through a skylight. I'm going to take a guess that you were trying to rob some place.

"Burglary. I went too quick. Straight in."

Have you done any time in prison here?

"Oh, aye. I've been up in that there Crumlin. Central Hotel."

Do you have any Catholic friends?

"Oh, aye. I know a few through the day centre."

What's the day centre?

"When you're put through the courts you've to go to a day centre, three days a week. You go to the sauna and that and do the weights and all."

We were both laughing now. There was something absurd about body-building for young criminals.

Did you ever have a Catholic girlfriend?

"I had one time. But I had to leave her. Cos I was getting too much hassle from *my* side. Getting so much stick. Like you're going out with a Taigue and that there. If you're walking into a disco and all it's, he's going out with a Fenian and all that there crap. So, I don't bother nigh going out with Catholic girls."

("Nigh" is the local pronunciation of "now".)

I was curious about his mobile phone. He asked me to turn off my tape-recorder. That phone was worth a lot of money to him. No. It wasn't stolen. It was well worth the rental. I didn't ask him what line of business he was in but I guessed that might be selling drugs. He told me he had done time in prison in Spain. That was for possession of cannabis. I told him it didn't bother me if he was selling dope in Belfast. I knew there was no demand for heroin here. He chose not to tell me any more.

His friend came out of the DSS. He would speak to me too. We stayed near the door so that we would be able to hear when his ticket number was called. Like the other man, he had been the victim of a punishment squad.

"I got me arms broke, like. That was 1989. And I had to clear off, tay England. And I've just come back to see my family, my friends. I've still got a steel plate in me arm."

Why did they do it?

"They said I was breaking into houses."

And were you?

"No. But that's the way loyalists are. They like to do things like that to people. To show an example. The area I live in, the Shore Road, it's all hard-core loyalists."

You're Protestant?

"Yeah."

He had a blue dot, what's called a borstal spot (in Belfast, a "borstal spat") tattooed on his cheek. Young people disfigure themselves in this way for bravado. It signifies a period in borstal or prison. I asked this man if he had a prison record.

"I have been in prison, aye. Been in a few times. Stealing cars. Breaking into places and that. Nothing serious. No assaults or nothing like."

So that's why the UVF punished you?

"I broke into places but it wasn't houses. It was shops. I don't break into people's houses. I break into shops, big warehouses and factories, but I don't do anything more like."

Tell me about the punishment you got. Was it terrifying when they took you out of your home?

"At the start it was. I was shaking and all like."

How did they break your arms?

He pointed to the iron covering on a drain in the gutter.

"With a grating. Off the road. They lie you face down. They had me arms out."

Jesus.

"I was in hospital for six weeks. I nearly lost me arm. I have a steel plate and all in it."

Do you think there can be peace in Northern Ireland?

"No. If one side get what they want the other side will just ... start."

If the republican side got what they want, would you accept that?

"No. To be truthful I wouldn't. Even though I don't like the paramilitaries, I still stay who I am. Protestant. That's not against Catholics. I had lots of Catholic friends in London. But if they say a united Ireland, I would take up arms."

Chapter Twelve

GALWAY

Rahoon Flats, 12 August 1992

It was wet, cold and windy. Unseasonal weather for August. I was waiting outside the community welfare office at the entrance to Galway Regional Hospital. The flat complex of Rahoon is a little way down the hill. Those flats are full of people on social welfare. The people of Rahoon attend this welfare office. My plan was to meet the people of Rahoon here. To be invited into those flats.

Things weren't working out. It was so wet and cold that people were running past me. Not waiting around for a chat. I was soaked as well. My fingers had gone white and numb. Time to be nice to yourself, Paddy. There's a cafe at the shopping centre down the road. Get a newspaper. Have a cup of coffee. Think out what you're going to do.

People from all over Galway come to this shopping centre but you can tell the locals who have walked over from Rahoon flats. Poor people have a look about them. Single mothers pushing prams. Their clothing is shabby. They smoke a lot. Their faces give them away too. I can't define it but there's a look about someone on low money.

There are lots of travellers in Rahoon. You can tell them

by their looks as well. Their style of dress. Weathered faces. Lots of children. Women gone to middle-aged fatness when barely out of their twenties.

The weather wasn't getting any better but I was determined to crack Rahoon. It was my kind of place. Probably not a private phone in the whole estate. Full of people whose voices were never before heard on radio.

When the rain eased I wandered into the flat complex. There are large blocks of four stories and some outlying, two-storey blocks. It's a shabby place, although Galway Corporation told me that a major face-lift was planned for the following year.

Who would I talk to? Still too cold and wet just to hang around. I hadn't yet learned that simply banging on doors would yield results.

A number of travelling men were working on bits of vans. You're a reporter? They kidded with me first. Talk to him. That fellah will give you some stories. But they were cautious of me or maybe just shy.

Michael said he'd love to talk. He brought me out of the flat complex to the caravan he was living in on the perimeter. Margaret, put on the kettle. We have a man here from RTE wants to see us.

Michael and Margaret were a young couple. They had one baby daughter and she was only out of hospital with her chest. It's the caravan, you see. The dampness. They're on the list for a flat or a house. They didn't like living in a caravan. They grew up in caravans but they didn't want it for themselves.

I was explaining that I would like to interview them on tape when there was a knock on the caravan door. Michael was called out. He looked pale when he came back in. I'm sorry but you must leave. And you're not to say anything that I said on the radio. What's the problem, Michael? Who was that at the door? I'm not saying. You have to go now.

231

No point in even speaking to Margaret, of course. These people were travellers, which meant that the man's decision was the only one that counted.

I made my way through the long, wet grass. Back to the flat complex. I was angry. I suspected it was some kind of tribal elder of the travelling community who had given Michael his orders. Or possibly some alleged traveller representative who wouldn't want me to speak to Michael and Margaret because that young couple might say the wrong thing. They were parents who wanted the best for themselves and their child. There was no mention of preserving ethnic identity or demanding ethnic representation on the local council.

Michael and Margaret were people whom everybody could understand and identify with. That's bad news for the ethnic politics brigade. They would rather keep travellers distant from journalists so that only the ethnic representatives would have the power to speak on their behalf.

When I'm angry I get determined. I'll get a programme from here. The single mums were good. Two of them stood out in the wind and rain talking to me. One was born into a family on social welfare. Another was hoping for better things out of life but parenthood had changed all that.

At the playground I met a woman with two small boys. She had a Scandinavian accent. She was on a Social Employment Scheme. She would love to tell me all about it. She gave me her flat number to call to later.

I was trying to figure out how the Scandinavian woman could be on a Social Employment Scheme. She couldn't have been on single parent's pay because you can only get an SES if you're on the dole. I remember a woman in Blanchardstown in Dublin who, after her husband's suicide, claimed dole money for herself and the children and got accepted on the SES. When her widow's pension came through she lost her chance at the SES because she was no longer counted as unemployed. The SES is used to keep jobless figures down.

The Scandinavian woman must have been claiming dole. Which meant she was on separate payments from her husband and separate payments meant he was a man who was unreliable with money. A wild Irishman. A musician, I'll bet. Or at least a bodhran-banger. There are loads of them in Galway. They hold a fascination for young European women. Great fun for a romance, I'm sure, but disastrous as husbands.

Her flat was on the top floor of one of the blocks. It was nice to get in from the cold.

"I am on the Social Employment Scheme at the moment. I started mine about eleven months ago, so it will be over in another four weeks time. I was on the long-term unemployment assistance. I was actually getting the money for my whole family. My husband, my two children and myself."

So you were signing for separate payments?

"Yes. And then my husband went to prison. I took over the signing."

This woman was not someone who would hold back on me. I was curious to know what her husband's crime was and I probably could have asked her that question straight away. But experience tells me that it's better to build up an interviewee's confidence by asking easy questions.

The government seems to be planning a further expansion of work schemes for unemployed people. Do you think that's a good idea? What did you feel about the scheme you were on?

"Personally, I think it is a good idea. At least if you have a job that you enjoy, which I have, luckily. And for me personally, with the two small children, I enjoy an opportunity to get away from home. Not to be stuck at home with the children all the time. And it gives me a small chance to eventually come back to work full-time, perhaps when the children go to school."

You have only four more weeks on the scheme. So you're back on the dole next month.

"Most likely. As it is, at the moment my marriage is breaking up. I have everything more or less upside down, so, even if I wanted, I wouldn't be able to look for work right now. But I'm hoping when the children start going to school then the experience of this scheme will do some good for me to find work."

I'm curious about your accent. Where are you from, please?

"I'm from Finland."

And how did you come to be in Ireland?

"I came on a working holiday and I met my husband and I came back and we got married. That's about five and a half years ago."

What do you think about living here in Rahoon?

"It's definitely not the best place. And it's not a very good place for children. And as I am living in the top floor flat with two small children it is very difficult. These flats weren't built for having children. The playing grounds aren't really much. This is a place where poor people are put. There are no corporation houses to get and we are people who can't afford anything private. I don't think you find many people in Rahoon who work. If they are working they are probably just waiting to get the money enough to get a mortgage and buy a house."

Does your husband agree with you that your marriage is breaking up?

"We got separated a few weeks ago. At the moment he is in prison. So I suppose after he comes from prison we have to see about things again. See what will happen. We are only a few weeks separated and it's nothing official, just he is away."

Will he be away for long?

"Six months."

What's he in for?

"Dangerous driving."

Tell me what you think about Irish men. Any different to men from Finland?

"I think people are the same all over the world ... probably the Irish society is a little bit more old-fashioned than the one I come from. Men where I come from are more inclined to help at home and do things like that. And to see women as equals. But still even in Scandinavia the women aren't equals yet. But it's a little bit more advanced in Scandinavia."

Your husband, is he the sort of man you'd meet in Finland, or is he a more traditional man?

"He is a very traditional man. Very traditional man altogether. Actually when I first met him I thought he was a little bit more modern than he proved to be in marriage. But I would say that is very, very usual with any other man, any man in the world."

She was laughing now. She seemed to enjoy remembering the years with her husband. But her face became pained, her voice stressed, when she answered the next questions.

Do you want to say what broke your marriage up?

"Alcohol."

On your part or his part?

"On his part. He is very badly ... the breaking is being done by me because I can't stand it any longer. He is very badly ... badly ... "

"Drink."

It was her little boy who said this. He was about three years old but he obviously knew what was distressing his mother.

"Yes drink, my son says. The alcoholism is ruining everything. It's impossible to live with an alcoholic in the long run. It's too destructive ... it's too hard emotionally and too destructive financially. That's what always happens with people who drink. They end up with broken up marriages, losing children. Unless they look for treatment which, unfortunately, my husband hasn't seen any reason to do yet."

If he listens to the radio in prison, is there anything you want to say? Is there still time to save your marriage?

"There's always time. He is the father of my children and we spent a few years together. And they weren't unhappy times all the time. So, of course, there's always a chance. But it's very much up to him now."

She told me her mum and dad in Finland knew her marriage wasn't going too well. But they didn't realise that she was living in poverty like this. I don't suppose Finland has got an equivalent of the Rahoon flats. There's not the unemployment there that there is in Ireland. She was welcome to go back to Finland if she wanted. Her family had a farm far in the north of rural Finland.

How sad, I thought. What an unlikely place for a young Finnish woman to end up. A welfare slum in Ireland. Trapped inside with two children on a wet afternoon. I asked her if she might go back to Finland if her marriage was finished. She wasn't prepared yet to close the door on her marriage.

Was she once impressed by her husband because he was a wild Irish bodhran-banger? No. He had no musical skills. She loved him and had happy times with him. But drink had ruined things.

For the first time she dropped her voice and spoke to me as if she were saying something she felt she shouldn't.

Perhaps it will help you to understand if I tell you my husband was a traveller.

It did help me to understand. Travelling men are very traditional men. The cultural gulf between a Scandinavian woman and an Irish travelling man must have been immense.

When I was in Copenhagen four years earlier I interviewed Danish women who had romances with hard-drinking, undomesticated Irishmen. Good for a laugh but there was unlikely to be a long-term future in those romances. Scandinavian culture gave women higher expectations than these Irishmen would reach.

Here in Galway I had met a Scandinavian woman who went the whole way and married an Irishman, a traveller, and had children by him. She made the act of trust that a woman makes in a man when she gives up her independence to have children. Once the ring was on her finger (or was it once the children were born?) the man's traditional values began to show. A fun romance. A disastrous marriage.

Before I left the flat I asked her again about going back to Finland. It seemed to me to be the best escape from the welfare ghetto called Rahoon.

Maybe she would go. Maybe she would stay. Her marriage wasn't over yet.

Chapter Thirteen

DROGHEDA

Rathmullen Estate, Co. Louth;
18 November 1992

Rathmullen housing estate is a welfare ghetto on the high ground to the west side of Drogheda town. I was knocking on doors. That week the government was paying welfare recipients the seventy percent bonus that had in the past been paid in the week before Christmas. Did people think it was a good idea or not to pay the bonus a month earlier than usual? This would be my opening line.

She was a single mother aged about twenty-five with two children. She brought me into the front room where most of the wallpaper had fallen off, revealing dampness and fungus behind. She was good-humoured and welcoming. She spoke with a Louth accent, a kind of Northern twang. What did she think about getting her Christmas bonus in November?

"Well we had no choice. Like we were told just we were getting it this week and that was it like. But it is too early to have it cos like I mean as soon as you get it it's gone and that's it."

You're a single parent. Was it your choice to raise the children on your own?

"Well I had no choice only to raise them on me own. I was going with a separated man. He was already married so I couldn't marry him."

And he's the father of both your children?

"No. The eldest fellah. I was going with another fellah as well but it just didn't work out."

But you had a baby by him as well?

"Yes but it was an accident. It wasn't planned. It just happened."

I'm always hearing about accidental pregnancy. You understood contraception?

"Well on him, the eldest, I was on the pill but I didn't know you couldn't take antibiotics. Like while you're on the pill the antibiotics stop it from working which I didn't know so that's how I got caught on his nibs over there. And this fellah here was a condom baby."

What's a condom baby?

"Using condoms and it busted."

Living here in Drogheda, is there still prejudice against single mothers?

"The thing that I find most is when I actually got my house there was ones that were married and cos they didn't get houses they said, oh yeah they can give them to the single people but they can't give them like to the married couples. But as I said, I done me time on the waiting list the same as what they did. And like what makes me laugh is the way they turn around and say they have kids for to get the money. Which is a load of bull. Like I mean a person on the dole is getting about fifty-five, sixty pound a week for themselves where a single parent has what, fourteen pound extra to raise a child and pay bills with? You don't just go to have a child just to get an extra fourteen pound. Because the fourteen pound doesn't cover yeh."

Do you feel bitter at all against the men in your life?

"Yeah. One of them anyway."

The first or the second?

"The second."

Why?

"Cos he lied to me."

She was laughing now. How did he lie?

"Well he's not from this country you see. And he told me the first night I met him the first thing I asked him was he married and he said no. But he was married all along."

You couldn't guess?

"No. Cos when I asked him the questions he didn't stumble over the answers. He just answered straight out which to me was genuine, you know? If he had've sat now and was trying to work out what to say I'd've copped on, you know?"

And you met him here in Drogheda?

"Yep."

And he's gone now?

"Yep."

Do you ever think he should help you with the maintenance of the child?

"We were just talking about that today to find out if I'd be able to get him to pay maintenance."

Is he earning any kind of money?

"He's a sailor. He's plenty of money. If he hadn't've lied so much I'd probably've just let it go. But like, after being so false about everything."

Could you find him?

"He's in Drogheda every so often."

Would he not be interested to meet his son?

"He met him. But it doesn't bother him."

Is he with his wife still?

"Yeh. But she knows nothing. If he doesn't give me any maintenance I'll go over myself and tell her if I have to. I don't care. Like I mean why should they get off scot free the whole time with it? It's not fair that we're left. Like I mean it's bad enough we have them for them and then we have to rear them on our own while he's off having a good time."

You know where he lives in England?

"He's not living in England. He's living in Norway."

So he would stay with you when his ship came in?

"Uh huh."

And you loved him?

"Mmmm."

I still feel you should have realised he was married.

"Well not when he asks you to marry him which he did. Like I mean he asked me to go over to Norway to live and I went and I sold off a load of me furniture and all in the house. I have to scratch now to get me furniture back into the house. Like when a fellah asks you to marry him you don't expect him to be married in another country."

How did you find out he was married?

"One of his shipmates."

That must have been some shock.

"Well it was after all the bull that he gave me."

Sorry. You're upset.

"No. I just want to kick the head off him when I see him again."

241

Chapter Fourteen

RELATIONS OF SEX OFFENDERS

Arbour Hill Prison, Dublin;
1 December 1992

The two women seemed unlikely companions. They were both in their mid-forties but one looked poor and the other didn't. The better-dressed woman's hair was dyed and set. The shabby one's hair was greying and limp. The smart one smelled of perfume and powder. Her companion smelled of cigarettes.

They spoke differently. The shabby woman had a working-class accent and was shy. The better-dressed one had a confident, well-educated, middle-class voice. She had a lot to say about visiting Arbour Hill prison.

"I'm very pleased here with the conditions in Arbour Hill. Most of the prisoners seem very happy. But there are things I would like to see changed here in Arbour Hill. For a start, when a person is put into prison, people are inclined to forget the families of the accused. There is no help for us outside. The only help we can get is if we have money to pay for a counsellor and have special counselling done. Now the majority of people here in Arbour Hill could not afford to pay for these services. The prisoners are well looked after in there but we're outside. We carry the sentence as well. There is no place we can meet and discuss our problems with other people. We are not really accepted in society."

When I heard that last comment I guessed that I was speaking with the relative of a sex offender. Arbour Hill is where they keep sex offenders.

In what way are you not accepted?

"We have nobody to turn to. There should be an organisation for us. There's an agency to help battered wives and organisations to help everyone else. But prisoners' relatives have no one to turn to when we are faced with this terrible situation when someone that we dearly love ends up in a prison."

How has it affected you?

"I have taken this very bad. Someone who I was very close to ... I have tried to get help. I was suicidal at one stage. I found I have nobody to turn to."

The man you were just in to see, how is he today?

"He was in great form today. Now I could come back next week and he could be very upset and stressed. People in here, in this prison, especially the ones like him with a very long sentence, what can you say to them? Today I'm really thrilled with him and I feel very happy that I came to see him which I do every week. Tonight I'll go home and I'll cry for three hours. I mean there are times when you could really break down."

Is it your husband in there?

"Ehm ... it's my brother. This lady's husband. These are his children. I think these long sentences are really ridiculous."

The prisoner's wife chose to stay silent. She let her sister-in-law do the talking.

Do you think he deserved to go to prison?

"In my opinion, no."

Was it a violent crime?

"Ehm ... it was, yes. But brought about through a lot of drink. It was a drink-related problem. He is not a violent man."

She had chosen not to tell me the type of crime. I had to try another approach.

Do you find that there's a social stigma attached to having a relative in prison?

"Of course there is a terrible stigma. I couldn't go and tell my next-door-neighbour that I have a brother in Arbour Hill. People will say about him that he's a ... people forget that there's goodness in every one of us."

Your neighbours don't know about your brother?

"My neighbours do *not* know."

Are you worried that your neighbours might know your voice on radio?

"Definitely not. They do not know it's me."

I guessed that this interview had just become redundant. I knew once her middle-class friends and relatives got to work on her that she would change her mind about it being broadcast.

How do you feel about the victim of your brother's crime?

"Oh, the victim of the crime. Well they get special counselling ... "

Was the victim a man or a woman?

"It was a woman. I know myself ... that lady is perfect today. But here we are, we're still suffering. We still carry that burden. We're suffering more, actually, than the prisoner or the victim. And another thing I would like to say, when somebody is accused of a crime, the way the papers refer to these people ... like they're human beings and they refer to them as beasts and animals and they're not fit to live among society."

Was it rape?

"Eh ... yes ... it is a rape case."

Well, rapists are despised. Inside and outside prison.

"Yes, I can accept that. But I don't think there's any need to say that someone is an animal. It's inhuman. I mean it's the families that suffer and nobody wants to listen to us. Nobody wants to know us. I mean little children are put down for a crime someone else has committed."

How are the children affected?

"They go to schools. You have to give your father's name, what they worked as. How do you tell somebody that your father is a rapist? The children know their daddy has committed some crime but they don't understand the meaning of the crime. And then they're faced with this all their lives. And with housing, or things like that, you have these people getting together and then they say, we can't have that family in beside us."

I must put it to you about your brother, that neighbours might be afraid of him because they think that if a man has raped once, he might rape again.

"Well I think this is very wrong. From what I have read, in the majority of cases, that crime is never again committed by those people."

I've interviewed rape victims as well. It seems to me that rape victims can continue to suffer for life ...

"Well possibly there may be a little bit of that but at least for them it's over. When the person is sentenced at least they can say, well now, he's been punished for what he did to me. But whereas he will always suffer for years. I mean, putting someone away for fifteen years. I think that was really outrageous. And now that girl is perfect. *Perfect.*"

A few days later I got a message from that woman to phone her. The number was in middle-class Rathmines. It was as I expected. She had talked it over with her family and she had thought better of doing the interview. She was distressed now and begged me not to broadcast it. I told her to relax. I wouldn't broadcast it.

She was right not to let the neighbours know about her brother. The previous year I interviewed a woman in St. Michael's Estate, Inchicore, whose husband was in prison for rape. A dirt bird, she called him. Do you go to see him in prison? I do in my shite. A few days later I had to go to see the man who was her new partner in life. His head was bandaged and stitched. Neighbours had attacked him with a metal bar. We heard your bird on the radio say you were a rapist. The man was a victim of confusion on the part of listeners.

I met a priest visiting Arbour Hill. He was in to see a man whom nobody else would visit. Had the man no relatives? That wasn't it. He had family, plenty of relatives. But none of them wanted to know him because of the nature of his crime.

A stout, red-faced woman with a London accent was in to see her son. She had travelled from Tuam to see him. She kept laughing. Rape. That's what he's in for. She didn't care what the neighbours thought. There was a smell of drink from her. I didn't broadcast the interview.

A cheerful Dublin woman spoke to me. She was too cheerful. It didn't seem right.

"I got on great. I was in visiting me son. It's a nice prison. They seem to have great fun. He has great friends in there."

Did I hear her right? Great fun. Great friends. We were talking about a prison for sex offenders. She went on about how nice the staff were. I asked her if her son ever got depressed in there.

"Well I don't think so. He could get depressed but I don't suppose he'd show it to me."

Is it a long sentence?

"He is doing a long time, yes."

Do you want to say what kind of crime he's in for?

"Well, I'll tell you the truth, I don't know much about it. Me family knows but they kept it dark from me. I never saw any papers nor nothing."

You don't know what your son is in for?

"A little. A bit. I just have hints and hints and I don't ask him. I let him tell me when he wants to. You know?"

Do you suspect what he's in for?

"Well I'm not sure if it's true now. No, I'm not. I don't really."

Okay. A lot of the people here have told me they were in visiting sons who are in for sex offences. Do you think it was something like that?

"It could have been. Because, ehm … he was one himself when he was young. Yeah. Yeah."

He was sexually assaulted when he was young?

"Yeah. When he was a child. In school … one of the Brothers, yeah."

Well … not everybody who is molested as a child goes on to be a child molester. Why do you think that … ?

"Well we were told that he'd be always curious as to what experience the other person got. And I think that's the way it was with him. And he had some drink taken. And he can't take anything. He's not into that. When you're drunk I suppose you're weak."

Did his offence involve children?

"Now that I don't know. I just know he was out drinking with friends and that's how it happened. I only get bits of everything. I don't get the paper or nothing. And I wasn't told anything a long time after."

She told me a hopelessly confused story about how her son was molested in Daingean, an approved school. She was vague on every point. She was only partly in touch with the real world. I didn't broadcast the interview.

I met a young woman. How did the visit go?

247

"Very well, grand. You get about half an hour. The prison wardens are very good, very nice."

What do you talk about?

"I just talk about what's going on outside ... you know ... home, the children."

What are his spirits like today?

"He's grand today. He wasn't when he first got the sentence. He got six years which he'll do four and a half years of. The first nine months were the hardest. The first Christmas was very hard. He couldn't accept what had happened. He'd never been in trouble before. It was just a one-off thing. It was hard for us and hard for him. He's a brother of mine."

Does it affect you on the outside?

"Ah yeah. Well you get very depressed. You're worried all the time he might do something to himself. It's hard to accept that you're going to be in there four and a half years."

What sort of offence is he in there for?

"Well he's in for a sexual offence. He was wrongly judged, I think meself. It was a girl he'd been going with. She has his child. He'd been in a relationship with the girl. How do you call that rape? When you're in a relationship with a girl I wouldn't classify that as rape. I think every second girl is going around crying rape, now, because of the system. There's husbands being done for raping their wives! When you get married, whatever goes on in your married life, that's the vow you take when you're being married. You just don't go crying rape."

Does it get him down still?

"He was very low at first. He was very sorry for what he did. He wasn't in his right mind when he did it. He had an awful lot of alcohol taken. The doctor says that his mind was disturbed at the time. How can you judge a person like that? I just don't think a person should be put away for

248

six years for something like that. Twelve months, maybe, but not six years. The stigma will always be there. I don't think it should go down as rape in the case of a relationship."

Did he beat her?

"Yes he beat her, but it was because he was drunk."

Does he suffer in prison from the stigma of being a sex offender?

"No. They're mostly all sex offenders in there."

Does it worry you that he's in there with them?

"No. Not particularly. At first it was just a matter of getting the right person in the cell with you."

You're his sister. You're very loyal to him.

"Well we're all rearing children. Nobody knows what's ahead of us. What our own children might turn out like. Everybody is rearing and they should stop to think before judging."

Do your mum and dad visit him?

"They're both dead. But my brothers and sisters are very bitter. They don't go to see him. But he's in for a long time and I hope they change their minds. Maybe one day they'll come to forgive him. Because it's affected him more so inside that the rest of the family don't want to know him. And that's very hard for him. I mean, we're outside. We've other people to comfort us. They've nobody to comfort them in there."

Why do your brothers and sisters not feel the same way about him as you do?

"That's their judgement. I don't really know. I hope one day they'll come to forgive him and one day they will come up to see him. It is very hard to be inside if the rest of your family don't want to know."

If he had robbed a bank, would they visit him in prison?

"Oh, yeah, definitely. If it had been a bank robbery,

yeah. It's just the word. Rape. There's a stigma. It's just that actual word. Rape."

A couple who had been in to see their son said they would talk. I did the interview in their car. The man spoke first.

"We're doing the sentence that he's doing in there. We're probably doing a harder sentence out here."

Can you explain that a bit more to me, the way that you are serving the sentence?

"We visit him every Tuesday, and we have from Tuesday to the following Monday then to just get over the last visit when we have to start all over again."

You're upset now having left him?

"We are very upset now, yeah."

"I agree with my husband about serving the sentence. It's very hard on the parents. It's hard on the whole family. It's hard on everybody concerned."

Has he much longer to serve?

"He has a long time ... I couldn't even talk about it ... a long time."

How is he when you're with him?

"He's in good form. He tries to make the best but I'm his mother and I know myself, he's upset when we leave, you know? It's hard, very hard."

Do you want to say the sort of offence he's in for?

"No."

"It's a bad offence."

"It's a bad offence he's in for."

You stood by him after this offence?

"Oh yeah, one hundred percent."

Do you think he was at fault?

"The last words coming out there ... I don't think I should be in, Da, but if I did what I did, I deserve to be here. I don't know if I did it or not. If I didn't do it there's a bastard out there who did do it."

"I blame society meself."

"The drug ecta ... eska ... ecstasy was found in his system. He hasn't an idea. He has no recollection whatsoever from the night."

He was on ecstasy and something else happened?

"Yeah."

There are a lot of sex offenders in there. Was it a sexual assault?

The woman answered.

"It was a sex offence, yeah."

Does that upset you very much?

"It does, yeah. It upsets everybody."

"Like my wife says, it upsets everybody. And he was very happy-go-lucky. There was no need for him at any time to have to do that. He has a girlfriend that stands by him."

How do your neighbours react?

"We're not interested. But we've had some good neighbours too. Neighbours came in to us, console his mother and myself. And made us ... brought us out, when we weren't going out. Made us go out."

"The parish priest visited my son and he come and visit us. It's heartbreaking. I won't see my son, and he won't see us, till Tuesday. And we're dreading Christmas. That's the worst time."

Will you get to visit him at Christmas?

"Well he doesn't want us to visit him on Christmas Day. He said to me, Ma, I don't want any suffering for you on Christmas Day."

"They have a party for themselves in there on Christmas Day. They all get different boxes of chocolates or whatever."

Do you think it would be a good idea for the two of you to get counselling to help you through this?

"Our doctor arranged a therapist for us. She cost us

251

thirty pounds an hour. We couldn't afford thirty pence an hour so we couldn't keep it up. When myself and my wife went in, her watch came off and after sixty minutes we're told, come back next week. But she was a great help. She made everything come out. No matter what was inside us that even we didn't know was hidden."

"It helps to talk. But for the prisoners inside there's nothing. They get tablets to calm their nerves and to help them sleep but they still have to wake up and face reality the next day. Just to sit and talk would help. Sitting here talking to you helps. But there's nothing for the prisoners. There used to be some kind of help in there for sex offenders but it's gone now."

Was there press coverage of your son's offence?

The woman answered first.

"You never get over that wounding. The Beast of Rathfarnham, they called him. You can't go to the shops. People are pointing their finger at you. And I mean, everybody is rearing children. Nobody knows what they're going to do tomorrow. It's very hard to go and face people. To do your shopping. Even to go to Mass. You don't want to go to Mass because people are pointing at you."

"Due to the bad press, they actually imprisoned us. The parents."

"And our younger children had to go to school. To have to go to school and face ... can you picture the effect of that on young children?"

With the tape-recorder off, the man told me how hard it had become to earn money since his son's offence. The line of business he was in meant that he worked in people's houses. Nobody was calling for his services any more. He didn't want his son to know this.

The next time I heard from that man was a year later. His marriage of twenty-seven years had broken up. His wife had been seeing another man. She had listed her lover's phone number in her note book under "Annie's Mother". He found out, beat up the man concerned and was facing an assault charge. He had done time in Mountjoy for a similar offence once before.

He was a sad and lonely man. His wife had left with the children. He was still seeing his son in prison every week. His wife had given up the prison visits. She couldn't take the pressure, she told him. For several months his son was in Cork prison so that meant paying for the train journey every Saturday. His son was back in Dublin now in Wheatfield. He would continue to see him. He was all he had.

Chapter Fifteen

TRALEE

Mitchell's Estate, Co. Kerry;
30 November 1993

It was still daylight in Tralee as I walked towards a group of travellers in Mitchell's Estate. The travelling families were bunched at one end of the estate. You could tell by the vans and caravans. A group of men stood around one of the vans. They saw me coming a long way off, the fellow in the hat. They were joking with each other. I think they probably knew who I was. I had tried to interview one or two of those men earlier at the dole. They had been cautious of me and had said no. Now I was on their territory and I was the one who was cautious. Not that I feared for my safety but I wouldn't get any good work done if I antagonised them. I was probably talking half out loud to myself as I rehearsed what my opening lines would be when I reached them.

I asked them if they thought paying the Christmas bonus in November had been a good idea. (This line had worked well a year before in Drogheda so I was using it again.) They met me with good-humoured banter. He's the man who'll talk to you. You should interview him. What, me? Don't mind him. Interview that fellah instead, you'd never shut him up. And so on. Okay men, I said. I'll be around the estate for the next few hours if you change your minds. You'll spot me, the fellow in the hat. Meanwhile I'll knock on some of these doors.

A woman aged about thirty answered. She was good-humoured and interested. Behind her glasses it was obvious that one eye had been badly injured at some time in the past. The flesh around the eye-socket was disfigured and the eye pupil was a tiny black dot in the grey iris. I know now that I had already subconsciously decided that she was one of the settled community, not a traveller. I was wrong. She explained to me later why I had made this mistake about her.

She told me her husband had gone years ago. Maybe she had a view on divorce? No. She'd be against that. She'd be too shy to speak on radio but I should come into the kitchen and meet her sisters.

They were both in their twenties and the older, red-headed woman did look like a traveller. She had freckles and the premature, middle-aged heaviness of a travelling woman. Broad-shouldered and fat-bottomed. Her young sister was slim and pretty with long brown hair.

The three sisters were lovely, calm and welcoming. A relief from the rough banter of the men outside.

Now here in Mitchell's Crescent in Tralee you tell me you're on Social Welfare. Did you get the Christmas bonus yet?

The red-haired woman spoke first.

"Friday, I'm getting it."

Is that a good idea to be getting it so early?

"I'd rather get it a week before Christmas with the kids and that kind of thing because when you get it too early you'd spend it, you know what I mean?"

What payment are you on please?

"I'm on a Widow's Pension. I get ninety-four pounds a week. That's for two children and myself."

You're a very young woman to be widowed.

"Too young altogether."

Do you reckon you'll stay on Widow's Pension?

"Oh I'll stay on Widow's Pension cos I don't believe in getting married again. I don't believe in anything like that."

Why not?

"Oh for the sake of my young fellows, for the sake of my children like. If I had got no kids I would, but for the sake of my two children I wouldn't. I don't believe in it."

Why do you not believe in it?

"That's the way we were brought up. That's our religion like. We don't believe in anything like that."

You say the way you're brought up. Your religion. Are you a Catholic?

"Yeah, I'm a Catholic, yeah."

And isn't it acceptable that if the husband has died you can marry again?

"No I don't believe in it, cos we're travellers you know and we don't believe in anything like that, like getting married again. Like we believe in staying a young widow and just rearing our two kids and that's it, like."

That seems to me to be very hard. Do you agree with your sister here?

This question was to the youngest.

"Yeah, I'm married and I'm separated and I wouldn't live with no one else."

Does your husband live here in Tralee still?

"No. He's from another part of the country, like."

And you're saying just because you've been married once that that'll be it?

"Yeah to me I wouldn't get up and live with no one else, even though I've got no thoughts of going into the House of God again and getting married. I wouldn't get up and do it anyway even if I had the authority."

She used the word "authority" in a strange, reverent kind of way. This was no mere secular authority. It was something sacred, mystical, rooted in the ways of her people.

Is that your religion again?

"It's just the way we were brang up like. We were brang up in our parents' home. My father is dead now the last eleven year, but when they were together they were together until death like, and she never took on with no one else like. So to me we've only one father or one husband."

You must have been a young woman when you married. What age were you?

"I was nineteen and I'm twenty-two now."

So even though you're separated, that's it now?

"Yeah."

If we have a divorce referendum next year will you vote in it?

"I wouldn't because of my children like. I've got two children and I wouldn't. The same as my sister I wouldn't."

Do your children ever ask about their dad?

"They do but they don't understand it that young. What can you tell a two-year-old and ten-month-old? What could you explain to them? They're too young to understand."

It seems to me that you and your sister are being very hard on yourselves. I'm not suggesting that you want to meet another man but if you did meet someone else, I don't see why you shouldn't form a home again?

"But when you have a home already, why want another home?"

And do you not miss the company of a man, or of an adult?

"You would like. But you'd get used to it. I was with my husband for only two year. If he treated me right I'd probably still be with him but unfortunately he didn't. What I went through in my marriage, I wouldn't go through it again with another man. I'd be afraid to make the same commitment to another man like I did with my first marriage. I wouldn't do that again and I wouldn't put my children through the tormentation I got and the hardship."

You say the hardship, do you mean he beat you?

"Yeah, so I wouldn't put my children through that."

You tell me that you're travellers. Is traveller culture different that way, do travellers marry only once?

The widowed sister answered this one.

"All travellers are not the same. Other travellers have their own opinion of life, you know what I mean? Just like the settled community. It all depends on how you feel yourself."

Have you always lived here in Tralee?

The younger, separated sister spoke now.

"I was reared in Tralee but I lived in England as well. And the difference between the two countries like, when you go to England, you're a person. No one would come up to you and say you're a knacker or a tinker. You're just treated as a person. Like when you're back here in Ireland and you go to a pub or a disco, they wouldn't say you're travellers but they say we've the right to refuse admission. It seems they have the right to refuse admission on us just because we're travellers. But they wouldn't come out and say that."

I was on familiar ground now. England, forever England. The refuge for unwanted Irish people. I've learned an awful lot about Irish culture, North and South, and its lack of tolerance, from the days I've spent outside welfare offices in London, Birmingham and Manchester.

Would your sister agree with that, that you would rather be in England?

"I would. I'd totally agree with her. I lived in England

258

for seven years and I came back for my brother's wedding there a year and a half ago. My husband died that night in a road accident. And I didn't want to come home but he kept forcing me the whole time and I'm here now since.

I don't go out cos they won't leave you in anyway in the first place, you know what I mean? So the place where my brother got his hotel in was a very dangerous place cos if he got it in the town, Tralee town, it would have never have happened. My husband would be still alive."

What do you mean about this hotel?

"It was out in the Limerick road. They had to go out miles for it. If it had been in the middle of the town or a few miles from the town you could get cabs there and you could come up home again after the wedding."

And you're saying because you're travellers you couldn't get a hotel here in Tralee?

The younger sister answered now.

"I know some travellers look for what they get because they don't treat a place right but you can't blame that on the whole travellers. You get some quiet travellers and some that are violent."

"You get that in the settled community too Bridgie, but you get more [of the] settled community who can take their drink without having an argument and you get more settled people who go home peacefully."

Bridgie, the younger woman, was annoyed at her sister here. The older, widowed woman was being critical of her own kind. A few weeks earlier there had been trouble in Glenamaddy, Co. Galway, when locals had attacked a pub used by travellers. In the subsequent media coverage the traveller position had been represented by the usual alleged spokesmen who saw groundless racism, on the part of the settled community, as the reason for bad community relations. Discussion on the behaviour of travellers was ruled out of order. These spokesmen bore me stupid. Here in Tralee I could hear real travellers discussing the problem with candour.

Why do you think, Bridgie, that publicans refuse travellers?

"Because we're classed as the rest of itinerants, violent and so on. Like if one traveller have an argument inside in a pub, well, like to me, if it was my bar, and one settled community had an argument, it's the one who caused the trouble I'd put out cos I wouldn't paint them all with the one brush. That way I wouldn't lose custom. But if one traveller have an argument in a pub that's everyone in the pub that's put out."

If you go back to England, Bridgie, where will you go?

"I'll move to Elephant and Castle in London cos when I was there I used to go out two nights a week with my husband but since I came home I never went out. I went away for a week last week over to my brother and I went out for three nights. They brought me out. They asked me, do you ever go out behind in Ireland? And I says, no cos we don't be served. Now you have to travel to London to go out and enjoy yourself, please."

"I feel the same way about that. That's not right. Like I'm by myself a young widow with two kids and I do deserve one night a week out here."

"Well I wouldn't rear my kids back here. There's nothing back here for them. What's back here only going through what their parents went through? Like I imagine a lot more for my children. I imagine I want to put them to school and know what it is to get education properly and stuff. Like the school I went to I got no education. I was put back to the back of the class. Any subject that came up that I didn't know I was made scribble. That's what I was made do. It was when I went to AnCo that I learned to read and write and when I started to go to travellers' meetings and going here and there about travellers. That's when I knew then, like, what I was and not to be ashamed of it. But they'd make you ashamed of what you are, which is wrong, because everyone has their own culture, like everyone has their own beliefs in God, you know?"

The eldest sister, the one with the glasses who had opened the front door to me earlier, joined us now in the kitchen. She told me she had married a man from the settled community and things hadn't worked out. They were living apart now. I asked her again if she would speak to me on tape. She agreed.

"The first bating I got now I was married an hour. I came out of the chapel, went down to reception, arguing. I'll never forget it. I wore a black eye. And from then on the bating started."

Do you have a view on legalising divorce?

"I want it. It would be not for the sake of getting it. I'd never get married again. I'd never trust again anyway. But there's an awful lot of people trapped in marriages that don't want to be trapped. I mean, if anybody goes to a battered wives home they'd take one good look at a woman and children. I was in two in Dublin and in Limerick and two in the North. If you go into a battered wives home you're not protected enough."

Did your husband come after you there?

"He didn't come after me. He just knocked at the door and took me home. Because as a traveller you're not to leave your husband. And we're not allowed take on again. Ever again."

Your sisters said that to me too. They won't take on again. You feel the same?

"No, no. Cos it's dirt."

Well hold on. Your husband has left you. If you meet another man why shouldn't you make another life for yourself?

"Yeah but why should my children grow up confused? That's dirt. I mean you can't grow up confused. He's not your father. He's a take-on. And it'll always be thrown in my face and if it don't be thrown in my face it'll be thrown in the lads' face through an argument."

On my tape I hear myself sounding shocked at the life-long self-sacrifice of these women to marriages that have long since ended. I felt these women were being very hard on themselves. Just as a few months previously I had discussed contraception with travelling women queueing at the Castle Street welfare office in Dublin. The same self-sacrifice by women had been evident there.

The sister with the glasses, as I told you earlier, had a badly scarred left eye. I asked her about that.

"It's gone. It's not totally blind but it's bad enough. I was seven weeks off having my last child and when I got badly baten I lost the child."

I see. And he hit your eye?

She laughed here and her sisters joined in the bitter laughter.

"Oh he didn't hit me boy, he went right in. He put it right out of my head. It was right out of my head."

Your sisters told me earlier that they get put out of pubs here in Tralee. How do you feel about that?

"Well I can walk in anywhere."

"Oh yeah, she can."

And why are you treated differently to your sisters?

Her voice dropped here and she looked a bit bashful.

"The pair of specs."

"She wears glasses. You'd never think travellers would wear glasses."

I realised now why I had presumed, without thinking, that she wasn't a traveller. The glasses had sent a signal to me that she didn't seem to be a traveller.

"Well the first time I came home with the specs, I was

ashamed. I wouldn't wear them. And they were all making a laugh."

"Tis like bags. She carries a bag and wears glasses but we don't carry no bag. We've plenty of babies hanging off us."

They were all laughing now. Making gentle fun of their sister's glasses and her hairstyle which was in a bob. True traveller women put their hair up in what I think they called a cook.

Then they got worried. Supposing their husbands heard them on the radio? They would be in big trouble. I asked the women about their husbands' radio listening habits. It seemed to be pop music stations so I told them I thought they would be safe enough.

I'll tell you one more thing that happened to me in Tralee. On the Wednesday night I stayed in Benner's Hotel. As usual when I'm away from home in a hotel I found myself in the company of commercial travellers. We're all there. Men in our thirties and forties propping up the bar, keeping each other company and drinking to pass the time when we'd all rather be at home with our wives and families. I've met a lot of sales reps over the years. They know each other well and are used to hotel culture. And I get on with them. Like most people who drive a lot, sales reps are usually good radio listeners so they tend to know my work.

There was a disco that night in Benners. There's a full bar and residents get in free. So we all sat at the bar as the young people of Tralee discoed away in front of us. I'd already had a few but I was in good form for a few more. I knew my work was done and I had only to get the train back to Dublin the next day.

One young woman was very noticeable. I'll call her Rose. An obvious name for a Tralee woman. Rose wasn't overly good-looking but she danced very well, making her flouncy dress seem much shorter than it was. I'd already spoken to her earlier that evening in a pub where there was a band playing. At closing time I put on my hat and coat. Rose approached me and asked if I was Garth Brooks. I could have said that I had been wearing a broad-rimmed hat long before Garth Brooks was ever heard of. I said no, but the hat was good for starting conversations. Then I headed back to the hotel.

And now Rose was at the disco. Rose approached the bar, picked me out from among the sales reps and asked me out to dance. I was never much of a dancer. I would have been more comfortable at the bar. After a polite few minutes I thanked her and went back to the men. One of the reps, a Corkman in his thirties, looked at me wide-eyed in amazement. He shouted over the disco music. C'mere boy. Dat's your hole.

What?

His arms stretched out, palms forwards. His eyebrows arched and his voice filled with concern at my lack of cop-on. Your hooaall. (Think of this in a strong Cork accent. Making hole a two-syllabled word.)

Ah no. I'm not looking for that.

Later on my Cork friend approached me again. He was drunk now. His tone had changed. He took on the sage tone of an older and wiser man. C'mere boy. You're right. Like you'd be in bed with your wan. And you'd wake up later and you'd be thinking about your wife and you'd be thinking about your kids' faces lookin' at ya and, c'mere boy, you'd feel lousy.

There was loads of emphasis on "lousy", to show just how bad you would feel.

Do you know, you sound like a man who's been there and done that?

You're right. But it won't never happen again.

Chapter Sixteen

Pawn Shop

Queen St., Dublin;
16 December 1993

There are four pawn shops in Dublin. I was at the one at
Queen Street, near the Smithfield fruit market. It's a small
shop in a tumbledown area. Like all the pawns, it has a
sign over the door with three metal balls. Nobody knows
the origin of the three-ball sign. There's a theory that it's
based on the family crest of the Medicis who, among other
things, were bankers. Maybe so. But I think the reason why
a visible symbol was used was because the pawn was
always a place for poor, illiterate people. Bank customers
could read. Pawn shop customers needed a sign that didn't
have to be read.

There's jewellery in the window going cheap. These are
the things that have been pawned and then abandoned.
Perhaps people couldn't afford to redeem their goods. Or
perhaps they just weren't bothered. Who wants an
engagement ring back if the engagement has been called off?

A man of about forty came out. As he unchained his
bicycle from the railings, he told me what he was in for.

"I pawned a ring for a tenner. For messages. For dinner

for the wife and kids. Until tomorrow when I get paid off the dole."

How much interest will you pay?

"Seventy pence."

Do you use the pawn a lot?

"Every week nearly. The day before dole day. It's me young fellah's ring. He doesn't mind. He knows that's the way it goes."

That man's story shook me. I was never in my life stuck for a tenner to pay for food. Even if I was in debt I could use my overdraft or credit cards. At the pawn I was meeting people who could never get that kind of credit. They went in with jewellery, television sets, snooker cues, musical instruments, anything that could be used to secure a loan. The pawn shop is a banking service for poor people.

Two middle-aged men came out. They smelled of drink.

"We were pawning a watch. Cos we're stuck for Christmas."

"We're just stuck for a few bob. We're out drinking. No money. We got twenty-five pound for the watch. There you are. There's the pawn ticket. Me wife bought the watch for me when I was married. Twenty-seven year ago. It's a very good watch."

Will your wife mind that you pawned the watch?

"You can't tell her. I'd be divorced if she knew. I'm going to get it out in the afternoon cos he's going up to get his dole and we're going to get it out."

How much interest will you pay?

"Fifty pence. Then get the whole lot back out."

It started to rain heavily. I ran into a pub around the corner in Smithfield. It was ten in the morning and the place was buzzing. Rounds of drink. Lots of laughter. Like Saturday night. There was a video on in the corner. A maggoty-looking zombie was strangling someone. Really loud screaming. I asked the barman if the place was always

266

this busy. Morning times, he said. Everyone is here after work in the market.

I saw the two men I had interviewed earlier. I got them a pint each, which seemed the polite thing to do. I got a cup of tea and joined them. They were both ex-British Navy men. Down on their luck now. Because of the government. That fellah Dick Spring. Going on his jet all over the place. I didn't bother suggesting that you would expect the Minister for Foreign Affairs to travel a bit. And that RTE. Useless fucking programmes. Okay men. I think the rain has stopped. I must get back to work.

I was glad to get out when I did. The drunks were still at the lay-down-the-law stage. The nasty stage would come next. They could keep that for their wives.

A young woman had cycled from Ballymun to pawn her rings. She would raise twenty pounds until she got paid on Thursday. She was a single mother. She pawned her rings most weeks. Her child had eczema. A lot of the creams for the child aren't covered by the medical card. But you can't let the child just itch, can you? I told her that I sometimes suffer with eczema. No. You couldn't just let that child itch. The difference is that I don't have to pawn anything to pay for the creams. I asked her if I could take her address in Ballymun. It's Christmas time, I said, and I'm long enough in this business to spot a story that gets a listener response. Sure enough, a member of RTE staff who heard the interview gave me fifty pounds to pass on to that single mum.

A middle-aged man came out of the pawn shop.

"My wedding rings is in the pawn and I had to renew my ticket. I hadn't got the money to take them out. I paid the interest on them, you know?"

What's your loan?

"Forty-two pounds. I paid almost a fiver to renew them. That's for the four months."

Was there something special you needed the money for?

267

"Mostly for food. And ... you know yourself."

With his right hand he tipped an imaginary glass to his mouth.

Drink?

"I have a problem with the drink, so. But what can you do about it?"

His tone was self-righteous. Like the people I've met at community welfare offices who look for emergency payments because they have a drink problem. After all, when you've paid for your drink you need money to feed the kids, don't you?

Are you married?

"Yeah. Five kids. They're all grown up."

How does your wife feel about you pawning the rings?

"She doesn't agree with it but what can she do about it? I need money for my side of the problem. She needs money for her side. The rings have to go into the pawn. What can she do? It's a problem I have. Simple as that."

Did you say your wife has a problem too? Is that drink?

"No. My wife never touched a drink in her life. She's a Protestant. From Scotland. Her problem is to cope with the money she's left with after me drinking."

Your drinking must make your wife very unhappy.

"It does make her very unhappy. Ah, she's ... kind of got over it a little bit now. She has to. I have a little drink problem, that's all."

Will you drink this week?

"When I get my labour Thursday, I will, to be honest with you. I owe my wife twenty pounds so she can have that. But there won't be a lot left. I mean, you have to have drink when the problem's there. The last job I had was with CIE. I lost that."

Because of drink?

"No ... not really. I was made redundant. That's what started me off on the beer. With the money I got I went off and blew it. Temptation. You know what I mean?

268

Temptation. What could you do?"

How long did the redundancy money last?

"Eight months."

This story made me think about another ex-CIE man I met years before in a bookie shop in Tallaght. He had taken redundancy so he could drink and gamble. And I once met a woman, collecting her children's allowance at the post office in Clonmel, whose alcoholic husband couldn't resist the offer of redundancy money. The opportunity to sit in a pub for several months just couldn't be passed up.

I asked the man at the pawn if his drinking had caused hardship to his family.

"Oh yes. I have to admit that."

Do you behave yourself when you're drunk?

"I'm told I don't. But I don't realise I'm doing it at the time if I have enough on me. If I'm just mild, I'd be okay."

What do you do when you have enough on you?

"Fight. I never hit my wife now. But just fight. Argue. That can be more worse than the hitting. You hit and it's gone. But argument can be worse on ... the mind."

He started on about the government. It's the government's fault that he was out of work. Dick Spring jetting around the place. (Spring was getting a lot of stick this morning.) He talked about how the country should be run. He was sober as he spoke. I thought about what he must be like with drink. When he's just mild. And when he has enough on him. I was glad when he left.

A woman of about forty wouldn't talk on tape. She used the pawn most weeks but her husband didn't know. But surely, it's to pay for looking after his family? No. She couldn't tell him. Sure you know the way that men are?

She was right there. I do know the way that men are. Look in any community welfare office in the country. The queue will consist mainly of women. A lot of them are lone parents but there are married women there whose unemployed husbands won't go to the welfare because of pride. So the wife is the one who has to queue up, often for hours, to look for help with an electricity bill or whatever. Likewise when the free beef comes from the EC each year you'll see women queueing with the food docket that the husband has got in the labour. Men have pride. Women with children don't allow themselves that luxury.

A young man had just got his jewellery back out.

"I only got twenty pounds. I could have got more but I was just stuck for twenty pounds on the day."

What did you need the twenty pounds for?

"Drugs. To be honest, drugs. That's it."

Do you often pawn for drugs?

"You'd have to sometimes because I don't want to be out robbing. Get locked up and you can't have your drugs."

When did you last take heroin?

"Yesterday. And I'll be going back down today to take some more."

An awful lot of drug addicts in Dublin have died. Mainly from the AIDS virus. Are you worried by that?

"I'm very careful of myself. I wouldn't use a syringe after anybody else."

Would you like to give up drugs?

"No. I'll be on drugs for life. I'm happy with that. I'm not a drinker. I'm not anything else. I'm happy with drugs."

A teenage girl came out.

"I got thirty-five pounds on two chains and two rings."

When will you get them back?

"Three or four months. I'll pay about a fiver. Then I'll renew the ticket."

("Ticket" was said like "tickah". A strong Dublin accent.)

Was there a special reason for getting the money?

"I'm going down to Cork to see me fellah in prison in Spike Island. He was the one that got me some of the jewellery so I have to pawn it now to go down and see him. He'll be lonely at Christmas now so I want to go and see him."

I was a bit disappointed when she told me her boyfriend's offence was joyriding. It would have made a better story if he was a jewel thief.

A woman in her mid-twenties seemed upset.

"I pawned me engagement ring here about four months ago and the ticket went missing. Apparently my engagement ring is gone now."

You lost your ticket?

"Yeah. I've been chasing it for a while and he said somebody must have taken the ticket and took it out on me."

Do you think that could have happened?

"Yeah, sure. Our flat was broken into. It must have been robbed on me then."

How much did you borrow on the ring?

"Forty pounds. I needed the money for a certain thing. People do it for fuel, ESB, for rent, for anything really."

What did you need the money for?

"I needed it for rent at the time."

Did your husband know you were pawning the ring?

"No. I didn't like to put pressures like that on him. I try to be open with him but I don't like to over-pressure him. Christmas is a great pressure."

Did he not notice the ring missing from your finger?

"Yeah, he did. I told him I didn't want to wear it around the house."

So you've told him now that you pawned it?

"I told him. I told him that I think I lost it. He said, I've got you ... the ring is gone ... but I've still got you."

It seems to me very unfair that you had to keep it from him ... I mean it's his money problem as well as yours. You're very self-sacrificing to have taken that strain on yourself.

"A lot of women are. They would be afraid. Their

271

husbands would blow up in their face. I know some women who have gotten beatings over it ... you know ... pawning stuff. I mean you can't go to your husband and say, I haven't got the money for the rent. A lot of men run to the pub when anything is wrong."

Would your husband do that?

"Yeah. It's normally to Mammy or the pub. Normally it's to Mammy and then, with Daddy, to the pub."

All of that has happened in your marriage?

"Ah yeah. On Friday now he's going to come into me pissed drunk after being with his father. I blow up at him. He says it's his one day out. I say excuse me, what about my day out? I don't go out. I'm stuck at home with the kids. I'm sacrificing all my time. If I could work I would, but with three children, it's hard."

Is it just once a week he goes out?

"Well it's accumulating now into a two-day, three-day thing. With Christmas coming up he feels stressful. He would like to have the money to give towards Christmas and he hasn't got it."

Do you think the strain will eventually break up your marriage?

"It has done, twice. We broke up two years ago. To be honest I took a nervous breakdown and ended up in St. Loman's. I tried to OD."

You say it's a strain on him. What can you do about that?

"All you can do is try to build him up. Get the kids to bed and sit down together, have a cup of tea, watch the TV. It's essential that you communicate. I mean, if anything happens to a bloke, who does he run back to but Mammy? But you must sit down and say to him, listen, it's okay. I don't think any less of you because you're not working. And I'm the one that counts. Nobody else."

Chapter Seventeen

DAYS IN HELL

Ballymun Flats, Dublin;
19 January 1994

The week of my marriage break-up was the worst week in my life. I was numb as I walked about Ballymun flats that Wednesday. I'd walked out on my wife and children less than twenty-four hours earlier. I had barely slept the night before in a B&B on the South Circular Road. But now I had to work. I had to get a programme on the air the following Saturday. For no particular reason I selected Eamonn Ceannt Tower to knock on doors and to see who would invite me in. I was trawling through the wreckage of other people's lives, as I had been doing for years. But it would never again be the same for me. When I meet people now who are separated I know something of the pain they have gone through.

How could anything else be important to me when fourteen years of marriage had just ended? How could I concentrate on work?

I climbed the landings of Eamonn Ceannt Tower. I knocked on all six doors on each level to introduce myself. I took a note of those that didn't answer. I could try again later. Most people said no, they had nothing to say to me. One young man brought me in to meet his wife and their baby daughter. Will you have tea? Yes, that would be lovely. A sandwich? No, thank you. I had no appetite.

He was a well-built fellow, big with strong arms and shoulders. He was good-natured and good-humoured. He had an easy confidence about him that, I guess, came from knowing that he could be as tough as the toughest of Ballymun if he had to. He was off the dole now for several months and had never felt better. You can provide for your family, not begging off anyone, you know? And better still, they were getting out of Ballymun. They had a loan for a house.

I couldn't tell him how I was hurting inside. He was so positive about things. He was in his early twenties and determined to make a go of his life. He was doing the best for his family. I was a few days short of my thirty-seventh birthday and I hated myself for what I had done to my family the day before. Everybody loves Jacinta. But I was the only one married to her. I couldn't take the stress any more of marriage when, for too long, I had loved another woman more than I loved my wife.

The interview wasn't bad. He spoke about how he had been penalised by higher rent and the loss of his medical card since he had taken a job. This would be topical with the Budget coming up the next week. Then he talked about what it was like to have a father a drug addict. My God! It's 1994. His dad was one of the hippy addicts. Not part of the heroin epidemic that hit working-class Dublin after the fall of the Shah of Iran in 1979. The kids of the hippy generation have grown up and can speak for themselves about the crap they got from the generation of parents who were going to change the world. I said I would be fascinated to hear about his experiences of his dad but he didn't want to talk about this on the record.

I kept climbing the stairs of Eamonn Ceannt Tower. This is so unreal. Memories of the previous day kept coming back to me in waves. I had told Jacinta a month earlier that I wasn't happy and I wanted to separate. I had tried to prepare her for the split. Jacinta asked me to give the marriage a real try before we threw it away and I agreed. The last month had been good and bad. We had lived more intensely with each other than we had done for many years. When she asked me if I really wanted to be with Deirdre, I lied. I told her I had often longed for Deirdre's company over these last few years and I still felt very attracted to her but that I wanted to leave because I was no longer happy in my own marriage. In fact I was more deeply in love with Deirdre than I had ever been.

So why didn't I tell my wife the truth about Deirdre? Cowardice? Yes. That too. But what's the point in telling your wife that you have been having a love affair with her best friend if you still think you might stay married? Telling about the affair would only make it harder to make the marriage work. Deirdre and I were absolutely crazy about each other but we both knew we had responsibilities and that neither of us wanted to leave our children. So our marriages had continued and our love affair continued.

Deirdre used to tell me that I would never be happy with her. She wouldn't want me if part of me was always going to be left behind with my wife and kids. She began to make her own plans for ending her marriage. She wanted to try to make a home of her own where she could still be a mother as best as she could. You stay where you are Paddy. We'll stay forever friends but be lovers no more.

The prospect of losing Deirdre was unbearable. I went back on to the familiar treadmill of feelings. Yes I love her. Yes I want her. But I love my wife and children too. And when we had children the deal was that we would both rear them. Could I bear the thought of breaking my wife's heart and my children's hearts? But then I would never stop thinking about Deirdre. Every thought I had I wanted to know what she thought. Every radio programme I made, every chapter of this book I wrote, I wanted to know what Deirdre thought. When I was with Deirdre I loved her. When I was away from her I looked forward to our next meeting or next conversation.

Something had to break. I don't want to talk about that yet. I'll tell you about the next person in Eamonn Ceannt Tower who opened the door to me. Her flat was high up in the tower block. I was glad to meet her. I had only one interview on tape and things weren't going well. She kept me at the door standing which was good because my tapes picked up the characteristic echo of the tower blocks, giving the listeners a sense of place. We spoke for maybe ten minutes about unemployment and about how her husband and herself were slightly better off since he was jobless. They had an asthmatic child and needed the medical card. But on a personal level, he had become depressed.

We talked about marital stress and how unemployment could aggravate it. I felt like a fraud. My own marriage problems had nothing to do with money. I told her what had happened to me the day before. She was sympathetic. Marriages don't always last, she said, and people can't be blamed for that. Then she asked me about legal separation and I was ashamed to tell her that my marriage break-up had been much more sudden, dramatic and ill-planned on my part. I explained how I had been in bed with Deirdre Tuesday lunch-time. Her husband was working down the country. It was a way of saying goodbye to each other before she moved out on her own. Don't leave your family Paddy, she had told me. You'll never forgive yourself. That's what she was saying to me in a naked embrace when her husband's key turned in the front door.

My interviewee in Ballymun wasn't impressed. She was worried that my marriage had ended by accident rather than by design. Deirdre had lost her home and children and so had I. And so now she didn't hold out a lot of hope for me and Deirdre. She said we would bitterly regret what had happened and would come to hate each other.

I was having a lousy day. None of the most interesting things were on tape. I had banged on every door in Eamonn Ceannt Tower and I had just two interviews. I kept thinking of the last twenty four hours and all the hurt I had caused. Deirdre's husband had ordered us both out of his bedroom and into the kitchen. He made coffee. Have some sugar in it, Paddy. You probably need it after the shock. He told Deirdre that she could go with me or stay with him and he would say nothing to my wife. But I knew that both our marriages were over.

Come with me now Deirdre. You have to leave here. I'll go to my wife now and tell her. Face up to the nightmare that I have avoided for too long. Deirdre hesitated for a minute or two. What about her children? My children? We'll have to work that out. I'm sure your children will always want their mum but you can't stay here now, no more than I can leave you now and try to go back to my wife as if nothing has happened. We left the house and Deirdre closed the door on her marriage.

And then I faced my nightmare. And it was a nightmare. When I called, Jacinta had been typing some of the tape transcripts for this book. I'm sorry my love, something awful has happened. I've been with Deirdre this lunch time. We were in bed together and her husband came home by surprise and found us. I can't live with you anymore now. I have to leave.

You bastard. I knew it. I always knew it. You told me you would try to make our marriage work but you haven't even tried.

The door bell rang and our six-year-old was home from school. Hi Mum. Hi Dad. He went to his toys as his mum and dad rowed in the next room. You bastard. Everybody told me there was something between you and Deirdre but I believed you and not them. You bastard.

She stormed out. I went to speak to our son. I explained that I wouldn't be living at home any more and he burst into tears. No Dad. He played with his Lego as if he could build up his little world again, shutting out the new reality he couldn't cope with. No Dad. Don't go.

My wife came back in. She had met Deirdre sitting in her car and had attacked her. You were only ever friends with me so you could get close to my husband. As I left she demanded the car keys from me. I told her they were on the kitchen table. I was leaving in Deirdre's car. I was glad Jacinta looked for the car. It meant she was already thinking realistically about life without me. Not just begging for me to come back.

I didn't want to work. I hated Ballymun. I hated its dreary tower blocks and high-rise welfare misery. The memories of the day before kept sweeping over me. My wife's anger. My son's pitiful crying. I pictured what my ten-year-old daughter's reaction must have been when she came home from school. I felt burned out inside. Deirdre and I had stayed in a B&B that night. Deirdre cried in her sleep, wishing for her children.

She had gone back to her house during the afternoon to see her kids. Their father had told them how he had found out about their mother's love affair. Her children are older than mine. Sixteen, fifteen and ten. She explained to them that she had longed to leave her marriage for a long time.

Deirdre's husband was no longer so calm. When Deirdre cried as she talked with her kids I put my arm on her and he reacted. Touch her again Paddy and I'll break your fucking arm.

The next morning Deirdre went to see her kids again. She told me to go to Ballymun and do what I always do. A very good job. You have a programme to get ready for Saturday. You're good Paddy. You're very good. Don't let yourself down. Those women in Ballymun will like you. There's nobody else can get on with strangers like you can. Go for it Paddy.

So yes, Deirdre, I was going for it. I hadn't had great success so far that day in Ballymun but I realised something about myself that I hadn't noticed before. I can cope with a bad day's work once I know that my lack of success hasn't been for want of trying. You're doing okay, Paddy, I told myself as I climbed the stairways of Ballymun. You're working hard. Perhaps all you need is a change of tactics. Or maybe just a change in your luck.

It was afternoon now. There would be more mothers home now that school was over. So back into the tower and up the stairs. I checked my notebook and knocked on doors where there had been no answer. A woman in her late twenties was interested in talking to me. She had a less pronounced working-class accent than most of Ballymun. She was articulate and had a lot to say. She brought me in to meet her ten-year-old son and she made us tea.

Joy spoke with some passion about living on welfare. She was tired of the fact that her social life revolved around cups of coffee in the homes of other welfare recipients. She was tired of being penalised for taking part-time work. That happened when she took a job in the women's hostel for a while. She was tired of welfare. She wanted to work.

Do you like living in Ballymun? No. She did not. She was born and brought up in Ballymun and she hated it. Her son was always bullied. I spoke to her son and I don't think I can ever remember such a plain-spoken ten-year-old. David had an accent more gentle than would be usual for the tower blocks. He talked about being picked on in the pedestrian underpass or another time being hung over the handrail on the stairway of Eamonn Ceannt. Those boys mustn't have a very happy home life, he said. Why else should they get any enjoyment out of hurting him or anyone else?

Well good for you David. You have the measure of them. I was moved listening to this calm, articulate young boy who wasn't going to let this bullying get on top of him. He was a child apart from the moment he opened his mouth. That alone would make him a prime target for bullies. I knew that only too well. Thirty years before I was bullied because I was an English child growing up in Ireland. I remember the Brothers setting the other kids against me. I was a good and precocious reader so they used to mock my accent. I remember I was asked to read a piece called "About Water". Do you hear him class? About wah-tah. About wah-tah. Mocking my London accent. What other kind of fucking accent did they think I would have? I was a London child, for Christ's sake.

The bullying reached its peak in 1966. We got daily talks about the 1916 Rising and its heroes. I knew I would be picked on going home from school. I would have a bloodied lip, or at least have my school books or myself rolled in the mud. But in the end, do you know I wasn't scared? They thought I was soft but I know now I was tough. Just like young David in Ballymun. Because of his gentle manner he had to grow up tough. Growing up tough, fearing no man, that's a lesson that stays with you for life.

Joy told me she was separated. What broke your marriage up? She asked what that had to do with social welfare issues. Fair enough, Joy. I'm being nosey as usual but I often find that people are on the welfare because of a marriage break-up. So I think it's fair to ask what was the cause of that break-up.

Joy told me that her husband had been unemployed which probably contributed to their splitting because they were with each other so much. The real reason was that she had simply outgrown him. No, there was no drink or drugs. Her father had been a heroin addict (another one!) and she didn't want anything to do with drugs. Her husband didn't beat her. He didn't gamble. She was just bored with him. They had run out of things to say to each other.

I told Joy my marriage was broken up too. It was hurting a lot. Especially losing the children. I told her about Deirdre. Joy said that when the person you are closest to in life is no longer your marriage partner then it's time for your marriage to end. For the sake of your spouse as well. There's never a good time and there's never a nice way to do it. But if Deirdre is where your heart is, then you were right to go with her. There should be no guilt attached to the fact that you have changed over the years. People marry with the best of intentions but people change. Joy seemed to understand a lot. She was making me feel a bit better. Then she asked me how long ago I had split with my wife. Yesterday.

Yesterday! You shouldn't be trying to handle interviews like this. You'll be too upset. No, I said. I'm okay. I told Joy how our split had been brought about. Not by a civilised and courageous talk from Deirdre and I with our respective spouses. The split had come when my lover's husband had found us in bed. I thought Joy would rebuke me as the soldier's wife had done but she didn't. What's done is done. She wasn't going to judge me. And you shouldn't be looking for a stick to beat yourself with. You have enough problems. Don't be so hard on yourself.

Joy told me that writing about my experience would be good for me. It helps to put things down in words. It will make you feel more calm and clear in your mind. Which is why these words have been written only days after the events they describe. Joy had a calming effect on me. I felt better as well for having a not-bad day's work done.

Ballymun flats, Dublin; the next day

Deirdre lost her job the day after she left her marriage. The result was that on the first day of our new life together Deirdre was on the dole.

It's you and me now Deirdre. We have no friends left. Come to Ballymun with me. I did a good day's work yesterday and I'll finish the job today.

Susan was on my mind. I'd met her five years before when I was interviewing single mums collecting their money at the post office in Ballymun. I never forgot her. I wonder how she is? If I could find her I'm sure she'd have something to say. Today I could do with somebody good. I'm just too tired to go door-knocking any more. I'd love to meet Susan again.

Outside the post office I started introducing myself. The women were shy of the microphone but wanted to chat. I asked about Susan. Was she still in Ballymun? I guessed she'd be the sort of person whom a lot of people would know.

Susan was still in Ballymun. Not at the address I used to have for her but nearby on the flats on Shangan Road. Ask anybody on the second block. They'll show you where.

We walked to Shangan. There were rats running around the stairways. Deirdre shivered. She doesn't like rats. Deirdre remarked to me that if she had left her husband and applied for housing, then Ballymun, or somewhere like it, is where she would have been offered.

The kids on Shangan escorted us to Susan's door.

How are you Susan? Great. Come in.

Susan looked well. As pretty as ever. Just a few days

short of her twenty-eighth birthday. Deirdre remarked to me afterwards about how much trouble Susan took over her appearance. Her hair, make-up and clothing all cared for. Her flat was comfortable and tastefully decorated. It was as if she were expecting visitors but no, Susan just likes to keep herself and her home presentable at all times. If I had been by myself I would simply have noticed how attractive Susan is. I don't have a great eye for visual details. It was Deirdre who pointed out the details to me afterwards.

Susan was pleased to see me, pleased to meet Deirdre. Call any time, she said. You're always welcome. She never got visitors from outside Ballymun.

Susan had a baby on her lap. That was a visual detail I couldn't miss. Five years ago Susan told me she was finished with men and finished with having children. Her one baby then would be her last.

I remembered as well that Susan had a lot of make-up on one cheek. That was to cover up a bruise given to her by her brother. And she was missing part of her front tooth. When Susan was a child her dad had tried to punch her mum and missed.

Why did you choose to take another man into your life?

"Well, at the time I didn't know. I suppose it's just being lonely, being on your own. You just want a bit of company. When someone comes along like, and they pretend they like you, you're just delighted to get a bit of company, and then you find they're someone that you didn't know. He wasn't using drugs at first when I met him, but then he started using drugs."

Did you find out straight away?

"Yeah, I did. It's been on and off like. It's been on and off all the time."

Do you love him still?

"Yeah I do in a way. People say I'm better off without him. Like my friends say it's more company I need but he's

283

no good for me. He doesn't help me out or he never minds the baby. I wouldn't leave the baby with him anyway."

Here in Ballymun you're very unlikely to meet a man who is able to say to you, come and marry me and I'll take you off the welfare?

"Ah janey, that's a dream. Around here it's a dream. Nearly all the fellahs around here use drugs. There's nothing else for them to do. They just go out and steal for their habit. My fellah will keep asking me for money but he knows I haven't got it. He goes out stealing to get money but I don't get any of it. Everything goes for drugs. Sometimes when he can't get anything he'll keep at me for money but I don't be able to give it to him. If I do, my bills just go short."

You are very unlikely to meet a man who is working here in Ballymun?

"No, not around here anyway. You can't go out to other places to meet people. You're just stuck here, like. You have your kids. This is your life. You can't go anywhere."

Could you get a man who was not a drug user?

"Well, I suppose I could but I'd have to go out of this place. But then I suppose there are junkies everywhere. They're the sort of people I attract."

Are you serious about that?

"Yeah, everyone you meet sort of uses you. They know the sort of person you are. If you're soft, they get around you and get things out of you. I keep taking him back. I say, I've had enough, I can't take anymore.

"Like he'll have to come off drugs and go and get help. He'll go and I'll just take him back then cos I feel pity for him. I don't want to see him out on the streets or anything. I know I would be better off without him. I can manage better on my own."

Is it just pity or is it, like you said, the company too?

"Pity and company. He wrecks me head ... but ... still I put up with it."

I remembered the day I first met Susan five years before. It was a hot, sunny July day. From the balcony of her flat we could see the gleaming sails of the yachts in far-away Dun Laoghaire. I had tried to excite some kind of jealousy in Susan for people with more money than her. But Susan remained unmoved. The yachts in Dun Laoghaire were no more relevant to her than were the mountains of the moon. I wondered again if Susan was happy with her lot in life.

You still seem a good-humoured person, very welcoming. You've put up with social welfare for years now. Did you ever wish for something better?

"Ah yeah. I had me last fellah and I always swore that if I ever got pregnant again I hoped it would be for a fellah that would be working, and for someone that would really like me for what I am, not just take advantage of me. Someone who would be there for the baby, working an' all, who would do everything for us but it turned out the opposite way."

You can't blame the young men for it. It's not their fault there's no work?

"No, not really. Even if they look for it there's nothing. A lot of them left school early. They haven't got an education."

You said you didn't mean to get pregnant again but you got caught. Are you glad that you have the second baby?

"Well I'm not glad. I wouldn't change him for the world. I love him and I wouldn't give him back. I got caught on the pill. I was using contraceptives since my other little fellah was born. The doctor said that after being on it for so many years I shouldn't have been caught, but I was. It was a big shock. Christmas Eve I found out I was pregnant."

The last fellow used to beat you. Does the father of

your second child beat you?

"No. He did once, but he wouldn't. I often jumped up and hit him when he would be going on, but he would never hit me back. When the baby was two weeks old he gave me a hiding, but like he was really out of his face and he said he doesn't remember what happened. I gave just as good as I got though. He left me badly bruised, but I still took him back again."

Where is he at the moment?

"He's gone out doing his usual job."

What's his usual job?

"He's gone to steal to buy drugs."

Does that upset you?

"Yeah it does, but what can you do?"

Do you have the police coming to the door looking for him?

"No. Not yet. He has warrants for stealing but they don't know where to find him."

What type of drug user is he? Does he use a needle?

"Yeah."

Are you not worried about the AIDS virus?

"I suppose I am but so far he has kept to himself, using his own needle. He hasn't been sharing with anyone. When I was pregnant, he was supposed to have hepatitis. I got a test done and they told me I was all right. If I found out he was using after anyone else there's no way I would have anything to do with him."

But you know what drug addicts are like, Susan. The only thing on their mind is drugs.

"Yeah, it does seem to take over their whole lives. They're just selfish. They don't care about anyone else. They don't realise what you're going through with your bills and the kids. All they're worried about is getting a needle into their arm."

Why are you putting up with this?

"I don't know. Everyone says, how do you put up with

it? Cos everyone knows what he's like. I say, I don't know. You just have to go on, you know what I mean? Put up with what happens and that's it. It's just a bit of company, you know, sitting here all the time. He'll go out in the day and sit in all night. Some days he won't go out at all, just sit around for the whole day."

What kind of company is he when he's been using drugs?

"He gets into a good mood when he does a turn on. In a good mood, goes around laughing and is nice to you. When he doesn't have that he won't talk to you at all. He'll just sit there and be in the height of it, waiting until he gets it. If he is like that you just try to get him the money to have a turn on just so as he'll talk to you."

The only rescue I can think of for you is a knight in shining armour to come along and propose marriage to you.

"I'll never get married. It would be nice, though, to have someone to be nice to you, treat you nice."

Susan's a beautiful girl, Deirdre said. Very beautiful. Very nice. Why the hell does she put up with that fellow? Deirdre could picture him. A little creep in a shiny track suit. Next time he's out of his face she would like to help him take a trip over the balcony. Tell him he can fly.

If only Susan could take more control of her life. She gets pregnant but just shrugs her shoulders and says, what can you do? Beaten up, what can you do? Hassled for money, what can you do?

Deirdre was chilled by Susan's attitude to AIDS. If her bloke got hepatitis there's every reason to think he's sharing needles. If she were to catch the virus, what would she say then? What can you do?

Chapter Eighteen

DERRY

Department of Social Security, Asylum Road,
8 February, 1994

I decided to speak with Northern Ireland Catholics. Sinn Fein said it was consulting the grass roots to see whether or not the war should be called off following the Downing Street Declaration. I decided to do my own consultation.

I needed a Catholic ghetto. I was in Belfast two weeks before so this time I chose Derry. I knew the DSS at Crown Buildings on Asylum Road, a steep hill on the west bank of the Foyle. I had worked there in 1990 and 1991. The people signing on there are from Catholic Derry – Bogside, Creggan, Shantallow.

You were just into the social security office here in Derry. How did you get on?

"Well I'm always received very well in here. I sign on every fortnight. I am actively searching for work. Unfortunately jobs in Derry are not that plentiful."

Do you like Derry?

"Yes, I do. I used to live in a border town and the atmosphere was different ... Derry is a friendly city. It is more like a village. Derry is a city by charter only."

Do you have any commitments here in Derry? Are you

married? Do you have children?

"Yes, I have children but they're adults now. My husband lives in another part of Ireland."

Are you divorced?

"No. It's a voluntary separation. A separation is not pleasant in any circumstances but if you can do it by agreement then the relationship can be on a humane level after the separation."

Was it you or your husband who decided to separate?

"It was me. There are people who live together for many reasons ... people who endure relationships because there are children. There are people who are content to be discontent. I decided that we would separate because I was not content to be discontent."

Can you tell me what broke the two of you up?

"There were a lot of factors ... to give you the romantic story ... I met a childhood sweetheart after thirty years and I took up a relationship again. Obviously there were underlying problems within my marriage that made me do that. It was a very hard thing to do. When you live with someone for X amount of years you know their every quirk ... their every whim ... how they are going to react to whatever you are going to tell them. You anticipate what they are going to feel and say."

Did your husband know that you had met this other man?

"Yes. He knew that I had met him but he did not know that I was having an affair with my now partner. I had to sit him down and tell him. That was the hardest thing that I ever had to do. I would have much preferred if I had been found out, rather than have to say to my husband, sit down I have something to tell you."

It must have put a gap between you and your husband when you had this other life that he didn't know about?

"Yes. I was in a fantasy world dreaming about my other

relationship. The dice was in my hands to throw, whether I was going to dream about it or whether I was going to do it."

Your husband must have been very upset when you told him.

"Yes he was. I was very upset watching him. I know he never had an extra-marital relationship. I know that he loved me. He depended a lot on me and this was like a bereavement. It was like a bereavement for me but it was much worse for him."

Did people judge you, saying you were a terrible woman to leave your husband like that?

"My husband's friends, relatives, thought it was the most catastrophic thing that they had ever heard tell of. On the other hand, when I told other people how I felt, the story of how I couldn't live a lie, they thought I was courageous."

I told this woman that my own marriage had broken up three weeks before. I understood her very well when she said that she wished that her love affair had been found out. I told her that, in my case, I didn't have to sit my wife down and tell her I was leaving. I was found out. Perhaps that's what I wanted. I knew when my lover's husband found me in bed with his wife I felt strangely relieved. A decision was forced on me.

The Derry woman, Louise was her name, talked to me about children. Hers were grown up by the time her marriage ended. She said it would have been wrong for me to wait around in a marriage until the children were older. Wrong for me. Wrong for my wife. Wrong, that is, unless you were content to be discontent.

I said how much I missed my wife and my children. The pain of separation is very hard to take. She said I was still a father. In later years, when the children were grown up, I could come to be a friend to my children. A father in a different way. You've gone through the pain, Paddy.

What you need to do now is to enjoy yourself.

I told Louise I was glad to hear that some people thought of her as courageous. Deirdre and I had nobody to stand up for us. Everybody seemed to have things to say against Deirdre in particular. As we drove to Derry the night before, Deirdre told me that she had come to understand the Bible story about the woman taken in adultery. She was stripped and stoned. Any passer-by could throw a stone at her. That's the way Deirdre felt. Stripped and stoned. That's how an adulterous woman is treated.

I liked Louise. She gave me her address. Next time you're in Derry, Paddy, call in and see me. I will Louise. Thank you.

One more thing I want to ask you Louise, do you think there can be peace in Northern Ireland?

"Yes, I do. That's everybody's hope."

Do you think Sinn Fein/IRA should accept the Downing Street Declaration?

"Yes, I do. But I think we in Ireland, Catholics, are right to be cautious because we have a history of being fobbed off."

The offer is clear that if there's to be a united Ireland, that must be by the wish of the majority here in Northern Ireland. Do you think the IRA should accept that?

"Yes, I do. Because that's democracy."

A young man was in to the DSS because his giro had been stolen. That's a hazard of living in a flat in a house in which everybody shares the same letterbox. He had been working in Germany until recently. He liked being back in Derry.

"Derry is a very friendly place, even with what's going on, you know."

Have you ever been affected by what's going on?

"I lost two brothers through the troubles. They were just in the wrong place at the wrong time. They were in a bar and the UVF came in and riddled everybody."

I'm so sorry. Which bar was that, please?

"That was up in Belfast. The Bridge Arms. It happened ten years ago."

What were your brothers' names?

"Patrick and Michael. They were seventeen and sixteen."

Do you think there will be peace in Northern Ireland?

"I think everybody wants peace. On both sides."

Do you think Sinn Fein/IRA should stop fighting?

"The way they're looking at it, a lot of young men have laid down their lives for what they believe in, but, at the same token, there's a Protestant majority here. You have got to compromise for them people as well."

The Downing Street Declaration says Northern Ireland stays British as long as the majority here want that. Is that acceptable to you?

"That's letting the people rule. That's democracy."

A man in his forties was tired of going on job schemes.

"It's going all over what I did before. The only thing is, it gives you something to do. When you're unemployed, all day, you've nothing to do. Where do you go, the bookies? Have a pint? You end up an alcoholic that way. I'm separated now, at the moment, through being off work ... and drinking."

Do you think there will be peace in Northern Ireland?

"I do. People are fed up with the troubles."

Do you want Sinn Fein/IRA to stop fighting, on the strength of what they have been offered?

"I'd love them to stop anytime. No matter what they're offered."

A young woman told me she was three years out of work.

"It's degrading when you can't do things that maybe your friends do. If you're in a social circle of people who are working, you find yourself left out. I'd like to think there's a job for me somewhere. Decent money. Decent house. No bills. A holiday once a year."

You're a single person?

"No, I'm married. My husband's on a job scheme."

Has the job scheme helped or not?

"Half and half. You get to the stage you're desperate. You'll do anything to get out of the house. Get rid of the sort of hate feelings you're feeling for your partner. You know, staring at them seven days a week. But at the same time you're doing a forty hour week for a pittance."

Do you have hate feelings for your partner?

"Well, you decide you don't like your partner every now and again, anyway. And with the added pressures of being unemployed, no money, stuck in, staring at each other. And there's only so many games of Scrabble you can play."

Do you think there will be peace in Northern Ireland?

"Not for a few years anyway. I think if it was actually down to the grass roots, to people on the street, then there would have been peace a long time ago."

Do you think the IRA should stop fighting?

"Oh yeah."

Are you Protestant or Catholic?

"I'm a Catholic."

Derry wasn't turning out the way I expected. I thought there would be a range of views as to whether Sinn Fein\IRA should, or should not, call off the war. I had been preparing myself for arguments in favour of the war going on. I found an overwhelming wish that Sinn Fein\IRA should call off the war and accept peace at the going price – that is, that Northern Ireland should stay British as long as the majority wanted that.

I asked a middle-aged man if he thought there would be peace in Northern Ireland.

"That depends ... what have you in mind when you say peace?"

At last. I knew I'd met a Sinn Fein\IRA supporter.

An end to the fighting and killings. That's what I mean by peace.

"Well if everybody recognises everybody's right to negotiate ... on a level playing ground. That means the privileges that have gone on for so long, and sponsored by the British Government ... it could have been over a long, long time ago had the British appreciated the damage they were doing by favouring one section of the community."

Okay. There's a lot of grievances to be addressed but, in the mean time, do you think IRA\Sinn Fein should call off the war?

He talked about B Men and British army harassment which he had known for fifty years. He spoke about this for several minutes. And because he hadn't answered my question I asked him once again if he thought the IRA should stop the killing.

"I would like to see an opportunity presented to Sinn Fein where they would have no opportunity other than to accept."

We know what's on offer. You can have a united Ireland if the majority here wants it. Do you think the IRA should stop the killing?

"Are we talking about a manufactured majority here? Or are we talking about a majority of Irish people?"

We're talking about a majority here in the North. Should the IRA stop the killing?

"Should they move back a step? Should they create another opportunity for another fifty years of gerrymandering?"

I think your answer to my question is no.

"My answer would be ... the situation I've grown up in, I think that would have to change before anything could change."

You don't want the IRA to stop fighting? That's what

you're telling me?

"I would like to see the British Government creating a situation where they [Sinn Fein\IRA] couldn't refuse."

The British Government isn't doing what you want, so you don't want Sinn Fein\IRA to stop fighting?

He was angry now.

"Well you keep emphasising about ... I would like you to address your questions to the British Government. And I would like to hear their response."

I'm not addressing the British Government. I'm addressing you. And I think what you're saying to me is that the IRA should not stop the killing until there's further concessions from the British?

"I would like the IRA to stop, but the situation is not conducive to them to stop."

So you don't want them to stop?

"They can't stop yet."

Hallelujah! I couldn't say I had a straight answer but it was as good as I was going to get.

In the weeks since Section 31 had been dropped I had listened carefully to Sinn Fein's approach to being interviewed. I had been rehearsing what my own response would be to Sinn Fein's evasions. This man in Derry gave me the only opportunity I got to grapple with the arguments against ending the war. His was a lone voice.

Two men, one aged about thirty-five, the other about forty, were standing across from the dole office. They were drinking cans of beer.

The younger man asked me what I was doing. I told him and he said he would like to talk to me.

"Being unemployed ... it sends you to the drink."

"It depresses you. You feel like you're a waster."

The older man was obviously drunk. His speech was slurred. I asked the younger man to talk to me again.

"You're getting up in the morning and you've nothing

to do. You've a whole day and you're trying to kill a day and you get fed up. I don't want to use unemployment for the reason for the break-up of my marriage but when you're sitting in seven days a week ... I'd rather work for my few pound. You feel like a man when you're out working. And when you come home, you feel like a married man. But when you're sitting in, seven days a week, you've nothing to talk about, you've no conversation ... how d'you get on? There's no, how d'you get on at work? Them things just go to the wall and then you start getting on each other's nerves. And then one thing leads to the other and it becomes a total turmoil."

"My marriage is broke up longer than his. It's the pressure of living broke up me and my wife. You can't get work and you can't provide. It's no wonder there's so many alcoholics in Derry."

I wanted to tell him that there's lots of alcoholics everywhere. Not just in Derry. These sad men sounded like men I've met at dole offices everywhere.

They were joined by a third man. A middle-aged skinhead. God, he looked rough. His face was scratched and bruised. He reached into the plastic bag that was at the feet of the other two men. He took out a can and the drunk lunged at him. Get your own fucking drink.

The skinhead backed off and the other two men talked to me again as if nothing had happened. I didn't stick around any longer. I'll be off, men. It's been nice talking to you. Thank you.